EXPLORING
THE GLOBAL ECONOMY

EXPLORING
THE GLOBAL ECONOMY

Emerging Issues in
Trade and Investment

Raymond Vernon

Published by

The Center for International Affairs
Harvard University

and

University Press of America

Copyright © 1985 by the

President and Fellows of Harvard College

University Press of America, ® Inc.

4720 Boston Way
Lanham, MD 20706

3 Henrietta Street
London WC2E 8LU England

Co-published by arrangement with the
Center for International Affairs, Harvard University

The Center provides a forum for the expression of responsible views.
It does not, however, necessarily agree with them.

Library of Congress Cataloging in Publication Data

Vernon, Raymond, 1913-
Exploring the global economy.

Includes index.
1. International economic relations.   2. Investments,
Foreign.   3. Government ownership.   4. East-west
trade (1945-   )   I. Title.
HF1411.V4394   1985   337   85-14895
ISBN 0-8191-4674-9 (alk. paper)
ISBN 0-8191-4675-7 (pbk. : alk. paper)

The Center For International Affairs Executive Committee, 1984-85

The Center for International Affairs is a multidisciplinary research institution within Harvard University. Founded in 1958, the Center seeks to provide a stimulating environment for a diverse group of scholars and practitioners studying various aspects of international affairs. Its purpose is the development and dissemination of knowledge concerning the basic subjects and problems of international relations. Major Center research programs include national security affairs, U.S. relations with Europe, Japan, Africa, and other areas of the world, nonviolent sanctions in conflict and defense, international economic policy, and other critical issues. At any given time, over 160 individuals are working at the Center, including faculty members from Harvard and neighboring institutions, practitioners of international affairs, visiting scholars, research associates, post-doctoral fellows, and graduate and undergraduate student associates.

Contents

Introduction

As one would expect of Ray Vernon, his twelve essays in this volume deal with an extremely broad range of topics: the international trading system, innovation and technological development, investment risks, multinational corporation strategies, regulation of multinationals, management of state-owned enterprises, the role of such enterprises in resource industries, U.S.–Soviet economic relations, the making of U.S. economic policy toward the Soviet Union. With two exceptions (which were published in 1979), they all originally appeared in the early 1980s. They reflect the wide-ranging interests of their author during those years. They also reflect, however, only a small portion of the diverse subjects on which he has worked during his career. In earlier writings, he also dealt with such issues as the regulation of security exchanges, commercial policy, the economy of metropolitan regions, most notably the case of New York, and the problems of economic development, most notably the case of Mexico. While many economists have tended to become more and more involved with technical issues of theory and methodology, Ray Vernon has been sensitive to the changing institutional environment of the real world. In the past twenty years he has pioneered the study of two major economic institutions which have played increasingly important roles in today's global economy—the multinational corporation and the state-owned enterprise. His recent thoughts on these subjects are well represented in this volume.

In all the areas in which he has worked, Ray Vernon's writings have left their mark, and not just in the minds of economists. For he is one of those rare economists who can produce serious economic analysis of serious economic issues in a form which non-economists can understand and apply to their own work. In the areas in which he has written, most notably recently with respect to multinational and state-owned enterprises, Ray Vernon has not only developed new concepts and theories, of which the product-cycle theory is only the most familiar, but he has also conveyed those ideas meaningfully to those of us in other disciplines working on related questions. For the past quarter-century his principal intellectual home has been the Harvard Center for International Affairs, and in the wide-ranging and often vigorous discussions that go on in that multidisciplinary environment, he has regularly made salient contributions to the illumination of economic and non-economic issues alike.

Ray Vernon brings to the analysis of economic matters a practical understanding of how and why human beings behave as they do in ambiguous
relationships and in complex organizations. This understanding derives not
only from his work as a thinker, researcher, and writer of note. It comes also
from his active engagement in a variety of public and private institutional
roles: as an official of the SEC and the State Department, a businessman, a
delegate to GATT, director of the Harvard Development Advisory Service, and
director of the Center for International Affairs. In the latter position between
1973 and 1978, he inaugurated a number of major improvements in Center
management and operations and with wisdom and determination sustained
the Center's research program during a period when foundation support for
international affairs was far less than it was previously or since. We at the
Center are honored by the opportunity to sponsor publication of this selection of Ray Vernon's recent essays.

> Samuel P. Huntington, Director
> Center for International Affairs
> Harvard University

Part 1

International Trade

1

Old rules and new players: GATT in the world trading system

Military planners, according to a time-worn cliche, are usually found preparing for the last war. Policymakers in the field of international economic relations can sometimes be accused of a similar bias. Today, the world's principal trading and investing nations are wrestling with the problem of how to maintain the benefits and minimize the costs that are associated with international trade. A critical question is how well the basic assumptions that underlay U.S. thinking in the formulation of the General Agreement on Tariffs and Trade apply today; and to the extent that new factors have appeared, what they may suggest about revising the terms of the existing trade regime.

The GATT's founding

The U.S. role

The end of World War II marked a new era in international economic relations. The war had helped push the U.S. economy into a position of unchallenged dominance in the international system. The country's economic weight and its position as the leader of a political and military alliance briefly endowed it with an extraordinary measure of influence over the rules and institutions that were established at the war's end. To be sure, other countries in the western coalition strongly supported one aspect or another in the package of newly created rules and institutions. But with hindsight, it is clear that the views of the United States on the nature of an ideal international economic regime were measurably different from those that typically prevailed in Europe and Japan, and sharply at variance with the views of most developing countries.

Perhaps the most pervasive factor that has distinguished the U.S. position from those of most other countries has been the deeply rooted preference of Americans for limiting the direct transactional role of government in international economic affairs. Tightly linked to that preference is the U.S. predilection for letting the market determine the direction of international

---

Reprinted with permission of the author from *Journal of Policy Analysis and Management,* vol. 4, no. 1, Fall 1984.

transactions. This set of preferences has been embedded in a system of governance that persistently limits the discretionary (hence to some extent arbitrary) power of its agencies, partly by requiring that each bureaucratic decision should be tested for its validity against some specified general rule.

The trade policy that the U.S. government adopted after World War II reflected all of these concepts. But the circumstances that led to its adoption at that particular time were in some respects quite unique. By 1948, Democratic administrations had been in power for sixteen years. As a result, a small group of antiquarian congressmen from the southern states had come to dominate many of the key committees of the Congress.[1] From those positions, this small group could express the historical preference of the south's cotton, tobacco, and apple exporters against high industrial tariffs and in favor of the promotion of exports. The influence of the southerners was bolstered by some distinguished survivors of the Wilsonian crusade at the end of World War I; centered mainly in the industrial and financial centers of the northeast, this group still believed firmly in the link between world trade and world peace. Finally, there were America's professional economists, projected by the New Deal and the special conditions of World War II into key planning positions in the U.S. government; this group, still smarting from its failed effort to block the passage of the Smoot–Hawley Tariff Act in 1930, was strongly committed to the neoclassical preference for open markets and nondiscrimination.[2]

Historical forces also explain the respective roles of the two political parties in the formulation of the postwar trade regime. In those years, as today, the Republicans were identified as the party of American business. Until World War II that identification usually carried the Hamiltonian connotation, a commitment to protect America's infant industries against European competitors. The Democrats, then as now, were a more diverse coalition, composed at the time of organized labor, southern agricultural interests, and northern internationalists. Where international trade policy was concerned, labor's attachment to the Democratic party was an anomaly, inasmuch as labor had traditionally been almost as protectionist as the industrialists. But labor's attachment to the Democratic party served to blunt its hostility to an open international trading system. Labor's ambivalence could be detected in 1934, when the first Trade Agreements Act was passed as part of a package of measures to fight the Great Depression, as well as in 1948, when the leaders of the AFL–CIO were closely identified with the nation's efforts to rebuild a destroyed Europe through the Marshall plan.

That was the background against which the U.S. planners after World War II attempted to frame a set of institutions and rules for governing international trade. Given their ideology and their outlook, their early plans placed heavy emphasis on a number of basic objectives: to outlaw international cartels; to bring down tariff rates; to phase out national licensing requirements that limited foreign trade; and to curb discrimination in the administration of trade regulations. These objectives—albeit much qualified and diluted—found expression in 1948 in a draft charter for an International Trade Organization, one of whose chapters would provide the basis for the General Agreement on Tariffs and Trade. The GATT, as numerous commentators have observed, was originally perceived as a stop-gap organization; the agreement was expected to do no more than provide the framework for international trade liberalization efforts during the period in which the ITO charter was being ratified. As it turned out, the charter never was ratified by any of the fifty-two countries that participated in its drafting. Other countries, viewing it largely as a U.S.-inspired document reflecting a U.S.-inspired ideology, saw no reason to take the lead in the ratification process.

Meanwhile, however, various groups in the United States were beginning to balk at some of the alien ideas that had been introduced in the charter's draft in the course of the negotiations.[3] These included various qualifications and demurrers regarding the rights of foreign investors, elaborate provisions for the negotiation of international commodity agreements, an approach to the restrictive business practices of state-owned enterprises that was more lenient than the approach applied to private enterprises, and a special tolerance for trade restrictions that were intended to promote economic development. By 1950, it became clear that the draft ITO charter did not represent a workable consensus. Besides, by that time, the U.S. foreign policy agenda was crowded with other more urgent issues, including the administration of the Marshall plan, the building of NATO, and the prosecution of the Korean war.

The death of the ITO left the much less ambitious provisions of the GATT to fill part of the breach. Enough of the U.S. ideology had been retained in its complex clauses covering the conduct of international trade so that U.S. policymakers could live with those provisions in reasonable comfort. The ideas of reducing trade barriers, avoiding discrimination, and settling disputes by discussion were still the paramount propositions of the agreement. And in the one major area in which U.S. domestic politics demanded import restrictions and export subsidies, that of agricultural commodities, the U.S. negotiators had tried strenuously to carve out the requisite exceptions to their own general principles, so that direct conflict between the GATT provisions and U.S. law could be held to a minimum.

The Congress, therefore, felt no strong need to block U.S. participation in the GATT. Indeed, in the years that followed, individual congressmen occasionally used the provisions of the GATT as an argument for modifying or abandoning some conflicting action that the Congress had under consideration. On the other hand, the GATT never acquired the legitimacy that would have been accorded to an agreement that had been explicitly approved by the Congress or to a treaty ratified by the Senate. Instead, the Congress tolerated the participation of the executive branch in the GATT, while occasionally ignoring and violating the agreement's provisions when they seemed to stand in the way.

GATT in operation

United States policies

Despite the equivocal character of U.S. official support for the GATT, the organization proved to be a pivotal instrument in the shaping and execution of U.S. trade policy during the three decades following its founding. In that respect, as we shall presently see, the United States was almost unique. In most other countries, the differences between the general approach embodied in the GATT and the national trade policies that they actually employed were much larger.

Not that other countries were necessarily in formal violation of the GATT. In addition to the U.S.-inspired exceptions applicable to agricultural commodities, the agreement's numerous escape clauses were sufficient to tolerate a considerable amount of deviation from its underlying concepts. Countries in balance-of-payment difficulties, for instance, could do very much as they liked to restrict imports and to discriminate among their trading partners. Countries that claimed developing-country status could use numerous provisions of the agreement to justify deviant measures.

At first, when European recovery occupied U.S. policymakers, the centrality of the GATT for U.S. trade policy was not very obvious. As long as the European recovery objective prevailed, the U.S. government devoted its energies mainly to helping the European participants in the Marshall plan shape a preferential system of trade relations among them, a system that discriminated systematically against the United States and other outsiders in the interests of promoting easier trade relations among the Europeans themselves.

Indeed, in those early days, GATT's main role was to organize and preside over a series of exercises that at the time seemed to border on a charade. The President from time to time requested and received limited powers from the Congress to reduce U.S. tariffs in order to carry out trade agreements undertaken with other countries. According to the norms of the negotiation that followed, all countries were expected to reduce their tariffs in roughly equal degree. In the late 1940s, however, practically all countries other than the United States and Canada were controlling their trade primarily by means of foreign exchange licenses rather than by tariffs; a reduction in tariffs, therefore, did not necessarily reduce the barriers to U.S. exports. Moreover, the question whether the various countries had reduced their tariffs in equal degree could never be resolved in terms that were theoretically defensible. The negotiators nevertheless devised various measures of each country's reductions, to be paraded before the U.S. Congress as proof of "reciprocity." Congress itself was content to take note of the outcome of those negotiations, expressing neither approval nor disapproval of the results.

The actions of the United States in those early days of the GATT rested on certain views among Americans that would soon be altered. One of these was the view—widely shared at the time by leaders in business, labor, and government circles—that the United States should play a role appropriate to the head of a worldwide coalition. Like any leader of a coalition, the U.S. government was prepared to overlook some of the peccadillos of its junior allies if this would promote the collective arrangement. A second view, reenforcing the first, was that the U.S. economy itself was practically invulnerable, at least from economic forces that were external to the country; that widely held view made it much easier to overlook the unbalanced character of the trade agreements.

As it turned out, these early acts of leadership paid off handsomely. By the middle 1950s, most European countries were in a position to abandon their discriminatory import licensing systems and to rely on tariffs for their trade protection. To be sure, the Europeans were not long in putting another system in place that discriminated against dollar goods, this time in the form of a customs union embedded in the provisions of the European Economic Community. The effect of that agreement was to eliminate tariffs in trade between the member countries and to establish a common external tariff, to be applied by the members to imports from nonmember countries including the United States. But the tariffs that were applied to U.S. goods by the Community's original six members reflected rates that had been drastically reduced as a result of the GATT-sponsored tariff negotiations.

The sense of the U.S. leadership that the country stood at the head of a world coalition remained strong through much of the 1960s. But the country's sense of economic invulnerability evaporated more quickly. Indeed, as early as 1956, the U.S. government was already belaboring Japan for its growing exports of cotton textiles to U.S. markets, and was already finding ways of restricting imports of oil and ores from other sources. And by the 1960s, American leaders were worrying over the steady decline in the country's gold holdings and over the competitive position of the U.S. economy as a whole.

As long as the United States saw itself in a leadership role, however, it was in no position to entertain seriously any general move to restrict its imports. The U.S. response to problems of increasing competition, therefore, mainly took the form of greater efforts to open up the markets of its trading partners, especially of the formidable European community. This was the chief impetus that produced the extensive tariff negotiations of the 1960s, the so-called Kennedy round; and it continued to provide enough momentum into the 1970s to produce still another round of tariff reductions, sometimes dubbed the Tokyo round. Piled on top of the tariff negotiations of the late 1940s and 1950s, these reductions cut the tariffs of the world's principal trading countries from levels that had characteristically run on the order of 20 or 30 percent to levels that were typically in the neighborhood of 5 percent. That reduction was an extraordinary achievement, quite unparalleled in the history of the world's trade relations.

From the U.S. viewpoint, however, GATT's achievements were largely submerged during the 1970s by a growing sense of dissatisfaction with the system. Increasingly, Americans chafed under what they perceived to be the asymmetrical impact of the GATT's provisions. That asymmetry could perhaps be tolerated as long as the United States saw itself steering the world toward a trading system that was compatible with its interests. But by the 1970s, the U.S. government no longer saw itself as the unchallenged leader of a new world trading system, nor would many other countries have acknowledged any such claim to leadership. One notable change was the slippage of the U.S. position in world trade; whereas U.S. merchandise exports in 1953 accounted for 29 percent of such exports from the industrialized countries as a whole, the analogous figure in 1970 had fallen to 19 percent.[4]

There was another element in the U.S. reaction, however. The United States saw itself as using the tariff as the principal instrument of trade control; other countries, however, were thought to be using various other means to control their trade, means that came to be known as nontariff barriers or simply NTBs. The GATT had operated effectively enough in reducing high tariffs; but its effectiveness in dealing with these so-called NTBs had yet to be tested. And there was considerable skepticism everywhere whether GATT could measure up to the test.

Accordingly, when in 1974 Congress gave the President fresh authority to negotiate for the reduction of trade barriers, it included a series of new emphases in the enabling legislation. The reduction of the offending nontariff barriers was stressed as an objective. More significantly, the President was instructed and authorized to take restrictive measures against countries that maintained "unjustifiable or unreasonable" import restrictions against the United States.[5]

The negotiations that the United States conducted under authority of the 1974 Act demonstrated that some fundamental shifts were taking place in U.S. policy. Some of the practices to which the U.S. government particularly objected, such as governmental subsidies and discriminatory procurement practices, were singled out for special negotiations whose results were embodied in separate codes. In ratifying the results, the U.S. Congress stipulated that rights under those codes would be extended by the United States only to those foreign governments that adhered to the codes rather than to all GATT members, a provision that the administration accepted. The inference was clear: The United States was prepared to accept major deviations from the nondiscrimination principle if necessary to make progress on these impediments to trade.

Since 1979, the sense that the United States was being unfairly treated in international trade has been prominent both in congressional deliberations and in executive pronouncements. The U.S. position has been that it confronts a world that bristles with nontariff barriers. With that conviction as a backdrop, the U.S. government has found it less difficult than in the past to square its ideological preferences for nondiscrimination and open markets with various ad hoc measures of trade restriction, including some measures that breached the principle of nondiscrimination. By 1980, according to one estimate, the U.S. industries that benefited from special measures of protection against imports—from so-called voluntary export restraints, trigger price devices, and the like—accounted for about 30 percent of the country's industrial output.[6]

Yet it would be a gross mistake to infer from such evidence that the United States had reverted to a simple protectionist position. On the contrary; although the American public at large was expressing protectionist sentiments, there was ample evidence that leadership opinion in the United States remained strongly wedded to open international markets.[7] By the 1980s, practically every major U.S. industrial enterprise and banking institution was organized on a multinational basis, with subsidiaries and affiliates all over the world. As a result, the common interest that management and labor once had shared in repelling foreign competition when it threatened home markets had disappeared. In the United States as well as other advanced industrialized countries, many managers and technicians were associating their well-being with the worldwide performance of multinational enterprises by which they are employed; labor, on the other hand, continued to see its interests in protecting the home market. More generally, those groups in the advanced industrialized countries from whom civic leaders are typically drawn—businessmen, bankers, academics, lawyers, and the like—came to identify their interests more strongly with open international borders than the population at large, creating a special set of problems for political decisionmakers.

European policies

To the extent that the United States succeeded in bringing down tariff barriers through the instrumentality of the GATT during the decades after World War II, its principal partners in the operation were the major countries of Europe operating either in their separate capacities or as members of the European Economic Community. Yet, as mentioned earlier, the main trade policies of the Europeans were preferential from the very beginning. The discriminatory trade liberalization schemes of the Marshall plan years were followed by the more enduring preferential arrangements associated with the European Economic Community. In addition to establishing a customs union among its members, the Community also developed a network of preferential arrangements with nonmembers. Free trade agreements were negotiated with each of the main nonmember countries in Europe, thereby eliminating tariffs on industrial products in trade with those countries. Bilateral trade agreements also were negotiated with various countries in North Africa and southern Europe bordering on the Mediterranean, providing for special trade treatment of their exports. Blanket five-year conventions were negotiated with several scores of poor countries located in Africa, the Caribbean, and the Pacific, former colonies of the EEC's members; these agreements also included wide-ranging preferences extended to the selected countries, along with various measures of aid.

The EEC's various preferential schemes were significant in at least two important respects. All told, they constituted a major departure from the nondiscriminatory world that the United States had been trying to promote through the GATT's key provisions. But they also provided a relatively rare example of a liberal trading system that had been created largely by discriminatory measures of trade liberalization. As a rule, discriminatory import regimes have usually proved to be highly restrictive of trade. In the case of the EEC countries, however, total imports rose from 12 percent of the EEC countries' gross domestic product in 1953 to 24 percent in 1980; and the relative increase in imports were due not only to a relative rise in trade within the customs union itself but also to a relative rise in imports from outsiders.[8]

To be sure, the EEC's liberalization policies did not extend to all products; even more than the U.S. case, agricultural products were protected by a special set of import restrictions and export subsidies. Nor was the EEC prepared to entertain preferential trade-liberalizing arrangements with all countries; an arrangement with Japan, for instance, would have been unthinkable. Still, the EEC's markets, measured by any historical or comparative standard, were opened wide to foreign goods.

The challenge to GATT concepts that the Community members have posed, therefore, has not been a challenge to open markets so much as it has been a challenge to nondiscrimination. But there has been another challenge as well. Governments in most European countries have been quite prepared to deal with problems of industrial development, economic adjustment, and export promotion by various ad hoc means: for instance, by creating state-owned enterprises and endowing them with capital and operating funds,[9] or by providing subsidies and extending preferences in various forms to their national producers.[10] In this respect, most Europeans reflected a political outlook and a historical tradition that were measurably different from those of the United States and that revealed the tenuous and incomplete character of the consensus underlying the GATT.

Japanese policies

Japan's participation in the GATT has served to emphasize even more strongly the limited nature of the GATT consensus.[11] As noted earlier, already by 1956 Japan's success as an exporter was testing the strength of the U.S. commitment to a nondiscriminatory trading system; *in extremis* the United States itself proved unprepared to follow the nondiscrimination principle to the letter. To be sure, the United States went to some lengths to avoid an overt violation of the GATT's strictures against discrimination; to achieve its purpose, the United States compelled Japan "voluntarily" to restrict its exports to the U.S. market. That disingenuous measure, it should be noted, may have weakened the GATT more than an overtly discriminatory import restriction would have done, because it seemed to legitimate the *de facto* avoidance of a basic GATT rule by a blatant subterfuge.

But Japan's participation in the GATT provided a second major lesson as well, a lesson already suggested by the reaction of the Europeans. GATT has been structured on the basis of assumptions that were largely consistent with the conditions of the U.S. economy—conditions in which the direct transactional role of government was limited, governmental institutions had little to do with the promotion or adaptation of business enterprises, and cooperative behavior by national enterprises was sharply limited through the operation of antitrust laws. The case of Japan illustrated how atypical the United States economy was in these respects. Although the numerous studies that scholars have recently produced of the Japanese economy differ in many details, almost all agree on a number of points that emphasize the differences from the United States.

For several decades before World War II, the Japanese government had had a major hand in stimulating, supporting, and coordinating the growth of private enterprise.[12] After World War II, the close ties between business and government continued. The institutions responsible for maintaining those ties included a ministry, MITI, that was charged with defining the country's development targets; a series of government-supported financial intermediaries that doled out credit on preferential terms to favored enterprises; and an extensive network of business organizations that interacted with the government to shape the required goals and produce the needed responses at the enterprise level. Apart from the United States, practically all other countries of the world also had developed some of the institutional features of the Japanese economy. But in the United States, such arrangements have been uncommon, except for a few exceptional cases mainly encountered in wartime. It is not surprising, therefore, that the GATT has largely failed to address the trade problems created by such institutions.

The Japanese case, of course, also has included some rather distinctive features of its own. Inside the country, Japanese enterprise has tended to organize itself in a number of clusters of interrelated firms. Until World War II, six or eight such clusters—the so-called zaibatsu—made up most of Japan's modern industry. After World War II, Japanese firms continued to be linked in a large number of clusters of a looser sort—the so-called keiretsu. One consequence of that structure was that most Japanese firms which were users of intermediate materials were linked to Japanese suppliers by vertical ties. In many cases, the intermediate materials were produced under conditions that generated substantial increasing returns to scale. As a result, Japan's aluminum fabricators normally acquired their metal from related aluminum smelters at home, Japan's automobile plants from related Japanese parts manufacturers, and so on. A study of the Japanese semiconductor industry suggests that returns to scale also have been a factor that explains the practices of Japanese firms of swapping specialty items with one another.[13] The Japanese case has driven home with particular force the fact that the structure of corporate relationships could significantly affect the propensity of a nation to import or export, a possibility that the GATT's founders did not address and the GATT itself did not consider.

The considerable gap between the U.S. perception of a GATT-inspired trading world and the Japanese perception of GATT's requirements explains in part the acute frustrations of the two countries in their quarrels over Japanese trade practices. From the U.S. viewpoint, Japan's record is commonly seen as one of extensive evasion; from the Japanese viewpoint, its record is one that compares quite favorably with that of other industrialized countries.[14] The size of that gap reflects in part the extent of the omissions, exceptions, and ambiguities of the GATT itself when measured against the U.S.-inspired conception of an open trading world.

Developing countries and socialist economies

The qualified nature of the developing countries' adherence to the GATT needs only a few words of elaboration.

Most members of the GATT claim developing status. Members in that category normally feel free to take any measures they think appropriate in their national interests. These measures have included widespread resort to import licensing, subsidies, and discriminatory trade regimes.

The size of the gap between pristine GATT concepts and developing country practices has been due to a number of factors. One of these has been the extent to which the GATT itself has provided for such deviations. Apart from the provisions applicable to all countries in balance-of-payment difficulties, a number of exceptional provisions have been fashioned especially to relieve developing countries from GATT obligations. Perhaps as important has been the fact that the institutions, practices, and values that typically prevailed in these countries with regard to the role of government have borne a closer resemblance to the Japanese model than to the American: Government-supported financial intermediaries have been extensive; industrial groups of the zaibatsu or keiretsu type, with local variations, have been ubiquitous;[15] government sponsorship of and participation in industrial development has been nearly universal. As a result, the actual practices of developing countries in the conduct of their international trade have had little in common with the system that the U.S. government had hoped to promote through the GATT.

The size of the gap between U.S. views and developing country views over the meaning and intent of the GATT has been underlined by efforts to have some of the newly industrializing countries, such as Brazil and Korea, accept some of the restraints that are embodied in the GATT's general rules, including restraints on the use of subsidies and on discriminatory trade practices.[16] Those efforts have now been going on for about a decade. One cannot say for certain that the efforts have been wholly fruitless; some of the newly industrializing countries have taken measures from time to time in the direction of trade liberalization. But the hostility generated by U.S. pressures has been monumental as compared with the meager results.

The participation of socialist economies in the GATT has been even more equivocal than that of the developing countries with mixed economies. The membership of several east European countries, the prospective membership of the People's Republic of China, and the Soviet Union's interest in obtaining observer status in the GATT have served mainly to highlight the irrelevance of the agreement's provisions for the conditions of a centrally directed economy. The provisions of the GATT that apply explicitly to the enterprises of socialist economies are in fact quite quixotic; their aim is to have enterprises in such countries behave as if they were independent entities responding to "commercial considerations," so that they are expected to buy from the cheapest foreign source and sell to the highest foreign bidder.[17] The fact that the enterprises are state-owned is acknowledged in only one important particular: The mark-ups of state-owned enterprises that import foreign goods for resale in the home market are analogized to a tariff and are therefore made subject to negotiation with other GATT members.

In actual practice, to be sure, the GATT signatories have exhibited a greater degree of eclecticism in dealing with centrally directed economies than the GATT's rules might suggest. They have largely ignored those provisions and have demanded other commitments of various kinds, such as commitments on the part of such countries to expand their foreign trade by some agreed amounts. But these commitments have only served to underline the fundamental point that the U.S.-inspired provisions of the GATT cannot usefully be applied in trade agreements with centrally directed economies.

Trade and traders

The fact that industrial structure can substantially influence trade behavior became sharply apparent in the decades before World War II. During those decades, the leading firms that dominated their respective national markets in various capital-intensive industries found themselves from time to time in costly rivalrous contact with one another in international markets. This was an era in which each national market in the new capital-intensive industries was characteristically dominated by only a firm or two, which accounted for the bulk of the country's foreign trade in the products of those industries.[18] In chemicals, DuPont, Imperial Chemicals, and I. G. Farben were overwhelmingly dominant in their respective markets. In electrical equipment, the leaders were only a little more numerous, including General Electric, Westinghouse, Thomson–Huston, Tokyo Shibaura, and Allgemeine Electrizitäts Gesellschaft. In aluminum, ALCOA, Pechiney, and later ALCAN dominated the world market. In copper, the international market was largely in the hands of America's Big Three plus Union Minière; and in oil, an equally small number was in control of the international side of the industry.

The new industries typically enjoyed substantial economies of scale; and because the leading firms commonly saw their positions in foreign markets as relatively insecure and transitory, they often dumped their products in the markets of rivals at prices that did not recapture their full costs. Soon, however, the leaders recognized the destructive consequences of such practices; and with that recognition came an era of cartel agreements, marked by the division of markets on national lines and by rules on the pricing of products that were sold across national borders. The power of these agreements during the 1930s was bolstered by high tariffs, by the extensive use of import licensing, and by the use of bilateral clearing arrangements with favored trading partners.[19]

After World War II, the international cartels that had been so ubiquitous in earlier years almost disappeared. To be sure, evidence occasionally surfaced after World War II that the institution of the cartel was not quite dead. In uranium, diamonds, and a handful of other products, restrictive trade arrangements still persisted. And the OPEC saga is too well known to require recounting. But these cartels were on nothing like the scale of the period before World War II. Moreover, there is considerable evidence—despite widespread impressions to the contrary—that the degree of industrial concentration in the mature product lines during the decades following World War II typically underwent a considerable decline.[20] With the risks of cartels and monopolies somewhat reduced, the role of tariffs, import licenses, subsidies, and the like took on added importance in shaping international trade. In this one respect, at any rate, the provisions of the GATT became more relevant rather than less. At the same time, however, other developments were reducing GATT's relevance.

One of these developments was the greatly increased role of the multinational enterprise. Although no precise data have been developed on changes in the relative importance of multinational enterprises in the conduct of international trade, it is clear that their role grew considerably in the decades after World War II and came to account for a greatly increased share of the world's trade. In the United States, for instance, 298 enterprises classified as multinational in structure were responsible in 1970 for 62 percent of all U.S. exports of manufactured products. Between 1966 and 1975 the majority-owned affiliates of U.S. firms located in foreign countries originated about one-third of U.S. imports.[21]

One reason why the growth of multinational enterprises introduces problems with regard to the relevance of the GATT's rules has to do with the underlying paradigm on which those rules are structured. These implicitly contemplate a world of buyers and sellers operating at arm's length across international borders, bearing costs that are primarily determined by the factor prices within their respective countries, and buying or selling in international markets on the basis of their position in the comparative advantage profile of their countries. In such a world, there is an objectively determined "right" pattern for international trade, which can be specified without regard to the structure of the firm.

In the abstract, the growing importance of multinational enterprises in world trade posed no particular threat to the GATT concept. On the contrary: Because multinational enterprises produced from a number of locations, they appeared to be in a relatively strong position to react more or less swiftly to changes in the cost structures of competing areas, precisely on patterns assumed in the GATT paradigm. In reality, however, various elements in the behavior of multinational enterprises served to demonstrate that the GATT's implicit assumptions regarding the behavior of international traders might be incomplete in various critical respects.

For one thing, the growth of the multinational enterprise appears to have increased the number of countries for which scale economies and learning curves were determining the patterns of international trade. Even before the era of multinational enterprises, governments in developing countries were insisting on their right to establish and protect various industries with large static and dynamic economies of scale, such as steel and chemicals. But the obstacles to acquiring the needed capital, technology, and access to markets and of putting them to work often appeared formidable. Multinational enterprises commonly seemed to offer an attractive way out because they were in a position to provide the required ingredients as a package; sometimes those resources came from within the multinational system, sometimes from foreign markets, and sometimes from within the developing country itself. What the multinational enterprises generally required in return was some expectation that they would be able to shelter their early output, which would be produced at high cost, from the competition of established producers. Developing countries often provided that shelter by import restrictions or by subsidies.

Once a multinational enterprise had established a production capability for any given product in more than one country, the existence of static and dynamic scale economies served to complicate its choices among various locations when expanding or contracting its production. Because the costs of the enterprise in each such facility were typically sensitive to the volume of production in that facility, it was not easy to specify how an enterprise would respond to any given change in comparative advantage. A multinational enterprise that was calculating the prospective benefits of setting up a facility in a new area, for instance, would have to take into account the possibility that one of its existing units in another area might be required as a result to cut back its production, thereby raising the average costs of that facility. Theorists have not yet developed any extensive hypotheses about rational behavior under such conditions on the part of multinational enterprises.[22] On the basis of empirical observation, however, there were suggestions that multinational enterprises have been less sensitive to factor-cost changes than national producers.[23]

Wherever multinational enterprises dominated in international trade, other factors came into play that were disturbing to the GATT assumptions. The available data demonstrated persuasively, for instance, that multinational enterprises with prior experience in any given area were much more strongly disposed to make added investments in that area than in areas in which they had no prior experience.[24] Moreover, with static and dynamic scale factors much on the minds of their managers, they have been sensitive to the moves of rivals when setting up new production or distribution facilities in major foreign markets. Extensive research on the subject offers strong support for the hypothesis that this sensitivity has led to follow-the-leader patterns in the investments of multinational enterprises; and that behavior, in turn, could easily produce patterns of trade that were quite different from those generated in a world in which locational decisions depended mainly on factor costs and markets.[25] In general, where static and dynamic economies of scale are important, the theory of international trade is somewhat underdeveloped not only in postulating the optimum behavior of the multinational enterprise but also in postulating the optimum behavior of governments. The theoretical basis for justifying GATT's emphasis on nondiscrimination and on the reduction of trade barriers becomes more uncertain;[26] accordingly, the persuasive power of the comparative advantage paradigm as a justification for lowering trade barriers loses some of its force.

GATT's rules have proved somewhat inadequate for dealing with the multinational enterprise for still another reason. Many governments have used the affiliates of multinational enterprises in their jurisdictions to impose various so-called performance requirements. Commonly, governments have offered special subsidies and tax exemptions to those enterprises they wished to attract and have shut out those unlikely to perform in accordance with governmental requirements. Those requirements, in practice, typically have included provisions for expanding exports and reducing imports.[27]

The influence of government performance requirements on the behavior of multinational enterprises, however, is probably even greater than their formal presence would suggest. Aware of the need to make themselves indispensable to governments, some multinational enterprises have been planning the location of their production facilities in ways that would reduce their vulnerability. Anecdotal evidence suggests that some have tended to develop organic links among their various affiliates in different countries that keep the affiliates dependent on one another for components or for markets. When coupled with performance requirements, that tendency may explain in part why the subsidiaries of multinational enterprises played such a substantial part during the 1970s in the striking expansion of manufactured goods exports from the newly industrializing countries.[28] At the same time, however, performance requirements have created a new impediment for maintaining an open nondiscriminatory trading regime.

State-owned enterprises

Another development that has tended to influence international trade during the past few decades has been the rapid growth in the role of state-owned enterprises. The trend has been especially strong in crude oil, copper, and iron ore, products in which state-owned producers have increased their share of international sales from practically zero in the 1950s to commanding levels in the 1980s.[29] In addition, state-owned enterprises have grown considerably in the import-substituting industries, especially in those industries that require large-scale capital-intensive facilities such as chemicals, metal producing, and metal fabricating plants.[30] Finally, there has been a tendency for governments to take control of the exportation or importation of some products critical for their economies, sometimes in order to exploit what monopoly or monopsony power they could muster, sometimes in order to simplify the administrative problems of taxing or subsidizing their importers or exporters.[31]

To be sure, governments have occasionally shrunk back the scope of their state-owned enterprise sector, rather than enlarge it. Cases of gross mismanagement or back-breaking cost have usually been influential in producing such reversals. But many governments do not see the state-owned enterprise as an exception or aberration in a market economy; instead, they tend to see such enterprises as an acceptable instrument of government, whose use depends more on empirical than on ideological factors.[32] Accordingly, it is doubtful that the occasional reversals foreshadow a countertrend on a large scale.

It was observed earlier that the basic concepts of the GATT could not easily be applied to the operations of socialist states. For similar reasons, the application of GATT concepts to state-owned enterprises in market economies proves to be exceedingly difficult. Remember that the basic GATT approach is to insist that state-owned enterprises must behave as if they were making their choices on the basis of commercial considerations alone. The fact is, however, that state-owned enterprises commonly receive their initial capital as a cost-free endowment, which is replenished as necessary when it is impaired by losses. Some shrinkage in the productive capacity of such enterprises may be allowed to occur, as evidenced by the state-owned steel industries of Britain, France, and Italy, but total liquidation is practically unheard of. In addition, it is inevitable that governments will attempt from time to time to use their enterprises for a multiplicity of purposes: to stimulate investment, to stabilize employment, to damp down inflation, to develop backward regimes, to subsidize exports, and so on. Managers of state-owned enterprises, therefore, cannot be expected to behave in ways that approximate those of the profit-maximizing, bankruptcy-threatened private manager.

The countertraders

In recent years, a variety of institutions have taken to arranging deals in which specified imports are linked directly to specified exports. Of course, bilateral deals between pairs of countries, balancing imports with exports, have a long history in international trade; and as long as such deals have been between two countries with balance-of-payment difficulties, the exemptive provisions of GATT have left them free to develop such arrangements. Contemporary versions of such deals, however, have not necessarily been justified on balance-of-payment grounds. And they have taken a variety of forms not previously encountered. Sellers of technology and equipment, for instance, agree to accept payment for their goods and services in the form of products from the buyer's economy. Sometimes, the products used in payment are produced in the very plant provided by the equipment seller, as when Levi Strauss received payment from Hungary in the form of blue jeans; sometimes, the products in payment come more broadly from the buying country, as in the case of Rumania's purchase of nuclear turbines from General Electric or Pepsico's swap of soft drinks for vodka with the Soviet Union.[33] When the relationship is for the long term rather than for a single isolated transaction, as in the case of mining or oil projects, prospective importers commonly lend capital to prospective producers on a long term basis, sometimes at terms more favorable than those available to an arm's length borrower; and such loans often carry a provision that forgives the producer portions of the loan to the extent that the lender has failed to buy specified quantities of the output. In some of these instances, the value of the products involved is determined by world market prices at time of delivery; but in other instances, where the use of world prices is impractical or undesirable, more complicated formulas are preferred.[34]

From the point of view of a GATT world, the difficulties presented by these countertrades can be formidable. One is the fact that no transaction can be judged by its own terms; each transaction is related to an offsetting trade. The price that Pepsico has paid for the vodka it brings to the U.S. market, therefore, cannot be determined without considering the price it receives for its soft drink in the USSR. The problem is exacerbated when long periods of time separate the offsetting transactions—when, for instance, a machinery export is paid for by materials imported many years later. The separation of the two transactions in time means that the marginal cost of the materials to the importer at time of importation may be close to zero. Moreover, in most of the cases in which a substantial period of time separates the offsetting imports from the original exports, the transaction is financed in part with public funds, thereby increasing the difficulties of measuring the transaction by the standards of the open market.

It is hard to estimate the importance of trades of this sort in world commerce. Japan's nine principal trading companies, which account for about 40 percent of Japan's exports and nearly 50 percent of the country's imports, make extensive use of countertrade arrangements of various kinds. So too do the western firms that engage in trade with members of the COMECON and the People's Republic of China. In addition, Brazil and Korea among others have been learning how to put together countertrade deals, especially in their transactions with other developing countries; Indonesia is making an effort to move in the same direction. Nevertheless, trade conducted on this basis probably represents only a small proportion of world trade, perhaps less than 10 percent. Besides, much of that trade probably involves multinational enterprises or state-owned enterprises or both. Accordingly, such trade does not necessarily enlarge the overall dimensions of the problem categories. But it does exacerbate the difficulties of applying GATT standards.

An overall appraisal

A considerable proportion of the world's trade is conducted on a basis that is substantially at variance with the U.S.-inspired concept of a trading world based on GATT principles.[35] Some of that variance is simply due to violations of the GATT, in letter or in spirit, which could conceivably be remedied by more vigorous enforcement of the agreement's provisions; voluntary export agreements, trigger price mechanisms, and various other disingenuous devices fall in this category.

But the problems lie deeper still. As suggested here, the institutions of international trade commonly march to a music that was not written for the GATT script. To be sure, despite all the obstacles, prices and costs continue to be relevant factors in international trade.[36] Moreover, the presumption that trade restrictions and subsidies will prove harmful to global welfare continues to be strong. Accordingly, the imperfect fit between GATT's underlying assumptions and the realities of international trade need not by itself be a sufficient reason for jettisoning the GATT's present approach.

Yet the risks of attempting to cling to the present GATT structure without some major modifications seem substantial. One reason why the risks seem so high is that other countries are no longer so readily prepared to accept the ethnocentric tilt that the United States was once in a position to implant in the GATT rules. The U.S. view that governmental restrictions or subsidies create "distortions" in world trade presupposes a concept of an ideal trading system that is not shared by many other countries and probably never was; and with the declining willingness or capacity of the United States to assert the leadership position, its ability to maintain that ideological tilt can be expected to decline. If maintained in its present form, therefore, the GATT seems destined to continue losing its persuasive power as an instrument for trade policy.

Another reason why revisions are needed is the special political sensitivity that attaches to certain categories of international trade. One such category is the sale of massive capital goods, such as a petrochemicals complex or a new subway system. Transactions such as these, which routinely involve government credit, countertrade, and state-owned enterprises, are often highly visible, being the object of vigorous hauling and pulling between governments; moreover, they commonly involve products with advanced technologies, products that exporting countries are usually especially eager to support.

Still another category of trade that is highly politicized, needless to say, involves the products of declining industries such as steel and textiles. The experience of the past decade suggests that governments are prepared eventually to allow such industries to shrink, possibly because any effort to retain them is so expensive; but governments are usually not prepared to allow them to shrink as rapidly as they might in the face of open world competition.[37]

The critical challenge for the United States therefore is to find a line of policy appropriate to the altered conditions of international trade.

A course of action

Three alternatives

Each of the alternatives available for U.S. policymakers is filled with risk. One alternative—the obvious one to which many U.S. policymakers are attracted—is to cling to the GATT's original principles, in the hope that other governments will eventually see those principles as the only ones that can be made to work in the long run.[38] The risks of that approach are too obvious to require elaboration. The odds are that the approach will fail to persuade other countries. And as that happens, a frustrated United States will be prodded into applying such unilateral measures of protection as its short-term interests seem to require.

The second alternative is no more promising than the first. This is the tit-for-tat approach, embodied in a number of different proposals that are being offered in the Congress and elsewhere under the general rubric of reciprocity. The details of the different proposals vary somewhat. But essentially they call for a unilateral determination by the United States whether a trading partner is providing access to its markets that is sufficient to meet the standard of full reciprocity; and, if the trading partner is found lacking, they provide for the imposition of new trading restrictions by the United States sufficient to restore the balance. This is obviously an approach destined to generate the lowest common level of market access. Moreover, because it entails a series of unilateral moves, it runs the usual risk of generating a downward spiral of restrictive action and restrictive counteraction. It is, in short, an approach that courts disaster.

The challenge is to develop a third alternative, with less risk and more promise than the two just described. It is not easy to define the third alternative in detail; but some elements are fairly evident. For one thing, we dare not proceed on the basis of unilateral action; international bargaining must continue to be central to the U.S. approach. In addition, the content of the bargains must be such as to contribute on balance to the promotion of open markets, not to the piecemeal closing of such markets. To achieve those results, we shall have to be tolerant of bargains that are less universal in country coverage and more eclectic in content than those negotiated under the GATT. One can picture agreements with the EEC and Japan on some trade subjects, agreements with a group of Latin American countries on other problems, and so on. Some of these agreements could cover such complex subjects as performance requirements, the behavior of state-owned enterprises, or trade in services, while others might be limited to more conventional subjects such as tariffs and export duties.

In some respects, an approach of this sort resembles that followed by the EEC, with its maze of multilateral and bilateral agreements formulated among its members and with outside states. In other respects, it is reminiscent of the various codes, such as those on government procurement and subsidies, that were concluded under the GATT's aegis in 1979. Despite these similarities, the approach raises a number of major questions that have to be tackled.

Relating to the GATT

To begin with, any search for a supplement to the GATT undertaken by the United States might be interpreted as a signal that the GATT was being abandoned. For various reasons, that kind of signal could have calamitous effects. The tariff truce that has existed over the decades among the world's principal trading countries could be undermined; and the GATT's role as a unique forum for airing trade quarrels and launching trade initiatives could be lost. Accordingly, we shall have to find ways to avoid destroying the GATT itself before any alternative has been created.

Whatever initiatives the U.S. government might undertake, therefore, must be formally linked to the GATT, even if the nature of the undertaking is quite foreign to the GATT's principles. Some formula must be found, for instance, for accommodating agreements that formally violate the nondiscrimination principle, so long as they contribute to the trade liberalization objective. The precedents for such cases are already numerous, including the various discriminatory trade arrangements of the European Community with nonmember countries, the innumerable discriminatory trade agreements among developing countries, the bilateral and swap arrangements of the centrally directed economies, and so on.

Developing U.S. bargaining power

Another obstacle to pursuing the third alternative is much more formidable, and the means for overcoming the obstacle much more risky. Other countries have to be persuaded that there is something to be gained in discussing problems with the United States such as those posed by countertrade, state-owned enterprises, performance requirements, trade in services, and so on. In attempting to persuade others to discuss such subjects, the United States no longer can draw support from its leadership position. All that is left as a basis for stimulating serious discussion leading to joint rules of the game is the anxiety of other countries that the United States may decide to join the game—that it may begin to use restrictive or supporting devices purposefully and on a scale that could constitute a threat to others.

To be sure, other countries have felt threatened in the past by U.S. actions outside of the traditional field of tariffs that seemed to restrict imports or promote exports. Long-standing governmental support granted to U.S. agriculture and the spill-over assistance that U.S. military procurement contracts have given to the country's commercial aircraft industry have been repeatedly noted. And the Export–Import Bank has not been slow to match the credit terms extended by other governments to their exporters of capital equipment. As a rule, however, these programs have been designed without foreign bargaining considerations in mind. Administrators of such programs have been obliged to stress transparency, public accountability, and responsiveness to the annual authorization and appropriation process of the Congress; and the President has not had the power, analogous to those he has exercised in the case of tariffs, to alter the provisions of such programs in order to bring them into line with international agreements.

Other countries have come to recognize, therefore, that the instruments which the U.S. government has fashioned for itself for dealing with international trade problems are relatively limited in scope, formalistic in application, and often not under the control of the executive. When protectionist threats arise, they come mainly from actions initiated by private individuals which the U.S. government cannot control, from legislation initiated in the Congress, and from the sporadic demands of the U.S. government for so-called voluntary export agreements. From the viewpoint of other governments, therefore, one conclusion seems fairly well indicated: Negotiating on such trade matters with the U.S. executive may be largely a waste of time. Until the U.S. negotiators seem in a position effectively to apply or to withhold measures that affect U.S. trade, it may prove difficult to persuade other governments to come to the bargaining table.

That conclusion carries a disconcerting implication. In order to increase the chances of effective negotiation, it may be necessary first of all to equip the U.S. government with more powers for the control or promotion of foreign trade than it now possesses, and to place the use of those powers more firmly in the hands of the country's negotiators. In effect, that was what the Congress originally did in 1934 when it authorized the President to negotiate internationally on the subject of tariffs. As in the tariff case, any such delegation of power would have to be subject to limitations and standards of various sorts. In that context it might be possible to stipulate that the new powers be used to negotiate in good faith for the expansion of foreign trade and services rather than for their restriction, or by other means to limit the risk of reversion to the tit-for-tat reciprocity approach. But some increased risk is probably inescapable.

Fingers on the trigger

Any effort to equip the U.S. government with powers sufficient to persuade other governments to come to the negotiating table courts all the risks that go with any international policy based on the principles of mutually assured destruction and negotiated limitations. In the case of trade policy, the problem is exacerbated by the fact that the Congress has usually insisted on placing more than one finger on the trigger; under U.S. law, for instance, both the Congress itself and private parties are in a position to force new trade restrictions over the resistance of the executive.[39]

It would be unrealistic to assume that the Congress would relinquish such powers to the executive. In an extraordinary case or two in the past, however, Congress has been willing to share such powers in ways that were consistent with effective negotiation. A hint of how this might be done is offered by the country's experience in negotiating a series of codes under the powers of the 1974 Trade Act. On most of the subjects covered by the codes, other countries were already uneasy about U.S. behavior, past or prospective. Under the rather extraordinary provisions of the Trade Act of 1974, members of the Congress tied their own hands in advance, undertaking to consider expeditiously and without amendment the results of any subsequent negotiation authorized under the Act. In return, selected congressmen took major substantive roles in planning and negotiating the codes. These codes, completed in 1979, covered the use of subsidies, government procurement practices, customs formalities, and a number of other subjects.

If Congress can be drawn into the negotiating process by some such formula as that in the 1974 Trade Act, there will still be the problem of curbing the power of individual firms to force restrictive measures on the U.S. government. In the case of trade policy, the power of the individual firm to compel government action stems from its ability under the law to initiate proceedings on the contention that imports were doing serious injury to the firm, or that a country was engaging in "unfair practices," or that goods were coming into the United States with the help of foreign subsidies or through dumping. Those powers must be curtailed if the U.S. negotiating position is to be strenthened. Yet it seems improbable that any of the required changes in U.S. law and practice will be adopted unless a considerable proportion of U.S. business is persuaded that the changes are desirable.

At the moment, the U.S. industries that see themselves as under the gun of foreign competition are bigger and more important than in the past. At the same time, the overall stake of U.S. business in reducing international barriers is also larger than ever before by a very considerable margin. In the past, U.S. business organizations identified with a specific industry have almost always directed their efforts in the field of trade toward restriction. Such organizations have done very little to institutionalize their interest in widening access to foreign markets. That lopsided emphasis has been understandable enough. Even though exports may be substantial and getting more so, the U.S. market is even more important for most U.S. firms. Besides, the U.S. government's efforts to liberalize trade in the past have taken place mainly through GATT tariff negotiations; these have been operations on so gargantuan a scale that the influence of individual firms or industries has generally been quite limited. For the most part, therefore, trade associations and

Washington representatives have proven their worth to their constituents not by seeking to open foreign markets but by seeking to close the U.S. market.

A critical question is whether trade negotiations that take place among smaller groups of countries, that cover narrower targets and more specific practices, and that are undertaken on a more frequent basis will be seen by U.S. industries as offering a greater opportunity for opening up foreign markets of specific interest to them. The same question could also be asked of U.S. labor unions, albeit with less optimism over the prospects of an affirmative answer. The answer to that question may depend in part on how effective the new agreements promise to be.

Improving enforcement

One of the critical questions in the formulation of international agreements is deciding how firmly to frame the commitments and how strongly to build the machinery for enforcement. In different international settings, the decisions of governments on this score have wandered all over the spectrum, producing agreements from vaguely formulated "codes of conduct" to the treaty provisions of the European Economic Community. When placed on that spectrum, GATT proves to be one of the more ambitious international agreements, relatively specific in some of its commitments and backed up by the threat of authorized retaliation against wrongdoers.

Still, GATT has always been a paper tiger, disappointing in its ability to compel adherence to its provisions. This has been partly because of the equivocal character of the U.S. role in the organization. GATT has been an organization subscribed to by the U.S. executive, not by the U.S. government, so that Congress has not felt bound by its strictures.

There is room for debate whether under any circumstances an international organization can reasonably be expected to exercise sufficient influence to restrain the action of the U.S. Congress on a subject with as much domestic sensitivity as that of import and export trade restrictions.[40] Still, there are various indications that Congress would respect trade commitments that it had had a direct hand in developing. For instance, Congress has rarely if ever altered any tariff rates that the President negotiated under the explicit authority granted to him in trade legislation; but it has readily enacted legislation that violated the GATT's general provisions—provisions that Congress regards as having been negotiated solely by the executive branch. It remains to be seen if Congress will also feel bound to honor the various GATT codes negotiated in 1979, such as those on government procurement and subsidy practices, which were negotiated explicitly with its advice and consent.

In any event, if Congress could be linked more directly to the negotiation of international trade agreements of the sort contemplated here, the possibility of developing a more effective international system of enforcement might be improved. The GATT system of adjudicating international trade disputes has not been wholly without success; but its limitations have been painfully obvious. The ineffectual character of the GATT's efforts has contrasted, for instance, with the respect that members of the EEC accord to the decisions of their own Court of Justice; the difference suggests that where the public good to be nurtured is sufficiently important to the countries concerned, effective international enforcement is not altogether out of the question. In the new network of agreements outlined here, it may be that some segment of the network could be linked to a process of enforcement that offers more hope than the present GATT pattern.

Reprise

It does not take long to realize that the case of the GATT is illustrative of a fundamental problem in the management of international relations which extends far beyond trade policy. Nations are no longer very manageable as economic units. Their external economic links have become vital to their national existence; and those economic links lie beyond their control to manage, except jointly with other nations. The problem is seen just as vividly in monetary and countercyclical economic policies as in trade.

This is a lesson that the United States finds more difficult to assimilate than most other industrialized countries do. One reason is that the external sector of the U.S. economy, until very recently, was of so little importance to the country. But that is hardly a sufficient explanation. Like a few other aberrant countries, including notably Japan, the United States embraces some values and institutions that are especially resistant to the fashioning of strong international regimes.

One such value is the strong American preference for the diffusion of governmental power and the extensive use of checks and balances. That preference means that the U.S. head of state, the President, will ordinarily prove incapable of speaking for the country on matters that greatly involve the domestic economy.

Another value that clashes with the development of effective international regimes is the distinctive U.S. view of the appropriate role of government, a view that balks at the selective intervention of the public sector in the management of the economy. That view is proving to be a formidable restraint on action at this stage. The stresses that are created by the growth of international economic links are highly selective in their effects: They are favoring managers over workers, aircraft over automobiles, agriculture over steel. And it is especially difficult for the United States to contemplate the selective national measures that might ease the adaptation process, whether taken unilaterally or in concert with other countries.

The result is that proposals which offer some slight chance of bridging the economic differences between countries at the present time, such as those suggested here, almost always seem radical in U.S. eyes, perhaps too radical for serious consideration. In the case of trade policy, however, the obvious alternatives are so bleak and so lacking in promise that the U.S. government may feel it has no choice but to seize the nettle.

Notes

[1]Barbara Hinckley, *The Seniority System in Congress* (Bloomington, Ind.: University of Indiana Press, 1977), p. 41.

[2]These points are developed in somewhat more detail in Raymond Vernon, "International Trade Policy in the 1980s: Prospects and Problems," *International Studies Quarterly*, vol. 26, no. 4, December 1982, pp. 483–510.

[3]William Diebold, Jr., "The End of the I.T.O.," *Essays in International Finance*, no. 16, October 1952, Princeton University, Princeton, N.J.

[4]Bela Balassa, "The United States in the World Economy," in Christian Stoffäes (ed.), *The Political Economy of the United States* (New York: North–Holland Publishing, 1983), p. 448.

[5]"Trade Act of 1974," Public Law 93-618, 93rd. Cong., H.R. 10710, Sec. 301.

[6]William Cline, *Exports of Manufacturers from Developing Countries: Performance and Prospects for Market Access*, Brookings Institution, Washington, D.C., 1982.

[7]See for instance John E. Rielly (ed.), "American Public Opinion and U.S. Foreign Policy 1983," Chicago Council on Foreign Relations, 1983, p. 24; also Council on Foreign Relations, "New Directions in U.S. Foreign Policy," New York, 1981, pp. 6–7.

[8]Balassa, "The United States in the World Economy," p. 451.

[9]The role of state-owned enterprises in western Europe is described in Raymond Vernon and Yair Aharoni, *State-Owned Enterprise in the Western Economies* (London: Croom Helm, 1981).

[10]S. J. Anjaria and others, *Developments in International Trade Policy*, International Monetary Fund Occasional Paper no. 16, November 1982, pp. 14–62.

[11]The Japanese and European approaches are summarized in "The Mercantilist Challenge to the Liberal International Trade Order," Joint Economic Committee, 97th Cong., second session, G.P.O., Washington, 1982, prepared by John Zysman and Stephen S. Cohen.

[12]Chalmers Johnson, *MITI and the Japanese Miracle: The Growth of Industrial Policy, 1925–1975* (Stanford, CA: Stanford University Press, 1982), pp. 83–156.

[13]Michael Borrus, James Millstein, and John Zysman, *International Competition in Advanced Industrial Sectors: Trade and Development in the Semiconductor Industry*, prepared for Joint Economic Committee, 97th Cong., 2nd. Sess., G.P.O., Washington, 1982.

[14]See for instance *Report of the Japan–United States Economic Relations Group*, January 1981, Washington and Tokyo, U.S. Government Printing Office, p. x.

[15]Harry W. Strachan, *Family and Other Business Groups in Economic Development* (New York: Praeger Publishers, 1976), pp. 34–39.

[16]Isaiah Frank, "The 'Graduation' Issue for LDCs," *Journal of World Trade Law*, vol. 13, 1979, pp. 289–302.

[17]General Agreement on Tariffs and Trade, Article XVII. See also Ivan Bernier, "State Trading and the GATT," in M. S. Kostecki (ed.), *State Trading in International Markets* (London: Macmillan Press, 1982), pp. 245–60.

[18]For a description of the leading cartels of the period, see Ervin Hexner, *International Cartels* (Chapel Hill: University of North Carolina Press, 1946).

[19]For a description of trade restrictions during this period, see W. S. Woytinsky and E. S. Woytinsky, *World Commerce and Governments: Trends and Outlooks* (New York: The Twentieth Century Fund, 1955), pp. 252–64, 267–78, 293–95.

[20]The evidence is summarized in my *Storm Over the Multinationals* (Cambridge, MA: Harvard University Press, 1977), pp. 73–82.

[21]Summarized in G. K. Helleiner, "Intra-Firm Trade and the Developing Countries: An Assessment of the Data," in Robin Murray (ed.), *Multinationals Beyond the Market* (New York: John Wiley and Co., 1981), pp. 31–55. Using a more relaxed definition of "foreign affiliate," according to other data summarized there, the import figure would be much higher, exceeding one-half of U.S. imports.

[22]A start in that direction is found in Mark Casson, "Multinationals and Intermediate Product Trade: A Computable Model," Discussion Paper no. 70, January 1983, Department of Economics, University of Reading, England. But the most comprehensive survey to date of the economic theory relating to the multinational enterprise, Richard E. Caves, *Multinational Enterprise and Economic Analysis* (Cambridge, England: Cambridge University Press, 1982), does not mention the subject.

[23]David J. Goldsbrough, "International Trade of Multinational Corporations and Its Responsiveness to Changes in Aggregate Demand and Relative Prices," International Monetary Fund, *Staff Papers*, vol. 28, no. 3 (September 1981), pp. 573–99.

[24]For strong statistical evidence on the point, see Raymond Vernon and William Davidson, "Foreign Production of Technology-Intensive Products by U.S.-Based Multinational Enterprises," Report to the National Science Foundation, no. P.B. 80 148636, January 1979, pp. 3–5.

[25]The supportive evidence on follow-the-leader behavior is summarized in Richard E. Caves, *Multinational Enterprise and Economic Analysis*, pp. 97–99, along with some minor dissents. For an exploration of the effects of this behavior on location and trade, see Raymond Vernon, "The Location of Economic Activity," in John H. Dunning (ed.), *Economic Analysis and the Multinational Enterprise* (London: George Allen and Unwin, 1974), pp. 96–97.

[26]Elhanen Helpman, "Increasing Returns, Imperfect Markets, and Trade Theory," Harvard Institute for Economic Research, Discussion Paper 921, October 1982.

[27]*Incentives and Performance Requirements for Foreign Direct Investments in Selected Countries*, U.S. Department of Commerce, Industry and Trade Administration, G.P.O., Washington, D.C., 1978. See also U.S. Labor–Industry Coalition for International Trade, *Performance Requirements: A Study of the Incidence and Impact of Trade Related Performance Requirements, and an Analysis of International Law*, Washington, D.C., March 1981, pp. 5–7.

[28]For data on the growth of exports of manufactured goods in Third World countries during the 1970s see *Development Co-operation: 1980 Review*, Paris, November 1980, p. 77. For evidence of the expanding role of U.S.-owned subsidiaries in such exports see Robert E. Lipsey, "Recent Trends in U.S. Trade and Investment," Working Paper no. 1009, National Bureau of Economic Research, Cambridge, MA, October 1982, p. 36.

[29]Raymond Vernon, *Two Hungry Giants* (Cambridge, MA: Harvard University Press, 1983), pp. 32, 39, 55.

[30]The data on this subject, though fragmentary, clearly reflect the trend. See for instance Leroy P. Jones and Edward S. Mason, "Role of Economic Factors . . ." in Leroy P. Jones (ed.), *Public Enterprises in Less-Developed Countries* (Cambridge, England: Cambridge University Press, 1982), pp. 17–47; also John R. Freeman, "International Economic Relations and the Politics of Mixed Economies," Working paper, MIT, Cambridge, MA, presented at Rio de Janeiro, August 9, 1982, pp. 1–4.

[31]See for instance M. M. Kostecki (ed.), *State Trading in International Markets* (London: Macmillan Press, 1982).

[32]Leroy P. Jones and Edward S. Mason, "Role of Economic Factors . . . ," p. 21.

[33]These transactions and others are cited in "Countertrade and Merban Corporation," Harvard Business School Case 0-383-116, 1983, prepared by David B. Yoffie.

[34]See *East–West Trade: Recent Developments in Countertrade*, OECD, Paris, October 1981; also *Analysis of Recent Trends in U.S. Countertrade*, USITC Publication 1237, U.S. International Trade Commission, Washington, D.C., 1982.

[35]In Samuel Brittan, "A Very Painful World Adjustment," *Foreign Affairs*, vol. 61, no. 3, Decem-

ber 1982, p. 546, reference is made without attribution to an estimate that in 1980, 40 percent of world trade was "managed."

[36]See Morris Goldstein and Mohsin S. Khan, "The Supply and Demand for Exports: A Simultaneous Approach," *The Review of Economics and Statistics,* vol. 60, no. 2 (May 1978), pp. 275–86; Irving B. Kravis and Robert E. Lipsey, "Prices and Market Shares in the International Machinery Trade," *The Review of Economics and Statistics,* vol. 64, no. 1 (February 1982), pp. 110–16; Jacques R. Artus and Susana C. Sosa, "Relative Price Effects on Export Performance: The Case of Nonelectrical Machinery," *Staff Papers,* International Monetary Fund, vol. 25, no. 1 (March 1978), pp. 25–47.

[37]For background on the governments' approach to the steel industry problem see Edward S. Florkoski, "Policy Responses for the World Steel Industry in the 1980s," *Steel in the 80s* (Paris: Organization for Economic Co-operation and Development, 1980), pp. 154–67.

[38]A thoughtful set of proposals that in general are based on such an approach is contained in C. Fred Bergsten and William R. Cline, *Trade Policy in the 1980s,* Institute for International Economics, Washington, D.C., November 1982.

[39]Such possibilities are especially present in the operation of Secs. 201 and 301 of the Trade Act of 1974. For a proposal to use Sec. 301 in its present form as a means of opening up foreign markets, see Bart S. Fisher and Ralph G. Steinhardt III, "Section 301 of the Trade Act of 1974," *Law and Policy in International Business,* vol. 14, no. 3, 1982, pp. 569–690.

[40]See for instance Robert O. Keohane, "International Agencies and the Art of the Possible: The Case of the IEA," *Journal of Policy Analysis and Management,* vol. 1, no. 4, Summer 1982, pp. 469–81, who argues for the inherent limitations in the power of international agencies.

2

Technology's effects on international trade: A look ahead

The main themes

In economics, technology is the catch-all category, the causal factor that defies easy definition. Identifying the role of technological change in international trade in the 1980s, therefore, turns out to be a tricky assignment, with ill-defined borders. In this paper, I have been obliged to draw such borders; but my choices cannot easily be defended. All one can say is that the borders as drawn include some powerful forces that promise to have major consequences during the 1980s. In substance, I offer the following propositions in the pages that follow.

The continued technological change promises to increase the availability and reduce the relative cost of channels by which technical information is communicated across international borders. That prospect could prove to be the most important single factor in shaping the international trade patterns of the 1980s. By reducing the cost and increasing the availability of information about sources and markets, it could sustain or even enlarge the margin by which the growth of international trade has exceeded the growth of world product in recent decades.

The 1980s, however, promise to be a period in which economic growth is slower than in decades past and threats of protectionism are more frequent. That prospect must be considered together with the fact that the relative cost of moving goods across international borders, when compared with the relative cost of transmitting information, is likely to rise. That shift in relative prices suggests the possibility that technical information and technical training will be substituted for the shipment of goods. Such a trend need not reduce the flow of foreign direct investment but it could reduce the level of international trade.

The prospect of slower growth and increasing protectionist threats suggests another trade-reducing possibility. Innovations in the advanced indus-

Reprinted with permission of the publisher from *Emerging Technologies: Consequences for Economic Growth, Structural Change, and Employment*, Herbert Giersch (ed.), Tubinger, Germany: Institut für Weltwirtschaft an der Universität Kiel, 1982.

trialized countries during the 1980s may lay greater stress on cost-reducing changes and lesser stress on the satisfaction of new wants associated with rising levels of income. This shift in emphasis seems likely to reduce both international trade and direct investment.

Another trade-reducing possibility is suggested by the fact that over the past few decades the national economic environments of the various advanced industrialized countries have grown more nearly alike in patterns of cost and of demand. As a result, the innovations induced in these environments will more closely resemble one another. Hence, trade between them based upon gaps in technology will be reduced although the effects on direct investment may well be indeterminate.

Finally, because more nations have acquired the requisite technological capabilities, innovations in the future will not be as geographically concentrated as in the past. Innovations originating within developing countries will generate some new opportunities for trade and investment among such countries based upon gaps in technology. But gaps of this sort will not last for long in any given product; the competitive advantages that they provide will rapidly be eaten away by the diffusion of the associated technology in the importing country.

Obviously, none of these propositions is self-evident, and it remains for the discussion below to present some of the evidence that supports them. More difficult than providing evidence for the existence of these technologically based trends in estimating the weights that each is likely to have in determining the future trade patterns. Beyond that there will also be the problem of estimating the power of other forces, less directly related to technological change, that will be operating in the 1980s to determine the patterns of international trade: among others, monetary factors, movements of population, war, the weather, and changes in demand. These factors, although partially independent of the technological variable, will ultimately affect that variable as well, with added effects on international trade. The observations that follow, therefore, should be seen as defining an agenda rather than providing the definitive projection with regard to the effects of technology.

Information as a stimulant to trade

We are on safe ground in asserting that during the 1980s there is likely to be a continued increase in the speed and efficiency of transmitting information across international borders.[1] It is a small step from that proposition to the assertion that these developments could stimulate the growth of foreign trade and foreign investment by reducing the special uncertainty, risk, and transaction costs that are associated with international transactions.

As a part of this general development, several more specific trends are worth mentioning. One such trend is the propensity of some firms to move toward the design and manufacture of world models for their products, especially in the fields of automobiles, electronic devices, and machinery (see Doz, 1980; *Automotive News,* 1979, p. 9). Not all firms in a given product line have been eager to exploit such possibilities; some have seen advantages in continuing to adapt their products to the distinctive requirements of each national market (see Doz, 1978). But in most industries, a few leaders could be found that were pursuing the world-model strategy.

The reasons for the seeming trend to world models are clear. The homogenization of consumer tastes and the globalization of industrial technologies, stimulated and facilitated by improved communication, have made such universal models feasible. At the same time, their development generates new opportunities for economies in design and in the manufacture of intermediates and components, not heretofore available to the manufacturing firms. In shifting to world models, however, many firms have been conscious of the need to avoid concentrating their production facilities in a small number of countries. Aware of the desire of most countries for exports, these firms have sought to bolster their position in foreign countries by situating the production of components or intermediates in a number of different countries and engaging in cross-hauling between the countries. To the extent that this tendency becomes stronger in the 1980s, it could contribute to an increase in foreign trade.

Still another type of international trade that could grow in the 1980s is that involving custom-made products or items with swiftly changing specifications. One of the significant limitations on such trade in the past has been the inability of entrepreneurs located in some national markets to communicate their plans, preferences, modifications, and queries to distant production points swiftly enough and accurately enough to ensure that the product would eventually be delivered in timely fashion and in accordance with specifications. Time has been of the essence in products with swiftly changing styles, while accuracy and responsiveness have been of the essence for custom-made products. Both categories could contribute significantly to the growth of foreign trade in the future.

Information as a substitute for trade

The expectation that information flows may prove to be an important substitute for trade in the 1980s, as we shall shortly see, is heightened by the expectation that the 1980s may prove to be a period in which economic growth is slow and threats of protectionism are common. But the expectation of substitution is based on a number of secular factors as well, which may be expected to operate even if growth is not slow in the 1980s.

Improving the channels

One such secular factor is the cost of communication, relative to transportation. That relative cost has been declining, and the tendency promises to continue during the 1980s as the availability of communication channels keeps growing. Evidence of the decline in costs is found in sharp reductions over the past few decades in the price of long-distance telephoning as well as declines in the cost of computer use and computer transmission.[2]

Of course, the communication of technological information as an alternative for trade depends on various factors other than the mere cost and availability of the communication channels themselves. Sources of such information must exist, as must receptors capable of searching out and applying the information. Evidence that both are increasing with some rapidity reinforces the expectation that they will be more extensively used.

One shred of such evidence is the fact that foreigners now make up a considerable part of the student bodies in schools of engineering and science located in the advanced industrialized countries. In the United States, for instance, in the years from 1970 to 1974, foreign students received 20.5 percent of all doctoral degrees conferred in the science and engineering fields (National Research Council, 1978, p. 47). In Europe in the 1970s nearly 50 percent of the university students in science and engineering were of foreign (although not necessarily of non-European) origin (UNESCO, 1976, Table 6). With foreign-trained scientists and engineers now stationed in considerable numbers over the face of the globe, foreign circulation of technical journals has never been higher, either in absolute or in relative terms.[3] Participation in international scientific congresses shows a similar trend. In the 1960–62 period, there were twenty-three such congresses with 33,100 participants; but in the 1975-77 period, fifty-two such congresses were noted with 59,700 participants (see National Science Board, 1979, p. 169). The consequences of this acceleration in the international exchange of information are sometimes evident in spectacular form such as the exploding of nuclear devices in India and China (see for instance *New York Times*, 1964; 1974).

Other data that suggest the acceleration in the international movement of technology are the figures on patents granted by various countries to foreign inventors. These figures are not altogether unambiguous in their meaning. The principal motivation of inventors in patenting outside their own countries is to ensure that others do not appropriate and apply the inventions in foreign markets that the inventors hope to exploit. Any such market can be supplied by the foreign inventor by way of exports; but it may also be supplied through a foreign subsidiary or by the licensing of an independent user in the foreign country. In any event, in the decades following World War II, measured both in absolute and in relative terms, the number of such foreign-owned patents rose rapidly in practically all countries. By the 1970s, most European countries were issuing a majority of their patents to foreigners; even in the United States, about one-third of the patents issued were going to foreign inventors.[4]

Sources and users of technical information

The international market for technological information is an amorphous entity, difficult to describe or measure. Still, however it may be defined, there can be no doubt that it has grown enormously in recent decades, with substantial increases in both the sources and the users of such information. Increasing similarities in the industry mix of different countries may be one reason for the expanded flow of information.[5] The effects of that trend in stimulating an international flow of technology have yet to be studied; but as a starting proposition, it seems reasonable to assume that these similarities are increasing both the needs and the proclivities of national industries for absorbing technologies generated in other countries.

Closely related to the growing similarities in industrial structure has been the proliferation in the number of firms in world markets that have mastered the technology of any given industrial line. Until World War II, in most industries with high technological content, the leading firms were organized in restrictive trading arrangements. Dupont, IG-Farben, and Imperial Chemicals dominated the world of chemicals; Merck, Bayer, Ciba, and a few others the area of pharmaceuticals; General Electric, Allgemeine Elektrizitäts-Gesellschaft, Thomson–Huston, and Tokyo Shibaura the field of electrical machinery; and so on. Restrictive agreements between them were sufficient to divide national markets for considerable periods of time (see for instance Hexner, 1946). It is a matter for debate whether these cartels tended to stimulate the international exchange of technology by freeing their participants from the fear of arming their prospective competitors, or whether the cartels tended to dampen technological diffusion by reducing the incentives for change. The judgment of most U.S. scholars was with the dampening hypothesis (for a representative view, see Edwards, 1976, pp. 32–41).

Today, however, areas of technology that are dominated by only three or four firms are rare. In many high-technology industries, to be sure, the number of firms found in any one country has declined through mergers, and this trend has created the widespread impression that the world's high-technology industries have become more concentrated in structure. But in many product lines the merger trend has been more than offset by the increasing capacity of firms to make effective offerings of their technology or of their products in foreign markets (for more details, see Vernon, 1977). As a result, the number of seemingly independent sources of technology in most high-technology industries also appears to have grown. This development in turn increases the probability that prospective independent licenses will find a source for the technology they require.[6]

There is a possibility, to be sure, that the increase in the number of seemingly independent sources of technology in world markets is no more than an interim stage, to be followed eventually by mergers on a world scale and much tighter world oligopolies. Here and there, indeed, one sees evidence of such a possibility: firms in the automobile, electronics, and aluminum industries among others form joint ventures across international borders (for discussions of the possibility, see Cotta, 1978, pp. 25–31). But it would take a considerable movement in that direction during the 1980s to offset the liberalizing effects of the opposite trend of recent decades.

The multinational enterprise

The idea that the transmission of information may become a substitute for trade, however, is suggested as much by the growth and spread of multinational enterprises as by the development of an international market for technology.

The multinational enterprise has been an important transmission belt for technological information, largely because of its ability to avoid certain obstacles that typically beset the prospective licensor and licensee who are doing business at arm's length. When independent parties are involved in efforts to arrange a transfer of technology, they ordinarily encounter special difficulties in arranging the transfer. As long as the technology is undisclosed or untested, the prospective buyer finds it difficult to assess its value. The buyer's uncertainties as to the price to be paid for the technology are matched by those of the seller. For one thing, market prices are not much of a guide. It is true that rival offerings of technology commonly occur; but each such offering usually embodies some distinct differences that make comparative pricing difficult. Moreover, the prospective seller cannot easily be guided by cost. In the sale of technology, marginal cost is generally close to zero. Opportunity cost may provide a guide, provided the seller is in a position to estimate the extent to which the buyer's use of the technology will limit the seller's opportunities in the future. That estimate, however, requires the seller to guess at the buyer's future effectiveness, as well as the buyer's dependability in honoring the constraints imposed by the license; and estimates of that kind are notoriously weak.

These difficulties are usually avoided, however, when the proposed transfer of technology is between the affiliates of a multinational enterprise. In that case the technology's contents are known, and the opportunity costs are of reduced importance or no importance at all; at the same time, most of the moral hazards associated with arm's-length transactions disappear.[7] The essential question then is whether the interests of the multinational enterprise as a whole would be served by a transfer between two affiliates in the system.

Several different kinds of studies indicate how multinational enterprises have been responding to that question. One group of studies seeks to answer the question: What type of enterprises show the highest propensity to establish producing subsidiaries in foreign countries? It has been demonstrated for firms in the advanced industrialized countries, for instance, that those in industries which engage in research-intensive activities have a higher propensity to develop a multinational structure than do firms in other activities (see J.E.S. Parker, 1978). Moreover, a recent study of fifty-seven U.S.-based multinational enterprises also has established the fact that a high proportion of the innovations introduced by them in their U.S. plants have been transferred soon thereafter for production in foreign sites.[8] Of the fifty-seven parent firms, those with a relatively high level of R&D expenditure made such transfers both more rapidly and more extensively than those with a relatively low level, suggesting that some proportion of the transfers do involve significant technological content. The same study provided some relevant details regarding 406 commercially significant innovations introduced in the period from 1945 to 1975. Of these 406 innovations, 35 percent were being produced in foreign subsidiaries within ten years of their U.S. introduction. Even more important in the present context, however, is the consistency of the evidence that the speed of such transfers has been steadily accelerating. Table 1 provides a picture of the speed-up in the thirty years between 1945 and 1975. (Not shown in the table is the persistent growth in the geographical spread of such transfers as well.)

Table 1. Transfers of 406 innovations by 57 U.S.-based multinational enterprises to their foreign manufacturing subsidiaries, classified by period of U.S. introduction, 1945–1975

		Percentage transferred abroad, by number of years between U.S. introduction and initial transfer				
Period of U.S. introduction	Number of innovations	same year or 1 year after	2 or 3 years after	4 or 5 years after	6 to 9 years after	10 or more years after
1945	34	8.8	14.7	2.9	11.1	45.3
1946–1950	79	11.4	15.2	10.1	14.1	39.3
1951–1955	57	7.0	5.3	15.8	25.4	32.5
1956–1960	75	16.0	21.3	16.0	20.0	18.7
1961–1965	63	26.9	17.5	14.3	7.9	8.1
1966–1970	64	28.2	17.2	12.5	6.2	n.a.
1971–1975	34	38.2	26.2	n.a.	n.a.	n.a.
Total	406	18.7	16.3	11.6	14.3	20.2

n.a. = not applicable.

Source: Vernon, Davidson (1979).

The same study offers a variety of indications that the propensity to transfer speedily and widely is closely related to the prior experience of the transferring firm, presumably reflecting a decline in the perceived costs and risks of successive transfers. The link shows up in a number of different contexts. Firms with a high proportion of exports transferred more rapidly and more extensively than those with a low proportion; firms with several product lines transferred more rapidly in the principal product lines than in ancillary lines; firms with many prior transfers moved more rapidly than those with few, and more rapidly to countries to which many previous transfers had been made than to countries in which the firm had less transfer experience. In short, the propensity to transfer appears to be a ratcheted response, growing as it goes.

All this may appear at first like persuasive evidence for the proposition that as multinational enterprises establish themselves abroad the tendency is to substitute information for trade. Yet insofar as past studies shed any light on the subject, they tell a more complex story—a story which on balance suggests that the creation and spread of multinational enterprise in the past may have stimulated international trade more than the opposite (see for instance Horst, 1979; Lipsey, Weiss, 1976; Stobaugh, 1976). How to reconcile these studies with the expectation that the transfer of information will tend to displace trade in the 1980s?

My conjecture is that the trade-stimulating or trade-repressing effects of multinational enterprises will depend in part on the extent to which future growth is based on the creation and introduction of new product lines, as distinguished from the expansion of sales in existing lines. As firms create new products and introduce them for production abroad, the early effects are commonly to stimulate international trade. In the early stages of production, foreign subsidiaries typically import components and intermediate products extensively from affiliates; uncertainties about the size of the market and about the reliability of domestic sources of supply tend to limit the depth of the commitment to local sources. But fragmentary evidence suggests that with the increasing maturity of the existing product lines in the subsidiaries, the commitment to local sources increases.[9] If that is the case, then with a slowdown in the flow of new product lines, the trade-creating effects of the subsidiaries' presence can be expected to decline while the trade-suppressing effects grow.[10]

What do we actually know about the role of new product lines in the expansion of multinational enterprises? Data on that point are available only for U.S.-based multinational enterprises, and only up to 1975. These indicate that the introduction of subsidiaries and product lines in foreign countries dropped off somewhat in the 1970s as compared with the decade of the 1960s (see Vernon, Davidson, 1979, p. 10). Nevertheless, the growth of these subsidiaries has been continuing at a rapid rate. During the 1970s, despite widespread nationalizations, the book value and the capital expenditures of foreign affiliates of U.S. enterprises paused only briefly in their swift upward climb.[11] With the decline in the introduction of new product lines, that growth must have been based in increasing degree on the existing lines.

One added group of studies of the behavior of multinational enterprises points to the same conclusion. This is a study based on a subset of thirty-two of the fifty-seven multinational enterprises referred to earlier, a subset that provided data with respect to both their foreign subsidiaries and their foreign licensees. Like the group of fifty-seven, the subset of thirty-two exhibited an accelerating tendency to transfer the production of new products to overseas subsidiaries. At the same time, however, as a given product line matured, transfers to independent licensees in that product line grew even faster than transfers to subsidiaries (Davidson, McFetridge, 1980).[12] On the secure assumption that independent licensees have lesser resort to the use of foreign components and intermediates than do foreign-owned subsidiaries, this finding adds still further to the trade-repressing picture.

The emphasis on cost-reducing technologies

In addition to the relative improvement in channels of communication, another major factor that may restrain the growth of foreign trade is an increased emphasis on cost-reducing innovations. In the years since 1945, the technological activities of industry in the advanced industrialized countries have been divided between efforts to reduce the costs or improve the quality of existing products, and efforts to satisfy new wants associated with rising levels of income.[13] As Table 2 suggests, firms in the advanced industrialized countries have been active in both categories. Of the 1,866 innovations covered in the table, 1,277 fell in factor-saving categories and the rest probably were addressed to new wants.

Table 2. Perceived advantages of innovations introduced in the United States, Europe, and Japan, 1945–1974

Perceived advantage	United States		Europe[a]		Japan	
	no.	percent	no.	percent	no.	percent
Labor saving	331	40.1	120	12.7	6	6.4
Material saving	175	21.2	444	46.9	32	34.1
Capital saving	58	7.0	104	11.0	7	7.4
Novel function	106	12.8	83	8.8	12	12.8
Safety	50	6.1	60	6.3	7	7.4
Other	106	12.8	135	14.3	30	31.9
Total	826	100.0	946	100.0	94	100.0

[a]Including Britain.

Source: Adapted from Davidson (1976, p. 214).

It is a familiar conclusion based on various pieces of empirical research that the nature of the innovation is influenced by the threats and opportunities that are present in the environment in which the innovator operates (see Vernon, 1977, pp. 41–46). The data in Table 2, in fact, are consistent with that hypothesis, showing among other things that U.S.-based firms emphasized labor-saving innovations and innovations with new functions more heavily than did their rivals in Europe and Japan. During most of that period, U.S. labor costs were higher than those of Europe and Japan, both in absolute terms and in relation to the raw material and capital costs that prevailed in the respective areas. At the same time, U.S. incomes per head were also at unprecedented new heights, running somewhat ahead of Europe and Japan.

As suggested earlier, however, the 1980s could well prove to be a period of slow growth in the advanced industrialized countries, a trend that would exacerbate the concern over the competition in manufactured goods emanating from developing countries. The competition generating the highest degree of concern presumably would be in products of a kind that had a considerable quantity of labor content. More strictly, perhaps, they would be goods whose labor-cost content was substantial relative to the price elasticity of demand for the individual firm's offerings; men's underwear more than high-style dresses, steel bars more than ceremonial masks.

That kind of concern among U.S. manufacturers is, of course, nothing new. In situations of this sort in the past, producers in the advanced industrialized countries have commonly responded by setting up production facilities in the developing countries in order to avail themselves of the low-cost labor in those areas. If the 1980s prove to be a period of slow growth and strong competition from developing countries, however, the risk of import restrictions will be somewhat higher than in the past. Uncertain whether import restrictions might be imposed, manufacturers may be more inclined to look for a technological response that can be applied in the home country. Labor-saving innovation is one of the obvious lines of response to the problem.

Innovations through labor-saving devices is hardly a new development, as the data in Table 2 attest. Characteristically, however, labor-saving innovations have created the basis for an increase in exports, rather than the basis for fending off imports; the linkage between innovation and exports, common in most countries, has been particularly strong for the United States (see for instance Wells, 1972). On the other hand, labor-saving innovation for defensive purposes has been common enough in Europe and Japan, and has not been altogether unknown even among producers in the United States. In the electronics industry during the 1960s, producers in the advanced industrialized countries had first responded to sharply increased competition in semiconductors by creating new plants throughout Japan and Southeast Asia (see Moxon, 1974). But during the 1970s, new advances in the manufacture and testing of microcircuits succeeded in greatly reducing the need for unskilled labor, a development that led to the reestablishment of plants in the United States (see Mojumdar, 1980).

In the 1980s, the swiftly growing robotics industry will lay the basis for a much more pervasive response of this sort (see for instance Groover, 1980; also Lipinski, Skinner, 1980). One reason for the anticipated response is the size of the expected savings. In a two-shift operation, for instance, the full cost of operating and amortizing a basic robot is said to run at only $3,000 to $7,000 per shift-year (calculated from Lipinski, Skinner, 1980, p. 36). At least as important, however, is the fact that the robot is distinguished from most labor-saving devices in the past by a critical characteristic, namely, by its effects on the scale of operations. The introduction of new labor-saving machinery in the past has usually required the firm to increase its scale of output and even to shift from batch processes to continuous processes (for a summary of the literature, see Gold, 1981). Robots, on the other hand, can typically be introduced on a one-worker-for-one-machine basis, without altering the scale or process of the plant.

The fact that the robot can typically be introduced without expanding scale or altering process has two implications for the competitive position of the firm. First, an important barrier that has commonly impeded the introduction of labor-saving devices in the past is avoided by the robot, namely, the uncertainties associated with introducing new processes and expanding production capacity. Second, in introducing the robot, the firm need not give up the flexibility in output mix that ordinarily goes with batch processes and short runs; indeed, the flexibility of the robot is sometimes greater than that of the labor it displaces. Such flexibility has been notoriously lacking in the large enterprises of the advanced industrialized countries in the past and has commonly been said to represent a source of their competitive weakness.[14]

These observations on the relation of technology to trade in the 1980s point to a larger generalization. Technological advances may be trade-creating in some circumstances, as in the first stages posited by the product cycle hypothesis (see Vernon, 1966); or they may be trade-suppressing, as in the conditions cited here. That possibility has of course been realized for a long time; for instance, exporters of natural products such as rubber have been constantly concerned that their products may eventually be displaced by synthetics. The possibility emerges again as we turn to the changing situation in trade between the advanced industrialized countries.

Technology–gap trade among the advanced industrialized countries

The point has already been made that the introduction of new products could contribute to the growth of exports from the innovating country, but that eventually such trade is likely to be displaced by production at a foreign production site. The argument in this section is that the propensity for new products to generate such trade may be on the decline, because the technology gaps that establish the basis for such trade are likely to be shorter in duration and less powerful in the competitive advantage they provide.

Until only a few years ago, the differences in the economic environment of the United States, Europe, and Japan were substantial; and as the data in Table 2 suggest, these differences pushed the industrial innovations of the three areas in rather different directions. In consumer goods, U.S. businessmen had traditionally concentrated on satisfying—some would say on creating, then satisfying—new high-income wants. The Europeans and the Japanese on the other hand had paid much more attention to the adaptation of products for lower-income needs, including the trimming of costs and prices as well as the improvement of durability. In producer goods, U.S.

businessmen had concentrated on finding substitutes for their high-cost labor, whereas the others had displayed a greater relative interest in material-saving innovations. As a result of these disparities, most U.S. innovative effort found eventual expression in new products, while the Europeans and the Japanese appeared to be devoting a larger proportion of their innovative effort to improving their productive processes.

These differences go some way toward explaining the special importance that product-cycle trade has had in U.S. exports over the past few decades. During practically all of that period, the U.S. economy was tracking ahead of its competitors both in per-capita income and in the pattern of its relative factor costs, covering terrain that the other industrialized countries would traverse some years later. As incomes and labor costs rose in the other countries, the demand for products that had already been created in the United States also grew; these changes eventually produced a mass market, for instance, for the electric light bulb, central heating, civilian aircraft, the drip-dry shirt, the numerically controlled machine tool, and the TV dinner. And for a time, as long as U.S. firms retained a significant technological lead and as long as no single foreign market had yet generated a high level of demand, some of these new needs could be more efficiently supplied by exports from the United States than by production within the foreign market.

By 1975, however, it was evident that several changes had occurred.[15] For one thing, the U.S. economy no longer presented its businessmen with an environment that was very different in income levels or in factor cost configurations from the environments of Europe and Japan. By 1975, the huge differences in per-capita income between North America, the various European states, and Japan had been greatly narrowed. At the same time, relative factor costs in the three areas had converged; the U.S. economy was no longer an economy in which the cost of labor relative to raw materials was strikingly high by comparison with Europe and Japan. The increased American reliance on imported raw materials and imported energy, coupled with the increased incomes of Europe and Japan, had practically wiped out the differences in factor cost patterns in the three areas.

The economic environments of the three areas have converged in still another critical sense. The home markets that businessmen confront in the three areas are no longer grossly disparate in size. In Japan, a sustained period of extraordinary growth has brought the size of its domestic market from less than 5 percent of the U.S. market in 1950 to over 40 percent in 1980, while in Europe a combination of rapid growth plus the European Economic Community has created a European market that is about equal in size to that of the United States.

These changes have meant that U.S. businessmen have lost a critical lead that they for so long had enjoyed. They could no longer count on being stimulated or threatened by their national environment sooner than their European and Japanese competitors. Indeed, in some respects, the position had been reversed. Out of necessity, the Europeans and the Japanese— especially the Japanese—had gradually been learning over the years how to respond to the distant stimuli generated by the U.S. market; not many American firms, on the other hand, had yet learned how to pick up stimuli emanating from the distant markets of Europe and Japan. By the 1970s, therefore, the Japanese could analyze the U.S. market's potential for absorbing such new products as civilian-band radios and videotape recorders and could introduce these innovations directly into the U.S. market; but analogous U.S. achievements were not easy to find.

Another basic change affecting the position of the U.S. economy as an innovational source has to do with prevailing expectations in the advanced industrialized countries. After many decades in which businessmen and technicians had automatically assumed that incomes would grow and that labor costs would increase in relation to other costs, the prospects in the 1970s were abruptly changed. The expectation that per-capita incomes would continue to grow was widely questioned; at the same time, energy took the place of labor as the factor input whose costs were thought likely to rise most. Once again, the implications of this shift were threatening to the American position. All at once, the innovational propensities of the Europeans and the Japanese became more relevant to world markets. The tendency to emphasize energy-saving and material-saving innovations and the tendency to generate austere versions of U.S.-created consumer products gave the Europeans and Japanese a leg up over their American competitors.

A priori, these shifts should be discouraging to product-cycle exports from the United States, inasmuch as wholly new products should be less common in the U.S. export mix. The effects of these shifts on the export mix of Europe and Japan to the United States should be more equivocal, being particularly sensitive to the trade classification system used by the analyst; improved versions of trucks, steel mills, and home-heating equipment emanating from Europe and Japan could prove indistinguishable in the statistics from like products emanating from the United States, and thus could come to be classified as intra-industry trade. We shall have to wait on more systematic analyses of these trade trends before the strength of the hypothesized shift can be said to be adequately tested.

There is a risk, however, of overestimating both the likely size and the likely duration of the decline in the product-cycle exports of the United States. Some absolute differences in size will continue to exist in the internal markets of the United States when compared with those of Europe and Japan. These differences are especially apparent in some of the high-technology industries, such as computers and aircraft engines, industries in which European governments persist in maintaining distinctive national markets. The differences are apparent as well in other activities relating to defense, such as extra-terrestrial travel and communication, and advanced applications of the laser; in such activities, the U.S. military establishment is likely to provide a market whose size cannot be matched in other countries. Activities such as these will continue to generate product-cycle exports of some presently indeterminate amounts.

Moreover, one special advantage that Europe and Japan have discovered in recent years can be expected to be transitory. This is their innovational bias toward the conservation of materials and energy, based on past conditions prevailing in their respective home markets. Now that U.S. businessmen and technicians confront similar conditions in their home markets, it is to be presumed that they will adjust the direction of their innovations to match those of their foreign competitors.

In gauging the relative capacity of the Americans for technology-gap exports in the future, the unexcelled network of foreign subsidiaries and affiliates of U.S.-based multinational enterprises could conceivably afford a major advantage. Various pieces of research in organizational behavior have demonstrated that messages which originate within an organization are likely to be communicated to other parts of the organization more efficiently than messages originating from outside (see for instance Allen, 1977; also Arrow, 1974, p. 42). With their networks in place, the U.S.-based enterprises appear in a strong position to be stimulated by the challenges of foreign markets.

So far, however, there is not much evidence that this unique facility has been used in that way. On the contrary; where major initiatives are involved, the impressionistic evidence suggests that most U.S.-based multinational enterprises are typically wired for one-way transmission of information and command, namely, from the center to the periphery (see Vernon, 1979, p. 264). But that characteristic could easily be the rational by-product of a long period of product-cycle dominance. With that dominance gone, the existing networks could conceivably be redirected to scanning foreign markets and absorbing the technological stimuli of those markets.

One must be cautious, therefore, in the assumption that U.S. firms will lose much technological ground to their European and Japanese competitors; the ground will certainly shift, but the U.S. firms may still be left with a visible competitive edge. If such an edge remains, however, it will rest not only on technologies originating in the United States but also on technologies generated in other markets. In that case, the associated production would probably take place in various affiliates of the enterprise, and would therefore be reflected in product-cycle exports from a number of countries.

Technology-gap trade affecting the developing countries

Trade between Europe, North America, and Japan that is based on a technology gap may well decline because of the convergence in the economic environments of those countries; but there will still be considerable differences between the economic environment of those countries and the economic environment of the developing world. Accordingly, it is easy to picture a continuation of technology-gap trade between the two groups.

Moreover, among the developing countries themselves, a fairly clear pecking order is developing in levels of technological achievement, an order that is compatible with the idea of technology-gap trade among the developing countries themselves. Mexico, Brazil, India, Hong Kong, Singapore, and a few other countries are increasing their exports of goods whose manufacture is technologically demanding;[16] in some cases, these exports have been adapted to the conditions of developing countries, such adaptations giving them a competitive advantage over like exports from the countries that were the original source of the technology. At the same time, the enterprises of these newly industrializing countries are setting up subsidiaries and licensees in other developing countries which act as a conduit for their adapted technologies. All these streams will presumably expand in time.

It is worth noting, however, that this kind of technology-gap trade is threatened by an obvious fragility. As a rule, trade based on a technology gap is vulnerable to the possibility that enterprises in the importing country will eventually absorb the technology and displace the foreign seller. In this case, the possibility is increased by the fact that the products involved have already been adapted in some degree to the conditions of developing countries. Such adaptation commonly tends to make the products or processes concerned less complex, more labor-intensive when in use, and more suitable for production in short runs. With such modifications, there is a presumption that indigenous firms will find the technology gap narrowed and the interval of their technological dependence shortened. When the gap is overcome, the advantage of the firms from newly industrializing countries will be overcome.

The question of weighting

Numerous factors affect the flow of international trade; technological changes represent only one category among several. Even within that category, the possibilities are diverse. In this paper, for instance, we have identified a number of quite distinct possibilities, technological in nature, that could easily have measurable effects on the trade patterns of the 1980s.

The problem for the prognosticator, therefore, is a problem of weighting—weighting the effects of various non-technological factors against those that are technological in origin, and weighting the effects of the various technological factors against one another. There have been times when a few of these factors have been so powerful in the foreign trade of a given country as to outweigh the others; the dominance of technology-gap trade in the exports of the United States in the immediate postwar period was one such case. But there is no reason a priori why a few factors should dominate or why the important influences should operate in a common direction.

The question of weighting is all the more critical because some of the technological forces that operate in the 1980s will very likely be trade-creating rather than trade-repressing in their effects, pushing against the general trade-repressing tendencies outlined in this paper.

On the whole, however, the technological factors reviewed in this paper seem to be biased toward the suppression of trade, rather than to its expansion. The substitution of technological information for trade itself operates in that direction. So, too, does the possibility that enterprises in the advanced countries will be emphasizing defensive technologies rather than technologies that are associated with the expansion of aggregate demand. The possibility of a decline in technology-gap trade points in the same direction. Indeed, it may be that forces of this sort already are beginning to affect the patterns of international trade.[17] But the hypotheses and speculations in this paper will have to be exposed to extensive test and quantification before such conclusions can be drawn with any assurance.

Notes

[1]See *Communications News* (1981); *World Business Weekly* (1981); *Electronic News* (1979); E. Parker (1981); Gassmann (1978).

[2]See U.S. Bureau of the Census (1980, p. 585); *Business Week* (1979, pp.124 f.); *Mini-Micro Systems* (1979, p. 65).

[3]Based on interviews with publishers.

[4]For Europe, see World Intellectual Property Organization (1977); for U.S., see National Science Board (1979, p. 218).

[5]To date, most studies have focused on intra-industry trade rather than on similarities in national industry mix (see Giersch, 1979, Ch. 2). But the growth in intra-industry trade strongly implies that there have been increasing similarities in national industry mix.

[6]These generalizations are supported by the findings of Stobaugh (1968). Stobaugh's data, covering nine major chemicals, demonstrate that as the products matured there were marked increases in the number of licensors of independent licensees.

[7]For an exploration of the advantages of internalization, see for instance Williamson (1975, pp. 82–105); Buckley, Casson (1976, pp. 32–65); also Arrow (1974, p. 33 passim).

[8]The results of this study, together with definitions and qualifications, appear in Vernon, Davidson (1979).

[9]For descriptions of this process of increasing commitment to local sources, see Leroy (1976, pp. 82 f.); Bilkey (1970, p. 113); Baranson (1969, p. 26); de la Torre (1970, pp. 128 f.); and Quinn (1969, pp. 150, 155). Shifts to local sourcing are also significantly affected by local content requirements, as shown in Bennett, Sharpe (1979, pp. 177, 182 f.).

[10]In a counterfactual world in which multinational enterprise did not exist, the same decline would probably also occur, as firms in the importing country absorbed the technologies needed for producing components and intermediate products. The observation in the text, therefore, is independent of the multinational character of the enterprises involved.

[11]Capital expenditures in foreign subsidiaries by U.S.-based multinationals, when deflated by the implicit price deflator for U.S. fixed nonresidential investment, show declines in 1975 and 1976; but thereafter such expenditures resume their upward trend. Calculated from Whichard (1981, pp. 39, 51); Lowe (1981); U.S. Bureau of the Census (1980, pp. 479, 572).

[12]Essentially the same finding for another sample is reported in Mansfield, Romeo (1980, p. 739).

[13]There is a strong tendency in economic theory to try to reduce all innovation to cost-reducing phenomena, but the effort often strains the limits of plausibility. For an interesting interchange between Wassily Leontief and John Chipman on the subject, see Vernon (1970, pp. 95–127, 132–42).

[14]See for instance *Business Week* (1980b, pp. 68–70; 1980a, pp. 58, 121). For a discussion of problems in obtaining production flexibility see Skinner (1969, pp. 136–45); also Abernathy, Wayne (1974); Porter (1980, pp. 289 f.) and Scherer (1980, pp. 214 f.).

[15]The argument that follows is developed at greater length in Vernon (1979; 1980).

[16]The subject is being explored by L. T. Wells, Jr., and will appear shortly in book form. See also Sercovich (1981).

[17]See for instance Blackhurst, Tumlir (1980, p. 15). The study shows that in the later 1970s there was a rapid shrinkage in the number of percentage points by which world export growth in manufactures exceeded world production growth.

References

Abernathy, William J., and Kenneth Wayne. "Limits of the Learning Curve." *Harvard Business Review,* vol. 52, September–October 1974, pp. 109–19.

Allen, Thomas J. *Managing the Flow of Technology: Technology Transfer and the Dissemination of Technological Information within the R&D Organization.* Cambridge, Mass., 1977.

Arrow, Kenneth J. *The Limits of Organization.* New York, 1974.

Automotive News. "New Wave of Auto Internationalism." August 6, 1979, p. 9.

Baranson, Jack. *Automotive Industries in Developing Countries.* Washington, 1969.

Bennett, Douglas, and Kenneth E. Sharpe. "Transnational Corporations and the Political Economy of Export Promotion: The Case of the Mexican Automobile Industry." *International Organization,* vol. 33, Spring 1979, pp. 177–201.

Bilkey, Warren J. *Industrial Stimulation.* Lexington, 1970.

Blackhurst, Richard, and Jan Tumlir. "Trade Relations under Flexible Exchange Rates." GATT *Studies in International Trade,* no. 8, Geneva, 1980.

Buckley, Peter J., and Mark Casson. *The Future of the Multinational Enterprise.* London, 1976.

Business Week. "The Supergrowth in Memory Chips." New York, September 3, 1979. "The Reindustrialization of America." New York, June 30, 1980 (1980a). "Foreign Competition Stirs U.S. Toolmakers." New York, September 1, 1980 (1980b).

Communications News. "Satellite Fulfills Communications Requirements of Smaller Countries." Vol. 18, no. 3, March 1981.

Cotta, Alain. *La France et l'impératif mondial.* Paris, 1978.

Davidson, William H. "Patterns of Factor-Saving Innovation in the Industrialized World." *European Economic Review,* vol. 8, 1976, pp. 207–17.

Davidson, William H., and R. G. McFetridge. *International Technology Transfers and the Theory of the Firm.* 1980, unpublished.

Doz, Yves L. "Managing Manufacturing Rationalization within Multinational Companies." *Columbia Journal of World Business,* vol. 13, no. 3, 1978, pp. 82–94. "Strategic Management in Multinational Companies." *Sloan Management Review,* vol. 21, no. 2, 1980, pp. 27–46.

Edwards, Corwin D. *Economic and Political Aspects of International Cartels.* U.S. Senate, Committee on Military Affairs, 78th Congress, 2nd Session, Washington, 1944, repr. 1976.

Electronic News. "Intelsat Gearing to Handle Increased Com Demand." Vol. 25, November 26, 1979.

Gassmann, H. P. "Data Networks: New Information Intrastructure." *The* O.E.C.D. *Observer,* no. 95, November 1978, pp. 10–13.

Giersch, Herbert (ed.). *On the Economics of Intra-Industry Trade.* Symposium 1978. Tübingen, 1979.

Gold, Bela. "Changing Perspectives on Size, Scale, and Returns: An Interpretive

Survey." *Journal of Economic Literature*, vol. 19, March 1981, pp. 5–33.

Groover, Mikell P. "Industrial Robots: A Primer on the Present Technology." *Industrial Engineering*, vol. 12, November 1980, pp. 54–61.

Hexner, Ervin, with the collaboration of Adelaide Walters. *International Cartels*. London, 1946.

Horst, Thomas. *American Exports and Foreign Direct Investment*. Harvard Institute of Economic Research, Discussion Paper No. 362, May 1979.

Leroy, Georges. *Multinational Product Strategy: A Typology for Analysis of Worldwide Product Innovation and Diffusion*. New York, 1976.

Lipinski, T. E., and C. S. Skinner. "Robotics." *Outlook*, vol. 3, Fall–Winter 1980, pp. 35–39.

Lipsey, Robert E., and Merle Y. Weiss. *Exports and Foreign Investment in Manufacturing Industries*. National Bureau of Economic Research, Working Paper Series, no. 131, May 1976.

Lowe, Jeffrey H. "Capital Expenditures by Majority-Owned Foreign Affiliates of U.S. Companies, 1981." *Survey of Current Business*, vol. 61, March 1981, pp. 34–39.

Mansfield, Edwin, and Anthony Romeo. "Technology Transfer to Overseas Subsidiaries by U.S.-Based Firms." *The Quarterly Journal of Economics*, vol. 95, 1980, pp. 737–50.

Mini-Micro Systems. "Projecting Prices for Bubble Memories." Vol. 12, July 1979, p. 65.

Mojumdar, B. A. "Technology Transfers and International Competitiveness: The Case of Electronic Calculators." *Journal of International Business Studies*, vol. 11, Fall 1980, pp. 103–21.

Moxon, Richard W. "Offshore Production in the Less Developed Countries. A Case Study of Multinationality in the Electronics Industry." New York University, *The Bulletin*, July 1974, nos. 98–99.

National Research Council. *A Century of Doctorates*. Washington, 1978.

National Science Board. *Science Indicators 1978*. Washington, 1979.

New York Times. "A Top Chinese Scientist was Deported by U.S." October 17, 1964, sec. 1, p. 10.

"Canada Says India's Blast Violated Use of Atom Aid." May 21, 1974, sec. 1, p. 1.

Parker, Edwin. "Communications Satellites for Rural Service." *Telecommunications Policy Yearbook 1981*, 1981, pp. 191–248.

Parker, J. E. S. *The Economics of Innovation*, 2nd ed. London, 1978.

Porter, Michael. *Competitive Strategy: Techniques for Analyzing Industries and Competitors*. New York, 1980.

Quinn, James B. "Technology Transfers by Multinational Companies." *Harvard Business Review*, vol. 47, no. 6, 1969, pp. 147–61.

Scherer, Frederic M. *Industrial Market Structure and Economic Performance*. Chicago, 1980.

Sercovich, Francisco C. "Brazil as a Technology Exporter." Inter-American Development Bank, April 1981.

Skinner, C. Wickham. "Manufacturing: Missing Link in Corporate Strategy." *Harvard Business Review*, vol. 47, no. 3, 1969, pp. 136–45.

Stobaugh, Robert B. *The Product Life Cycle: U.S. Exports and International Investment*. Harvard University Dissertation, Boston, 1969.

Nine Investments Abroad and Their Impact at Home: Case Studies on Multina-

tional Enterprises and the u.s. Economy. Cambridge, Mass., 1976.

Torre, José de la. "Exports of Manufactured Goods from Developing Countries: Marketing Factors and the Role of Foreign Enterprise." Unpublished DBA thesis, Harvard Business School, 1970.

UNESCO. *Statistics of Students Abroad.* Paris, 1976.

U.S. Bureau of the Census. *Statistical Abstract of the United States: 1980.* Washington, 1980.

Vernon, Raymond. "International Investment and International Trade in the Product Cycle." *The Quarterly Journal of Economics*, vol. 80, May 1966, pp. 190–207.

(ed.). *The Technology Factor in International Trade.* A Conference of the Universities–National Bureau Committee for Economic Research held in October 1968, Universities–NBER Conference Series, 22, New York, 1970.

Storm over the Multinationals: The Real Issues. London, 1977.

"The Product-Cycle Hypothesis in a New International Environment." *Oxford Bulletin of Economics and Statistics*, vol. 41, 1979, pp. 255–67.

"Gone are the Cash Cows of Yesteryear." *Harvard Business Review*, vol. 58, 1980, pp. 150–55.

Vernon, Raymond, and W. H. Davidson. "Foreign Production of Technology-Intensive Products by U.S.-Based Multinational Enterprises." Report to the National Science Foundation, January 1979, Doc. No. PB 80 148638.

Wells, Louis T., Jr. (ed.). *The Product Life Cycle and International Trade.* Boston, 1972.

Whichard, Obie G. "Trends in the U.S. Direct Investment Position Abroad, 1950–79." *Survey of Current Business*, vol. 61, February 1981, pp. 39–56.

Williamson, Oliver E. *Markets and Hierarchies: Analysis and Antitrust Implications.* New York, 1975.

World Business Weekly. "Survey: Communications." Vol. 4, no. 22, June 8, 1981, pp. 29–32.

World Intellectual Property Organization. *Industrial Property, Statistics for 1975.* Geneva, 1977.

Part 2

International Investment

3
Sovereignty at Bay: Ten years after

The author of *Sovereignty at Bay,* musing in public about his opus after ten long years, faces one very special difficulty. Practically every reader remembers the title of the book; but scarcely anyone will accurately recall its contents. For after its publication, like Aspirin and Frigidaire, the label (but not the contents) became generic. Robert Gilpin identified a "Sovereignty at Bay model," subscribed to by visionaries devoted to the proposition that the nation-state was done for, finished off by the multinational enterprise.[1] Seymour J. Rubin lustily attacked the visionaries; Lincoln Gordon ably provided supporting fire; Fred Bergsten was only a step behind. Even Walter B. Wriston turned briefly from his labors at building one of the world's biggest banks to cast a few stones in the same general direction.

Meanwhile, the themes of *Sovereignty at Bay,* if they were ever learned, were half-forgotten in the heady pursuit of more vulnerable quarry. Only the author and a few of his more attentive students would remember the argument of his final chapter, which concluded somewhat lugubriously:

> The basic asymmetry between multinational enterprises and national governments [that is, the capacity of the enterprises to shift some of their activities from one location to another, as compared with the commitment of the government to a fixed piece of national turf] may be tolerable up to a point, but beyond that point there is a need to reestablish balance. . . . If this does not happen, some of the apocalyptic projections of the future of multinational enterprise will grow more plausible.

Roots of the multinationals

Because *Sovereignty at Bay* was one of the earlier works in a stream that would soon become a torrent, much of the book was devoted to chronicling and describing the phenomenal growth and spread of multinational enterprises. Interwoven in the history and the description, however, were inevitably some hypotheses about causes. Some of these, although still bearing a

Reprinted with permission of the publisher from *International Organization,* 35, 3, Summer 1981.

51

touch of novelty in 1971, seem hackneyed today—suggestive, I suppose, of their validity and durability. The increased efficiencies of communication and transportation, which had been reducing the costs of learning and the costs of control, were given appropriate credit as expeditors of the multinationalizing process. Oligopoly was recognized as a near-necessary condition for breeding multinational enterprises, a conclusion that simply reaffirmed a point made ten years earlier by Stephen Hymer.[2]

Two kinds of oligopoly that seemed particularly relevant in explaining the spectacular growth of U.S.-based multinational enterprises in the postwar period were expiored with special attention. (The subtitle of the book, after all, was "The Multinational Spread of *U.S.* Enterprise.") One was the oligopoly based upon the special technological capabilities of the participating firms, while the other was the oligopoly based on the sheer size and geographical spread of the operating firms concerned, as in the oil and metals industries. In that context, a number of hypotheses were elaborated, which later would be tested and retested in various contexts. The most widely known of these, particularly applicable to the technology-based oligopolies, came to be called the product-cycle hypothesis. I shall have more to say about that concept in a moment. But there were other propositions, which also were exposed to considerable testing in subsequent years, such as the follow-the-leader hypothesis.

These various concepts purporting to explain the growth and spread of multinational enterprises have stood up about as well as one could have hoped. The follow-the-leader hypothesis has been adequately confirmed in one or two solid studies.[3] As for the product-cycle hypothesis, there have been numerous confirming and elaborating studies,[4] as well as a few important qualifications, reservations, and demurrers.[5] On the whole, the concept seems to have had considerable utility in explaining past developments and predicting future ones.

However, what has changed—indeed, changed quite dramatically—is the applicability of the product-cycle hypothesis in explaining the present behavior and the likely future behavior of multinational enterprises based in the United States. As an explicator and predictor of U.S. performance, the product-cycle hypothesis had particular applicability to the conditions of, say, 1900 to 1970; this was a period in which the income levels of U.S. residents were higher than those in any other major market in the world, in which U.S. hourly labor costs were the highest in the world, and in which U.S. capital and raw materials were comparatively cheap. That set of unique conditions, it was posited, had been generating a stream of innovations on the part of U.S. firms responsive to their special environment. And as the income levels and relative labor costs in other countries tracked over the terrain previously traversed by the U.S. economy, U.S. innovations found a ready market in those other countries. These innovations were thought to provide a oligopolistic handhold that gave U.S. firms their dominant position in many markets of other countries.

But even as I went to press with *Sovereignty at Bay,* there were a few signs that the pattern might be losing its explanatory force for the United States. A section captioned "Toward Another Model" presented speculations about the consequences that might ensue as U.S. incomes and labor costs became more closely aligned with those of Europe and Japan. In that case, U.S.-based enterprises would no longer have the advantage of doing business in home markets under conditions that were precursors of those which eventually would appear in Europe and Japan. Accordingly, the innovational lead that the Americans had enjoyed in earlier decades could be expected to shrink.

I cannot say, however, that I had the prescience to realize how rapidly the factor cost configurations of the various national markets would be brought into alignment, speeded by the rise in raw material prices, by the increasing nominal cost of capital, and by the weakness of the U.S. dollar. In my speculation about the growth of European and Japanese investment in the United States, therefore, the tone was hypothetical; there was no sense of conviction that the trend would soon develop. Intellectually, readers were put on notice; glandularly, they were not forewarned.

It was only in the latter 1970s that the convergence in the factor costs of the principal exporting countries had developed sufficiently to prompt me to reappraise the relevance of the product-cycle concept as an explicator of U.S. behavior.[6] As a result of that reappraisal, I concluded that the product-cycle concept continued to have some utility, explaining some of the trade and investment patterns visible in various countries of the world; but its utility in explaining the behavior of the U.S. economy had measurably declined.

Effects of the multinationals

When *Sovereignty at Bay* was published in 1971, the advocates and the opponents of multinational enterprises were already locked in furious combat. Several dozen propositions about the consequences of the operations of these enterprises had been advanced by both sides. One of the objectives of *Sovereignty at Bay* was to test the leading propositions of the opponents with such data as could be mustered for the purpose.

The issues involved were too numerous and too diverse to be effectively reviewed here. At the time when *Sovereignty at Bay* was published, however, it seemed clear that both sides were grossly overreaching in their arguments; some cases were consistent with their sweeping hypotheses, some were not. Even more often, the asserted effects of the operations of these enterprises, whether benign or destructive, could not be supported by the evidence. The classic Scotch verdict—not proven—seemed more justified than any.[7]

By 1977, however, numerous researchers all over the globe had published a great many additional studies of the multinational enterprise. Some of these studies cast new light on the issues that had been dealt with tentatively in *Sovereignty at Bay*: typical of such issues, for instance, were those relating to the technological transfer activities of the multinationals. The piling up of such evidence moved me to publish a second book on multinational enterprises, which appeared under the title of *Storm over the Multinationals*.

The added evidence reviewed in that book went some way to confirm the fact that simpleminded propositions about the effects of multinational enterprises were as a rule highly vulnerable. On the basis of the new work, it was possible to speak with somewhat greater assurance about some of the economic and political effects of multinational enterprises; but those effects were not simple. The caution with which I had approached such questions as the balance-of-payment effects, income-distribution effects, and employment effects of multinational enterprises in *Sovereignty at Bay* seemed justified by the conclusions of *Storm over the Multinationals*. Generalizations on some points are possible; but they must be framed with due regard for the vast differences in the activities of the multinational enterprises. Numerous variables determine the economic effects of the operations of individual firms, including for instance, their innovative propensities and their marketing strategies. Both the uninhibited broadsides of writers such as Barnet and Müller and the more restrained generalizations of scholars such as Robert Gilpin suffer from this lack of differentiation.

Threats to the multinationals

With the acuity that goes with hindsight, I might better have entitled my 1971 volume *Everyone at Bay,* in the spirit of its closing lines. But there would be some overreaching in such a title; I could hardly claim to have foreseen the spate of expropriations and nationalizations of the foreign properties of the multinational enterprises that occurred during the first half of the 1970s. My chapter on the raw materials industries, in fact, was written in a tone of complacency that must have been insufferable at the time to some of the worried managers of the international oil companies. The mood of that portion of *Sovereignty at Bay* is captured in the final paragraph of the raw materials chapter:

> Strong initiatives on the part of the governments of less developed countries to control the key factors in the exploitation of their raw materials are likely to continue. And as they do, the capacity of host governments to participate in management will increase. It is another question, however, whether the host countries will feel that their 'dependence' on the outside world has declined simply because their management role has increased. As long as the product requires marketing in foreign countries, dependence will presumably continue in some form.

Yet, as one reads the raw materials chapter with the hindsight of 1981, the argument for the increasing vulnerability of the oil companies is all there, carefully laid out under a heading dubbed "The Obsolescing Bargain." The oil-exporting countries, it was pointed out, no longer needed the oil companies as a source of capital; their taxes on the sale of crude oil were already providing a sense of independence on that score. Nor did the oil-exporting countries any longer feel shut away from access to the technology of oil exploration and exploitation; too many independent companies were bidding to provide that information and expertise. In the latter 1960s, the principal remaining source of vulnerability of the oil-exporting countries and the principal source of strength of the international oil companies was the companies' control over the channels of distribution.

What prevented me (and practically every other scholar at the time) from fully applying the lesson of the obsolescing bargain to the situation of the oil companies was our inability to appreciate that a profound shift in the supply–demand balance was taking place, which might reduce the need of the oil-exporting countries to rely on the marketing channels of the multinationals. Most of us took the chronic weakness of oil prices during most of the 1960s to mean that supplies were more than adequate. Accordingly, it was hard to contemplate that demand would soon grow so rapidly that the oil-exporting countries would feel free to cut their umbilical cord to the international oil marketers. Nor do I think that many analysts in the oil industry itself were aware of the dangers of an oil shortage at the time.

To be sure, by the latter 1960s, some thoughtful executives in the industry were deeply worried. Some were expressing alarm over the deterioration in their negotiating position, as Libya and other countries gleefully used the independent oil companies to leapfrog over one another in a continuous escalation of their terms. But so far as I know, nobody in the 1960s foresaw the great bulge in the demand for Middle East oil that would soon undermine the majors' position.

Looking back at the text of *Sovereignty at Bay* after ten years, I am frustrated by the fact that the analysis comes so close, while not quite drawing the key conclusion. The weakening of the international oil oligopoly during the 1960s is accurately enough portrayed; the appearance of the state-owned oil companies and the emergence of OPEC are appropriately chronicled. But it was not until a year or two later that I fully appreciated the key role played by the independent oil companies in weakening the position of the majors and in strengthening the negotiating hand of the oil-exporting countries. And it was a few years after that before it became evident that the period of weakening prices in the 1960s had been masking a shift in the supply–demand balance.[8]

No two persons will draw quite the same lessons from the experiences of the oil market during the 1960s and 1970s. The lessons that I draw, I suspect, will not be widely shared.

One of these is that any five-year projection of the supply–demand balance for world oil is inherently subject to gross margins of error, margins so large as to encompass both the possibilities of painful shortage and the possibilities of disconcerting glut. The importers of oil, of course, are justified in acting as if they expected an acute shortage, simply because the consequences of a shortage are so much more painful than those of a glut; prudence, therefore, demands that we act as if a shortage were inevitable. But whenever I review the various projections of supply and demand in the world oil market that are being circulated today, I am persuaded that today's projections are just as vulnerable as those of fifteen years ago.

A second conclusion, based as much on other raw materials as on oil, is that the concept of the obsolescing bargain does have a certain utility in analyzing the changing position of the multinational enterprises engaged in any given product line. Accordingly, wherever the conventional wisdom of any market turns from an expectation of shortage to an expectation of glut, I anticipate in accordance with the obsolescing bargain concept that the position of the multinationals will be somewhat strengthened.

And a third conclusion is that, for phenomena as complex as the role of multinational enterprises, scholars may be as vulnerable as laymen in speculating about the shape of future events. If scholars do their work well, their predictive models may be better crafted than those of the layman—more fully articulated, internally more consistent, more firmly based on earlier events. But scholars, perhaps more than laymen, must live with the risk of neglecting or overlooking what may prove to be the controlling factor that determines those future events.

The problem of multiple jurisdiction

As the title *Sovereignty at Bay* suggests, the book was much more concerned with the interests and attitudes of governments than with the aspirations and fears of the multinational enterprises themselves. Insofar as the title was justified, the justification rested on the validity of three propositions: that most governments, reluctant to give up the advantages they perceive in inviting multinational enterprises into their jurisdictions, will continue to permit a significant part of their national output to be accounted for by the affiliates of such enterprises; that the policies of any affiliate of a multinational enterprise are bound to reflect in some degree the global interests of the multinational network as a whole, and hence can never respond singlemindedly to the requirements of any one national jurisdiction; and that the network of any multinational enterprise cannot escape serving as a conduit through which sovereign states exert an influence on the economies of other sovereign states.

After ten years, I see no strong reason to modify any of these propositions. During those ten years, some foreign affiliates of multinational enterprises were nationalized, while other foreign affiliates were liquidated or sold on the initiative of their parents. But, all told, these withdrawals were only a minor fraction of the new advances that multinational enterprises were making all over the globe. In 1979 alone, for instance, U.S.-based multinationals increased their foreign investment stake by $25 billion, of which $18 billion was in developed nations and $7 billion in developing countries. Indicative of the resilience of such enterprises to the buffeting they had received only a few years earlier was the fact that nearly $4 billion of the $7 billion build-up in developing countries was in the form of fresh money remitted by the U.S. parent, while the remainder consisted of the reinvestment of past earnings.

To be sure, there have been some changes during these ten years in the identity of the world's multinational enterprises. Those based in Europe and Japan have gained a little in importance relative to those based in the United States. Moreover, the world is beginning to see enterprises of this sort that have their home bases in Spain, Brazil, Mexico, India, Hong Kong, and other such locations.[9] But these changes simply add to the sense of vitality and durability of the multinational structures.

At the same time as there have been some marginal shifts in the identity of the multinational enterprises, there have also been marginal alterations in their business practices. U.S.-based enterprises as a class have grown somewhat less reluctant to enter into joint ventures with foreign partners than had been the case in earlier decades. Multinational enterprises from all countries have proved increasingly flexible in taking on management contracts, acceding to so-called fade-out clauses, entering into partnership with state-owned enterprises, and involving themselves in other ambiguous arrangements.

The proliferation of such arrangements raises the question whether the various affiliates of multinational enterprises continue to respond to a common global strategy and to draw on a common pool of resources to the same degree as in the past. The available signs point in many directions. Some observers insist, for instance, that when the subsidiaries of multinational enterprises enter into partnerships with state-owned enterprises, they often manage to increase the degree of their control in the local market rather than to diminish it.[10] The increased prevalence of joint ventures and other ambiguous arrangements suggests that the authority of the parents of the multinational networks over their affiliates is being diluted. But other developments seem to be pushing in the opposite direction. For instance, there has been a constant improvement of software and communication systems for the command and control of distant subsidiaries, a trend that places new tools in the hands of headquarters staffs. In addition, the multinational enterprises in some industries, including automobiles and machinery, have been pushing toward the development of world models for their products, a trend that requires increasing integration among the production units of the multinational enterprises concerned.

I anticipate that, in the end, the generalizations will be exceedingly complex. We may well find, for instance, that in many firms control over the finance and production functions has increased, even though the physical location of these activities has been dispersed. We may find, too, that in the selection of business strategies some multinational enterprises have opted to develop maximum flexibility and adaptation toward local conditions while others in the same general product line have opted for the maximum exploitation of global economies of scale.[11]

Still, I would be surprised if on balance multinational enterprises had greatly reduced the degree of central control over their global operations. For insofar as multinational enterprises have any inherent advantages over national enterprises, those advantages must rest on the multinational character of their operations, that is to say, on their multinational strategies and their common resources. Multinational enterprises, therefore, may have no real option; by giving up their multinational advantages, they may be destroying the basis for their competitive survival.

If multinational enterprises continue to pursue some elements of a global strategy and to draw on a common pool of financial and human resources, then the problems of multiple jurisdiction will continue to play a considerable role in their operations. At times, affiliates of such enterprises will be marching to the tunes of a distant trumpet being played from the ministries of another government or from the offices of another affiliate. Some cases of this sort are well enough known; the occasional forays of the U.S. government's antitrust division in attempting to break up international restrictive business practices that affect the U.S. economy have received particular attention. But these well-publicized cases are on the whole less important than those that are less transparent. Multinational enterprises with an affiliate in Germany, for instance, will have to entertain the demand of German unions for more output and more jobs, expressed through the hard-won rights of *Mitbestimmungsrecht*; responding to such pressures, the parent enterprise may be obliged to reduce the the the output of its Brazilian subsidiary, thereby exporting Germany's unemployment to Brazil. For multinational enterprises with an affiliate in Mexico, the insistence of the Mexican government that the local affiliates must import less and export more may lower the output of these networks in Barcelona and Detroit. And India's insistence that foreign parents should charge their Indian subsidiaries nothing for their technology could lower the income taxes and export earnings of the parents of those subsidiaries operating from their bases in other countries.

Since 1971, the problems of multiple jurisdiction generated by the existence of multinational enterprises have grown. More than ever before, governments are telling the affiliates of multinational enterprises what they must do or not do as the price for their right to continue in business. As the world's overt trade barriers have diminished, these commands have become a principal weapon of many governments for pursuing a beggar-my-neighbor economic policy. Accordingly, when I published *Storm over the Multinationals* in 1977, I developed the jurisdictional issue in considerably greater depth than in *Sovereignty at Bay*. But the second book was launched under the shadow of the first; whatever the second book had to say, it was commonly assumed, had already been said in *Sovereignty at Bay*.[12] The heightened emphasis on the jurisdictional issue in the second book, however, seems appropriate to current circumstances.

So far, jurisdictional conflicts have been contained by the fact that not all governments are systematically playing the beggar-my-neighbor game, and by the added fact that multinational enterprises have a strong incentive for muffling the effects of the game within their respective networks. My assumption has been, however, that the number of players and the intensity of the game will gradually increase. In that case, if multinationals are to avoid being the instruments through which national jurisdictions are brought into repeated conflict, the sovereign states must be willing to agree on some international regime that can reconcile their interests. Any such agreed regime would presumably do two things: it would specify the rights of multinational enterprises in and their obligations to the international community; and it would delineate and restrain the jurisdictional reach of the governments involved, wherever an important clash in national jurisdictions might be involved.

Since 1971, there have been dozens of projects for achieving international agreement with respect to the multinational enterprises. Most of them have included proposals to restrain the multinational enterprises in various ways; a few have proposed some guarantees for the multinational enterprises as well; but until very recently, most have neglected or avoided the pervasive problem of conflicting jurisdictions.

Indeed, some of the international actions and international proposals that have been launched since 1971 have seemed carefully designed to preserve the contradictions rather than to resolve them. The member countries of the OECD, for instance, have adopted a set of declarations proposing that each government should grant national treatment to foreign-owned subsidiaries in its jurisdiction, thus acknowledging the national character of such subsidiaries; at the same time, these governments have paid obeisance to the applicability of international law in the treatment of foreign-owned subsidiaries, whether or not such treatment conformed with national law, thus acknowledging the foreign element in the subsidiaries' identity. In a similar obfuscating mood, the developing countries, as a rule, have simultaneously insisted upon two propositions: that foreign-owned subsidiaries, being nationals of the host country, were subject to all the obligations of any other national; but that such subsidiaries, as the property of foreigners, could rightly be denied the privileges of other nationals.

I can find only one functional area in which governments have made a serious effort to reduce the conflicts or resolve the ambiguities that go with the operations of multinational enterprises.[13] The industrialized countries have managed to develop a rather extraordinary web of bilateral agreements among themselves that deal with conflicts in the application of national tax laws. Where such laws seemed to be biting twice into the same morsel of profit, governments have agreed on a division of the fare. Why governments have moved to solve the jurisdictional conflict in this field but not in others is an interesting question. Perhaps it was because, in the case of taxation, the multinational enterprises themselves had a major stake in seeing to the consummation of the necessary agreements.

So far, the world has managed to stagger on without effectively addressing the many facets of jurisdictional conflict and without directly acknowledging the inescapable fact that the behavior of any affiliate is unavoidably influenced by external forces. The various sovereigns direct their commands at a unit in the multinational network; the unit responds as it can, giving ground to the sovereign if it must; the other units in the network adjust their operations to the new situation, spreading the adjustment cost through the global system. As long as there is no overt acknowledgment of what is going on all the parties can pretend that the jurisdiction of each sovereign is unimpaired.

The future of the multinationals

Lincoln Gordon would agree, I think, that his one-time proposal for a tract entitled "Multinationals at Bay" would not arouse much interest today. The tumult of the 1970s over the multinational issue has lost some of its stridence. The incidence of nationalizations in developing countries has declined dramatically. Kolko, Williams, Barnet, and Müller seem somehow out of date, while the various scholars of *dependista* theory seem a bit jaded. The U.N. Centre on Transnational Corporations has developed a businesslike air, more akin to the professionalism of the Securities and Exchange Commission than to the prosecuting fervor of the Church Committee.

In retrospect, it appears that the numerous threats to the multinationals that were launched in the 1970s—the spate of nationalizations, the codes of conduct, the U.S. legislation against bribery, the demands and resolutions of the General Assembly—were fueled by a number of different elements. One of these was a manifestation of a much larger phenomenon, namely a pervasive revulsion in much of world against the effects of industrialization, against the symbols of entrenched authority, and against the impersonal tyranny of big bureaucracies. Embodying all of these unfortunate attributes and burdened besides by the sin of being foreign, multinationals were inevitably a prime target of the period. A second factor that explained the attack on the multinationals, however, was the inexorable operation of the obsolescing bargain; as shortages appeared in various raw materials, multinationals lost the bargaining power that their marketing capabilities normally afforded.

The revulsion against bigness and bureaucracy that exploded in the late 1960s and early 1970s may have been ephemeral; but the process of the obsolescing bargain is not. From time to time, in the future as in the past, one foreign-owned industry or another will lose its defensive capabilities; and when that happens, some of those enterprises will be nationalized, joining the plantations, the power plants, and the oil wells that have been taken over by governments in years past.

But the future is no simple extrapolation of the past. Some forces seem to be speeding up the process by which the bargain between governments and foreign investors becomes obsolescent. At the same time, other forces seem to be diffusing and defusing the underlying hostility that gives the process of the obsolescing bargain some of its motive force.

The expectation that agreements between governments and investors will be breached even more quickly in the future than in the past is based on various factors. In reappraising their bargaining positions, governments are better informed and better equipped than they have ever been. Perhaps more to the point, opposition forces that are bent on embarrassing their governments have more information and more expertise. Besides, according to evidence presented in *Storm over the Multinationals*, governments are finding that in many lines of industry they have an increasing number of options for securing the capital, technology, or access to markets they require. Accordingly, although multinational enterprises taken as a class continue to account for a considerable share—even an increasing share—of the economies of most countries, individual multinationals have nothing like the bargaining position they sometimes held in the past.

Yet governments seem constrained to use their increased bargaining power in more ambiguous ways. Instead of outright nationalization, they seem disposed to settle for other arrangements, such as arrangements that make a gift of some of the equity to favored members of the local private sector or to an expanding state-owned enterprise, or contracts that allow the multinationals to manage their properties without formal ownership. Perhaps the increase in ambiguous arrangements is due to the decline in the power of the individual multinational enterprises; being less threatening, they are less to be feared. Perhaps, too, the ambiguity is due to the increasing power of the private industrialists in some countries who prefer to squeeze the foreign goose rather than to strangle it;[14] or to the unceasing struggle of the managers of some state-owned enterprises to weaken the control of their national ministries.[15] It may even be that the hostility of some countries to the multinational enterprises of others is being blunted by the growth of their own homegrown brand of multinationals.

Whatever the precise causes may be, I anticipate that business organizations with the attributes of multinational enterprises will not decline and may well grow in their relative importance in the world economy. Anticipating that development, I am brought back to what I regard as the central question. How do the sovereign states propose to deal with the fact that so many of their enterprises are conduits through which other sovereigns exert their influence?

Perhaps they will not deal with the problem at all. There is plenty of evidence for the proposition that nations are capable of tolerating ambiguity on a massive scale for long periods of time. And there are numerous cases in which scholars, peering into the future, have mistaken bogey men for monsters. But I am betting that the problem is real and its emergence as a political issue close at hand. In any event, it is this problem that invests the title *Sovereignty at Bay* with its real meaning.

Notes

[1]Robert Gilpin, *U.S. Power and the Multinational Corporation* (New York: Basic Books, 1975), p. 220. Be it said to Gilpin's credit that although he ascribes the phrase to me, he does not list me as one who subscribes to the model. Others, however, have been less careful in their attributions.

[2]S. H. Hymer, *The International Operations of National Firms: A Study of Direct Foreign Investment* (Cambridge: MIT Press, 1976), based on his 1960 thesis.

[3]See F. T. Knickerbocker, *Oligopolistic Reaction and Multinational Enterprise* (Boston: Harvard Business School, 1973). His subsequent work on the hypothesis, unfortunately never fully published, went even further in confirming its utility.

[4]The number of such studies by now is very large. Illustrations are: L. T. Wells Jr., ed., *The Product Life Cycle and International Trade* (Boston: Harvard Business School, 1972); J. M. Finger, "A New View of the Product Cycle Theory," *Weltwirtschaftliches Archiv* 3, 1, 1975; M. P. Claudon, *International Trade and Technology: Models of Dynamic Comparative Advantage* (Washington, D.C.: University Press of America, 1977); Seev Hirsch, "The Product Cycle Model of International Trade," *Oxford Bulletin of Economics and Statistics* 37, 4 (November 1975), pp. 305–17; Hiroki and Yoshi Tsumuri, "A Bayesian Test of the Product Life Cycle Hypothesis as Applied to the U.S. Demand for Color-TV Sets," *International Economic Review*, October 1980, pp. 581–95.

[5]For instance: W. B. Walker, *Industrial Innovation and International Trading Performance* (Brighton, England: Sussex University, 1976); and Kiyoshi Kojima, "A Macroeconomic Theory of Foreign Direct Investment," *Hitotsubashi Journal of Economics* 14, 1 (June 1973).

[6]Raymond Vernon, "The Product Cycle Hypothesis in a New International Environment," *Oxford Bulletin of Economics and Statistics* 41, 4 (November 1979), pp. 255–67; and Raymond Vernon, "Gone are the Cash Cows of Yesteryear," *Harvard Business Review*, November 1980, pp. 150–55.

[7]For a review of many of these issues and a well-balanced critical appraisal of my views, see T. J. Biersteker, *Distortion or Development? Contending Perspectives on the Multinational Corporation* (Cambridge: MIT Press, 1979).

[8]Those points are developed at some length in two later publications. See Edith Penrose, "The Development of Crisis," in Raymond Vernon, ed., *The Oil Crisis* (New York: W. W. Norton, 1976), pp. 39–57; and Raymond Vernon, *Storm over the Multinationals* (Cambridge: Harvard University Press, 1977), pp. 83–87.

[9]A book on this subject will shortly appear under the authorship of Louis T. Wells, Jr.

[10]This is a subject that is just beginning to be researched. For an analysis covering Brazil, see Peter Evans, *Dependent Development: The Alliance of Multinational, State, and Local Capital in Brazil* (Princeton: Princeton University Press, 1979).

[11]Patterns of this sort are being researched by Yves Doz at INSEAD, Fontainebleau.

[12]See for instance, C. P. Kindleberger's review of *Storm over the Multinationals* in *Business History Review* 51, 4 (Winter 1977), pp. 95–97.

[13]Nevertheless, there are glimmerings of some additional action eventually on the subject. Reference to the problem appears in a composite working draft of a code of conduct for multinational enterprises, prepared for consideration of an intergovernmental working group under the sponsorship of the U.N. Centre on Transnational Corporations; see Working Paper No. 7, November 1979, paragraph 56. But the prospects for action are not very great.

[14]See for instance Evans, *Dependent Development*.

[15]Yair Aharoni, "Managerial Discretion," in Aharoni and Vernon, eds., *State-Owned Enterprises in the Western Economies* (London: Croom Helm, 1980).

4

Organizational and institutional responses to international risk

My mandate is to deal with the organizational and institutional responses that foreign direct investors have developed in their efforts to deal with international risk. The boundaries of that mandate are not very sharp.

One problem in drawing the boundaries is to define institutional response. By implication, some responses to risk exist that are thought to be separable from institutions; I have had some difficulty in picturing what those responses may be. I hope I shall be forgiven therefore if, from time to time, this discussion wanders beyond the organizational and institutional dimensions into areas that some would regard as economics.

A second problem in drawing the boundaries of this chapter has been to decide which of the many different types of international risk could usefully be addressed. In one respect, the decision on boundaries is easy. This chapter is concerned both with the risks that arise from the investor's ignorance and with the risks that arise from random error. In other respects, however, the boundaries are less easily drawn. Direct investment internalizes a set of international transactions that otherwise would be conducted at arm's length with independent buyers and sellers, and one major purpose of this internalization is to avoid some of the risks that exist when dealing with such independent parties. Accordingly, a direct investment commonly represents a response to certain kinds of international risk. An exploration of this phenomenon seems almost indispensable as a preliminary for exploring the responses to the risks associated with the direct investment itself.

Direct investment as a response to risk

The desire of managers to internalize certain transactions as a way of avoiding risk is a phenomenon that is encountered in domestic as well as

This paper profited considerably from the reactions of Brian Levy and L. T. Wells, Jr. to an earlier draft. Stephen Baral and Jack Dulberger assisted in the research.

Reprinted with permission of the publisher from *Managing International Risk: Essays Commissioned in Honor of the Centenary of the Wharton School, University of Pennsylvania*, Richard J. Herring (ed.), Cambridge, England: Cambridge University Press, 1983.

international settings, occurring most commonly when the number of firms in the market is small, when the surrounding environment is uncertain, and when the representations or commitments of the parties concerned are difficult to verify or enforce.[1] Nevertheless, numerous writers have observed that the internalization of certain transactions is likely to be especially important as a risk-reducing measure when the transactions straddle national boundaries (Caves 1973, p. 117, Buckley and Casson 1976, pp. 33–59, Casson 1979, pp. 45–62).

Establishing the foreign subsidiary

The drive for internalization, it is generally agreed, stems from the firm's view that there is some marked imperfection in the market for the product or service concerned, a view that stimulates the firm to create its own internal market and to accept the narrowing of choice that is commonly involved in that decision. Two types of industry in which such internalization is particularly common are the exploitation and processing of oil and minerals and the development and application of advanced technologies. Not surprisingly, therefore, these industries prove to be heavily overrepresented among foreign direct investors (Vernon 1971, pp. 4–17, United Nations 1978, pp. 45–46).

In the case of raw materials, large indivisible costs and high barriers to entry keep the numbers small. The entry barriers are created in part by the difficulties of achieving agreements with host countries on the terms of entry and in part by the size of the capital commitment needed to finance the extensive developmental work and infrastructure that go with the launching of large raw material projects.[2] Meanwhile, the dispersed location of overseas operations and the tenuous links among the participating parties create uncertainties and hamper fact finding to a degree that is especially acute.[3]

The entry barriers that are typical in the technologically advanced industries are of a different kind, but are commonly no less formidable. They are created by the fact that a considerable expenditure of money and time is commonly required while firms accumulate the necessary knowledge, skills, and reputation that may be necessary for the effective marketing of the product. Like the raw material industries, too, the high-technology firms typically incur developmental costs in the launching of new businesses that are relatively high when compared with the actual costs of production (Freeman 1974, p. 126, Hochmuth 1974, pp. 145–69, Brock 1975, pp. 27–41, 57, Measday 1977, pp. 266–68, Parker 1978, pp. 112–19). After beginning production, individual firms characteristically experience a persistent decline in production costs that appears to be a function of their accumulated production, a fact that represents an added deterrent for newcomers (Hartley 1965, pp. 122–28, Abernathy and Wayne 1974, pp. 74–141, Conley 1981).

Both the firms in the raw materials industries and those in the high-technology industries, then, begin with large sunk costs on which they hope for a return. The importance of reducing uncertainties in industries that have such a cost structure has been sufficiently explored. Firms in such industries place more than the usual stress on avoiding variations in output, inasmuch as small variations in output can generate disproportionate swings in their return on investment. But there are some differences in the two types of industry as well.

In the raw materials industries, the firm's problem of securing a stable return on its sunk commitments is exacerbated by the fact that a relatively high proportion of its operating costs is also fixed. Variations in output generate disproportionate fluctuations in net profits. Accordingly, a persistent objective in the strategy of firms in these industries has been to find ways of stabilizing the demand for their output and to safeguard themselves against interruptions in the supply of needed materials.

On the demand side, of course, the price elasticities of aggregate demand for an industrial raw material such as iron ore or crude oil are typically fairly low, especially in the short run. Individual firms, however, face a demand curve that is considerably more elastic than that of the industry as a whole, so that the risk of losing customers in a declining market can be fairly substantial. Insurance, in this case, takes the form of acquiring tied customers who do not have the option to shift their sources of supply.

On the supply side, the integrating imperative is just as obvious. Because of high barriers to entry, the suppliers are usually limited in number. For the processor that does not control its own source of supply, any large increase in price or outright interruption in supply, whatever its cause, can be dangerous. But a particularly disastrous type of price increase or supply interruption is one initiated by a supplier that also controls processing facilities downstream, that is, a supplier that is also a competitor in the processor's market.[4] In that case, the supplier may be found taking over the customers of its unintegrated rival.

Events in the oil industry over the past decade have provided occasional illustrations of such a risk turned into reality. At various times during the 1970s, as multinational sellers were faced with reduced supplies of crude oil, they cut off practically all of the unintegrated processors that they had previously supplied, while continuing to supply their own downstream processing facilities and distributors (Commission of the European Communities 1975, pp. 144–45, OECD 1977a, pp. 23, 25, Levy 1982).

Nevertheless, the fact that such risks exist in the oligopolistic industries that process raw materials does not mean the risks always lead to vertical integration. Such integration has a cost. It requires an investment of capital, which has to be justified in terms of expected yield or an equivalent reduction in risk. Moreover, the capital investment entails risks of its own, which may outweigh the risk-reducing aspects of the investment. Besides, the flexibility of the integrated units is reduced as compared with unintegrated competitors; in times of easy supply, the integrated entity is inhibited from turning to cheaper sources of supply and in times of tight supply is restrained from abandoning its captive markets for markets in which profit margins are higher.

Why then is vertical integration so pervasive in the raw material industries? The strong tendency toward vertical integration seems to derive from the fact that, in an industry that is only partially integrated, there are always some participants who see themselves especially exposed by that fact; as long as a partial state of integration exists in the industry, a new move toward vertical integration on the part of any firm withdraws a source of supply or a potential customer from the market and thereby increases the perceived risks of those that remain unintegrated. Accordingly, any movement toward integration seems likely to snowball, until all the actors have rendered themselves equally invulnerable by integration.[5] If the markets concerned are global in scope—a situation that clearly exists for oil and aluminum and exists in part for copper and steel—the interactions between the firms will also be global in their reach.

The high-technology industries, as I have already suggested, face a set of risks that differs somewhat from the raw material industries. The challenge to the raw materials industries is to secure a firm link to supplies and markets, a challenge to which it commonly responds with vertical integration. The challenge to the high-technology firm is to secure a reliable return on its unique skills or knowledge. Unlike firms in the raw materials industries, however, those in the high-technology industries rarely exhaust the static and dynamic scale economies that can be exploited at any given production site, so that the costs of setting up another production point can sometimes be fairly high; besides, the relative unimportance of freight costs usually reduces the advantages of creating multiple production sites (Vernon 1977, p. 51). In addition, some high-technology firms such as those in the aircraft industry have been influenced in part by a desire to stay close to the military authorities in their own country, in order to avoid questions of divided loyalty or of security.

Nevertheless, risk-reducing considerations have pushed the firms in high-technology industries to set up overseas subsidiaries for a portion of their foreign business. The most obvious risk leading to direct investment has been that, as the technological edge of the firm is eaten away, foreign countries may begin to bar their products in favor of producers on their own soil.[6] Faced with that risk, firms in high-technology industries have commonly chosen the subsidiary alternative.[7]

But that response, as a rule, has not put an end to the risks to which the firms in high-technology industries have been exposed. The first move of such firms into foreign production sites has usually been limited, consisting of a facility designed to serve the local market. Countries with bargaining power, however, have sometimes obliged foreign firms to develop a more substantive response. In such cases, some firms have responded by establishing a world-scale plant in an important foreign market and shipping some of the output to other countries. That response has been particularly strong in the automobile industry, generating a shift in the location of production facilities, including a shift from the facilities at home; this development is very likely increasing the international flow of components and automobiles (Jenkins 1977, pp. 213-16, Bennett and Sharpe 1979, pp. 177-82, Frank 1980, pp. 102-5).

Once again, therefore, the avoidance of risk has contributed to the growth of foreign direct investment, as enterprises have shuffled their production facilities among countries in an effort to protect their access to the markets that otherwise might be denied to them.

Follow the leader

What the discussion suggests so far is that the foreign direct investment of any firm may represent a response to threats of various kinds. One such risk is that competitors may imperil the foreigner's access to a raw material or a market by making investments of their own. That response, as it turns out, follows some predictable patterns.

Consider a world market, such as the market for nickel or aluminum, dominated by half a dozen leading firms, each capable of observing the main moves of the others. The price elasticity of aggregate demand for the final product, the processed metal, is low; the marginal cost of production in relation to full cost is also low. The challenge for the industry, therefore, is to ensure that no participating producer upsets the existing equilibrium by cutting its prices and enlarging its market share. If that should happen, there is a risk that other producers will also be obliged to cut their prices, thereby reducing the rent for the industry as a whole.

Now assume that in those circumstances, one of the participants, troubled by the risk of being cut off from its existing sources, nevertheless undertakes the development of some new mining properties in a remote corner of the world where no such mining had previously taken place. In circumstances of that sort, history suggests that the other members of the oligopoly are unlikely to be totally ignorant of the geological characteristics of the new areas. In the typical case, they will have some information based on local folklore, observation of outcroppings, or even systematic borings. But the information will be grossly incomplete, thus placing a heavy discount on the value of the most likely estimate. What is the optimum response of the other members of the oligopoly?

Consider the nature of the risk that the others face. The quality of the initiating firm's information is not clear; it may be good or bad. If bad, it may burden the firm with a cost that will have to be absorbed in the rent generated by its other operations. But if good, it may eventually arm the leader with a source of ore whose low cost or strategic geographical location poses a threat to the stability of the oligopoly. If other members of the oligopoly are risk avoiders, they will want to learn about the new location as rapidly as possible. If the acquisition and processing of information take time, the firm that is slow to respond faces the risk of being preempted by the hastier action of a rival firm. Accordingly, the risk avoiders are likely to turn their limited facilities for information-gathering to an examination of the new location, even if that means curtailing their search in other directions.[8] Indeed, some firms may want to commit themselves to the new territories even without all the requisite information. The propensity to move will be enhanced by the expectation that if a sufficient number of members of the oligopoly make a similar move and if all of them eventually prove mistaken, the oligopoly will pass on part of the cost of the error to buyers in the form of higher prices. Hence, the follow-the-leader pattern.

On similar lines, risk-avoiding members of an oligopolistically structured industry will be expected to pursue one another into any substantial foreign market in which one of them has set up a producing subsidiary. In this case, the risk of preemption will be particularly great, inasmuch as the first entrant can be expected to urge the government to impose restrictions on any further imports and to limit the number of foreign producers allowed to set up production facilities in the country. The followers may possess little knowledge about the market's potential; projections about future demand may be inescapably subject to large error, but if the number of possible entrants is limited and if the aggregate demand for the product is thought to be inelastic, the followers can contemplate the possibility of cutting their collective losses by raising the prices.[9]

The urge of members in a tight oligopoly to maintain their relative positions in the industry, even if it entails some risky investments, stems in part from their desire to avoid what they perceive as an even greater risk. There is a common conviction among enterprises in oligopolistic industries that the enterprise is in special danger when its cash flow is diminishing in relation to that of its rivals. Behind that fear lie some strong assumptions about the efficiency of the capital markets. Internal capital is usually thought to be much cheaper than external capital; indeed, external capital is commonly viewed as a scarce, rationed commodity. (See Stigler 1967, pp. 287–92, Eiteman and Stonehill 1979, pp. 346–75. See also the various essays in Heslop 1977.) If oligopolists must match the moves of their rivals in order to maintain equilibrium, those with a reduced cash flow may therefore find themselves out of the competitive running. Worries such as these led a Ford executive to say:

> If we don't spend the money, our products will not be competitive. We will not get 25 percent. We will get 20 percent. And if you fall back and take two or three years to recover, soon it will be 20 percent, then 18 percent. Then you can't spend money fast enough to catch up again (*New York Times,* December 4, 1975, pp. 1, 9).

Although the quotation goes back to 1975, it suggests a certain prescience regarding the conditions that would prevail in the automobile industry six years later.

The recognition that enterprises tend to move in unison in their foreign direct investments is hardly new, having been advanced as a behavioral proposition at least a quarter of a century ago (e.g., Barlow and Wender 1955, pp. 146, 149). In manufacturing, the evidence is quite extensive and systematic.[10] Now and then, the pattern is so pronounced that it pervades an industry. Outstanding examples have been the wave of investment in semiconductor and microcircuit production in Southeast Asia during the 1960s and the leapfrog patterns of investment among the soap companies and the soft drink companies in Latin America during the same period.

In the raw materials industry, the available data are only impressionistic, but cumulatively they carry some weight. In oil, a surge of investment in the years before the 1930s carried the leading British and American oil companies to the lands surrounding the Gulf of Mexico, from Venezuela to Texas. In the two decades after World War II, another surge of investment greatly expanded oil investments in the countries surrounding the Persian Gulf. Similar waves of investment were to be seen in metallic ores: bauxite investments in the Caribbean area from 1950 to 1965; copper investments in Chile from 1947 to 1958, and in Peru from 1955 to 1960; and iron ore in Venezuela from 1946 to 1960, and in Liberia from 1960 to 1965.

The fact that rival members of an oligopoly tend to move together into a new geographical area, of course, does not conclusively demonstrate that a follow-the-leader pattern exists. A rival possibility, not to be dismissed, is that all of them have been stirred to action by a common stimulus: by the pacification of a hitherto unsafe area, by the appearance of a new consumer market, or by some other such factor. But the empirical evidence is fairly strong for concluding that the follow-the-leader factor is important.

Some of the most obvious illustrations of linked behavior are found in the occasional agreements in the raw material industries under which rivals have explicitly given up the right to act independently. The red-line agreement of 1928 among the world's leading oil companies was one such case. This agreement covered a large portion of the Middle East and remained in force for a decade or two; under its terms, each enterprise undertook not to develop any new fields in the indicated territories except in partnership with the others (see U.S. Federal Trade Commission 1952, pp. 65–67, Jacoby 1974, pp. 29–30, 34–36).

In a very different time and place, other strong illustrations appear of the importance of linkage among members of an oligopoly, albeit not in the form of agreements or consortia. In many markets of the developing world during the 1960s, the leading automobile companies scrambled with one another to set up producing facilities. In at least two cases, that of Argentina and South Africa, the number of firms prepared to enter the scramble and the amount of capacity they were prepared to put in place were so far in excess of prospective market demand as to suggest strongly that some of the investors were reacting to the decisions of the others (Baranson 1969, pp. 46-047, 53, Sundelson 1970, pp. 243, 246-49, and Jenkins 1977, pp. 39-42, 56-58). The seemingly nonrational behavior of the firms could be explained in a number of ways. The explanation I find most plausible, however, is that they were driven by a desire to hold down risk, defining that risk in the terms suggested earlier.

More systematic evidence that the follow-the-leader phenomenon reflects a risk-reducing reaction on the part of the participants in an oligopolistic industry is found in the Knickerbocker study mentioned earlier (1973, pp. 111–44). Knickerbocker found that the degree of the parallel behavior of U.S. firms in any industry was positively correlated with the degree of concentration in that industry—but only up to a point. The strongest patterns of parallel behavior were found in industries in which three or four near-equal firms were the leaders; in industries with an even higher concentration—say, one or two dominant firms, surrounded by a fringe of lesser enterprises—parallel behavior was not as strong. Knickerbocker also found that parallel behavior was a little less pronounced in firms with a relatively high level of technological inputs, where product differentiation was important, than in those with lower technological content. These added bits of information contribute marginally to the credibility of the follow-the-leader hypothesis as a factor in explaining foreign direct investment patterns.

The exchange of threats

Researchers also claim to see risk-reducing objectives in other seemingly imitative investments of the multinational enterprises. It has repeatedly been observed, for instance, that the U.S.-based industries that were generating the highest rates of foreign direct investments in Europe were much the same as the European industries that more or less simultaneously were investing in the United States (Hymer and Rowthorn 1970, pp. 80–82). One explanation for this behavior is provided by the so-called exchange-of-threat hypothesis. Threatened by the establishment of a foreign-owned subsidiary in their home market, the response of the leading firms in that market is to set up subsidiaries in the invader's home market. This cross-investment conveys a warning to the invading firm that any excessively energetic efforts to compete in the foreign market may be countered by similar efforts in the home market of the invader.[11]

The two-way flows of foreign direct investment in the same set of industries, moreover, may serve to reduce a somewhat different kind of risk, namely, the risk of lagging behind in the global technological race. In many oligopolistic industries, a limited number of multinational enterprises encounter each other in competition in many different national markets. In the computer mainframe industry, IBM, Fujitsu, and Siemens are world competitors; in chemicals, ICI, Dupont, and Rhone-Poulenc cross paths in international markets; and so on. Most multinational enterprises, however, do the bulk of their research and development within their home market (Samuelsson 1974, Ronstadt 1977, pp. xiii–xiv, 2, Lall 1980, pp. 102, 119–20); and most of these enterprises are greatly influenced by the conditions of the home market as they develop the niche that differentiates their products and processes (Davidson 1976, pp. 207, 216, Franko 1976, pp. 27–44). The U.S. stress on labor-saving, mass-produced products, for instance, was traditionally based on the high cost of labor and the absolute scarcity of artisan skills (see Habakkuk 1962, ch. 3 and 4, Rosenberg 1976, ch. 1 and 3; also Rosenberg 1969, pp. 17–18).

One risk for multinational enterprises in industries with rapid innovational change is that their rivals in other countries, exposed to different conditions in their home markets, may develop a technological lead that will eventually prove threatening elsewhere. American automobile manufacturers, for instance, were eventually threatened by the Japanese mastery of small fuel-saving automobiles, a capability that the Japanese originally developed largely in response to the special needs of their own market. Aware of the risk of falling behind, some multinational enterprises have maintained a constant surveillance over their rivals in other countries and have sought licenses for foreign technology whenever they felt the need (Abegglen 1970, pp. 117–28, and Ozawa 1974, pp. 52–56, 67–80). But some have preferred to acquire subsidiaries as a technological listening post in the territory of their rivals (Franko 1971, pp. 8, 14–15, 23, Michalet and Delapierre 1975; see also Vernon 1980, pp. 150, 153–54, and *Business Week* 1980, pp. 55, 59, 121). When that has occurred, the multinationalizing process has been the firm's response to a risk generated by the action of its competitors.

Joint ventures as risk reducers

Once a firm has determined that an international investment may be desirable as a means of reducing risk, it is still faced at times with the possibility of going it alone or investing in partnership with others. The choice among the various alternatives is commonly affected by questions of risk. But once again, the risks to be avoided are of various kinds.

Consortia of foreigners

For reasons already discussed, firms in the raw material industries typically place a high premium on reducing the risks of the unforeseen, such as wars, strikes, and earthquakes. But in operations in which scale economies are large, such diversification can be costly, especially on the part of the smaller firms in the oligopoly. The solution is for such firms to multiply their sources by joining others in a number of consortia. (For aluminum, the subject is fully explored in Stuckey 1981.) That response has had the effect of producing various consortia composed of firms engaged in the common exploitation of a raw material in a country that is foreign to all of them.

Consortia of this sort in raw materials industries, however, also respond to another risk that has already been noted: the risk that a rival firm might be in a position to upset the stability of an oligopoly by securing its materials at an especially advantageous cost. This second motive is, of course, difficult to distinguish from the first.

Some consortia in the raw materials industries, however, are formed with still a third group of risks in mind, namely, the category that is usually described as political risk. In practice, political risk can be of many different types. It can arise because of a host country's hostility to some specific foreign country and its nationals; or because of a host country's hostility to foreigners in general, irrespective of nationality; or because of a host country's efforts, without hostility to any foreigners in particular or in general, to improve an existing bargain.[12]

Whatever the variety of political risk may be, a consortium composed of foreigners of different nationalities is ordinarily seen as reducing the risk. If the risk to be reduced is a host country's hostility to one country, the consortium can be seen as diluting the exposure of any firm that is based in that country. If the risk is a deterioration in the position of foreigners in general, without regard to any particular country, the consortium can be seen as a counterforce that may be able to enlist the support of a number of different governments.

Although consortia among foreigners also are to be found in the manufacturing industries, especially those that require large-scale and heavy investment, such consortia are relatively uncommon. Occasionally, consortia of this type are imposed on the manufacturing firms by host governments. Foreign automobile producers in Peru and Mexico, for instance, have been compelled to merge their production activities in order to reduce the number of automobile types in the country and to achieve some obvious economies of scale.[13] But the reduction of risk is also a factor in such consortia.

One reason why consortia among foreign firms are less common in manufacturing than in mining or oil production is that manufacturing firms generally have better ways of diversifying their portfolios of direct investment. Although some foreign-owned manufacturing subsidiaries produce goods for export from the countries in which they are located, most market the bulk of their production within the host country (Vaupel and Curhan 1973, pp. 376–77, Curhan, Davidson, and Suri 1977, pp. 392–93, 398–99, Tables 7.2.1 and 7.2.6, U.S. Department of Commerce 1977, pp. 318–19, Tables III.H.1 and III.H.2). Firms in manufacturing, therefore, can often diversify their market risks by setting up subsidiaries in a number of different countries, relying on transportation costs or protective devices in each market to buffer them from outside competitors. Firms engaged in extractive activities, however, typically sell their products in world markets, so that high-cost production sites represent a real handicap. With fewer locations from which to choose, the raw materials firms find themselves obliged to turn more often to the consortium possibility in achieving adequate diversification.[14]

Finally, if the factors specified thus far were not enough to explain the lesser use of consortia by manufacturing firms, the nature of their strategies would provide a sufficient explanation. Unlike the raw materials producers, manufacturers commonly build such strategies on product differentiation, building up distinctive trade names and unique services to customers as their route to success. The consortium approach in any market, combining the offerings of rival producers, would be incompatible with a product-differentiating strategy.

Joint ventures with local firms

When manufacturing firms take local partners with an eye to reducing risk, the risk they generally have in mind is political risk. To be sure, multinational enterprises have a number of other reasons for setting up joint ventures with local stockholders. In some cases, they have no choice; host governments lay down and enforce a joint venture requirement (Turner 1973, United Nations 1973, pp. 83–84, Robinson 1976, United Nations Economic and Social Council 1978, pp. 22–23). In other instances, the decision to take a local partner may free the subsidiary of various discriminatory restrictions, such as disqualification from selling to government enterprises or borrowing from local banks. In still other cases, the joint venture may represent the right decision on the part of both partners simply on the basis of the classic choice of a profit-maximizing firm. It may allow both partners to put slack resources to work in a single entity; it may allow each of the partners to earn returns on their investments that were higher than their respective opportunity costs; and it may reduce the risks to the multinational enterprise of securing local distribution channels, while reducing the risks to the local distributor of securing assured supplies (Dubin 1976, pp. 27–43, Radetzki and Zorn 1979, pp. 57–61). The objective of reducing political risk, however, is ordinarily of some importance in such arrangements (see especially Franko 1977, p. 29, Pfeffer and Nowek 1976, p. 332, Caves 1970, pp. 283–302, Hogberg 1977, pp. 6–25, Tomlinson 1970, p. 5).

Apart from the direct testimony of businesspeople, the sense that risk reduction must be playing some significant role in the decision to set up joint ventures is supported by a number of studies of the behavioral patterns of the multinational enterprises. Two analyses, when interpreted in tandem, point in that direction. One of these studies offers strong evidence for the view that, as manufacturing firms gain experience in manufacturing in any market, they tend to assign a lower level of risk to that market. The second study concludes that the less experienced the firm, the higher its propensity for entering into joint ventures with local partners.

The first study, linking experience to perceived risk, covered the introduction and subsequent dissemination of 406 new products by fifty-seven large U.S.-based multinational enterprises during the period from 1945–75 (Vernon and Davidson 1979). In the early decades of that period, the firms were slow to establish production units for these products abroad. But the products introduced in the latter decades were produced abroad with much greater alacrity and in many more locations. By breaking down the data by firms and products, the factors that contribute to this trend became more evident. For instance, firms with a high proportion of exports transferred more rapidly and more extensively than those with a low proportion; firms with several different product lines established production sites abroad more rapidly in their principal product lines than in less important lines; firms that had made many prior transfers responded more rapidly than those that had made only a few; and all firms responded more rapidly in countries to which they had made many previous transfers than in countries to which they had made a smaller number.

The study that links experience levels with the propensity to enter into joint ventures consists of an exhaustive analysis of the behavior of the 2,800 foreign manufacturing subsidiaries of 186 U.S.-based multinational enterprises over a fifty-year period. In various ways, the data linked increased foreign experience with a decline in the propensity of the firm to use joint ventures (Stopford and Wells 1972, p. 99).

More suggestive evidence on the connection between risk and joint ventures comes from another direction. It has been commonly observed that for any foreign-owned enterprise the risk of nationalization rises as the firm loses its capacity to offer a scarce resource to the host country, such as technology, capital, or access to foreign markets (Vernon 1971, pp. 46–52, Krasner 1978, pp. 138–42, Jodice 1980, pp. 204–5, Kobrin 1980, pp. 65–88). At the same time, several studies suggest that firms that appear to be in a relatively weak bargaining position in relation to host governments, that is, firms that have little to offer the country, tend to use joint ventures more than firms in a strong bargaining position (Stopford and Wells 1972, pp. 120, 150–56, Fagre and Wells in press).

Most of the studies cited here are less than conclusive, being dogged by difficult problems of multicollinearity and multiple causation. But cumulatively they lend a considerable degree of plausibility to the hypothesis that risk avoidance is a substantial factor in the decision of foreign-owned enterprises to take local partners.

Joint ventures with state-owned enterprises

A special category of joint venture that has grown somewhat in recent years is partnerships between foreign firms and enterprises owned by the state. The oil-processing industires of the oil-exporting countries contain numerous examples of such enterprises (Ghadar 1977, pp. 17–46, Turner and Bedore 1979, pp. 13–36). But they are found in many other industries as well.

The reasons for such arrangements have been fairly well studied.[15] From the viewpoint of foreign partners, many of the reasons for entering into agreements with state-owned enterprises are the same as those that argue for local private partners: freedom from special restrictions, access to local resources, and protection from political risk. Foreign firms generally assume, however, that each of these factors gains a little strength when the partner is a state-owned enterprise. Whether the foreigner actually acquires greater immunity from political risks by entering into partnership with the state, however, seems quite uncertain; when enough experience develops for researchers to explore the question adequately, the likelihood is that a complex answer will emerge.

One difference between partnerships with private local firms and partnerships with the host state lies in the evolution of the local partner's interests over time. In a significant proportion of the joint ventures, the private partnership interest is held by a large number of local stockholders,[16] who commonly have even less power than public stockholders in the United States. In other cases, local stockholdings are more highly concentrated and fewer in number, but many of these stockholders, having received their equity interests as a gift, are content to play a passive role and to provide the protective coloration the foreigner has bargained for. Only a fraction of these joint ventures, therefore, represent active partnerships.

Managers of state-owned enterprises, on the other hand, generally find themselves much more actively involved in their partnerships with foreigners. Being exposed to the political process in the home country, state managers are often torn between buffering the foreign partner against political pressures in order to maintain the partnership, or swallowing up the foreign partner's interest in order to demonstrate their national commitment. In the Middle East oil industry, according to one study, those motivations have shifted over time in predictable patterns, ending characteristically in the nationalization of the foreigner's interest (Bradley 1977, pp. 75–83, and Ghadar 1977, pp. 25–27).

To be sure, oil may not prove to be a representative case, especially because of the period covered in existing studies. In other times and other industries, state-owned enterprises may see advantages in clinging to a foreign association, especially if technology or foreign market access is needed. But the recent history of the oil industry does suggest some of the difficult judgments that foreigners have been obliged to make when contemplating the use of joint ventures as insurance against risk.

Other arrangements for avoiding risk

In an effort to reduce some of their various risks, firms have often been pushed to establish foreign subsidiaries, and, in an effort to reduce the risk to their subsidiaries, they have sometimes been compelled to enter into joint ventures. But there have been instances in which no subsidiary, whether joint venture or wholly owned, has seemed able to reduce their risks on balance. Such subsidiaries simply appeared to be substituting one set of risks for another—the risk of expropriation, for instance, for the risk of preemption by a competitor. Faced with such unpalatable alternatives, enterprises have sometimes groped toward some intermediate arrangement hoping to minimize both kinds of risks. These intermediate arrangements have commonly involved long-term contracts of various sorts.

Such contracts have taken a variety of forms. In both raw materials and high-technology industries, some long-term contracts have authorized and obligated foreign firms to exercise managerial functions over extended periods (Bostock and Harvey 1972, Fabrikant 1973, Smith and Wells 1976, pp. 45–49, Zorn 1980, ch. 12). Some of these arrangements have contemplated cash flows for the foreign firm whose discounted value was not very different from the expected stream generated by an analogous direct investment. In fixing the appropriate discount rate, of course, either stream would have to be recognized as subject to risks of various sorts. But in some of these cases, one would probably have been justified in discounting the anticipated income from fees paid under managerial contracts at lower rates than those applicable to the streams anticipated from foreign direct investments.[17]

Yet long-term contracts simply substitute one set of risks for another. In practice, long-term contracts for the sale of raw materials have often turned out to be nothing much more than a statement of intentions on the part of the parties. Critical elements of the contract, such as prices and quantities, have been subject to repeated renegotiations. In their efforts to reduce uncertainties of this kind, one party or another has sought to introduce various kinds of sanctions. Buyers of raw materials, for instance, have made loans to raw materials producers with provisions for immediate repayment whenever the producers failed to deliver specified quantities, and producers have insisted that buyers must forfeit their rights to interest on such loans whenever the buyers failed to accept specified quantities.

Despite such provisions, large elements of uncertainty have remained. Buyers have been accused of delaying the arrival of their vessels in order to avoid picking up shipments of bulk cargoes; sellers have been accused of stimulating their governments to impose export embargoes in order to avoid delivering their products. Moreover, businesspeople have had reservations about the enforceability of their contracts, especially when enforcement could only be achieved through the use of foriegn courts.

For firms in the high-technology industries, long-term contracts have typically taken the form of a licensing agreement with independent producers in foreign countries. Such licenses have normally been written with various restraints. These restraints have sought to ensure that the licensee would not impart the information acquired under the license to an unauthorized third person; that the licensee would confine its use of the information to some specified geographical territory; and finally, especially when the licensee was authorized to use the licenser's trademark, that the licensee would produce the product in accordance with some specified standards. Each of these conditions, it is apparent, is aimed at reducing the licenser's risks: the risk of unauthorized appropriation, the risk of competition among license holders, and the risk of impairment of a valued trademark through inadequate quality control.

But long-term licenses, like long-term bulk purchase contracts in the raw materials industries, have had their limitations. Licensers have been aware that licensees can often disregard the contract because the sanctions for violation are notoriously limited. Information that has once been divulged cannot be retrieved; the licensee, therefore, may have little or nothing to fear from losing the licenser's goodwill. On top of that, if the foreign licenser is obliged to pursue its remedies in the home courts of the licensee, court orders directing the licensee to observe the terms of the contract and money damages for breach of contract may prove difficult to obtain.

Apart from the possibility that the courts may not be blind to the foreign nationality of the licenser, there is also the possibility that the underlying legal position of the licenser may be weak. A licenser that holds a strong patent position on an invention in its own home market will sometimes find that the patent protection on the same invention issued by foreign governments is much less secure (Maier 1969, pp. 207–31, Horowitz 1970, p. 539, Penrose 1973, p. 768, Scherer 1976). Moreover, in recent years, various developing countries have adopted laws outlawing the geographical restraints and other restraints that licensers have heretofore found useful to impose on their foreign licensees, further reducing the usefulness of that approach (OECD 1977b, UNCTAD 1979, pp. 24–39, also Naryenya-Takirambudde 1977, pp. 71–73).

Perhaps the most tenuous arrangements for the avoidance of risks in host countries entail payments that in U.S. law and practice would be classified as bribes. The justification for condemning bribes can sometimes be couched in rational terms. In a country whose officials do not solicit bribes, for instance, the foreign offerer of a bribe contributes to the destruction of a public good—the competitive market—an act that could conceivably be costly to all those in the market, including the offerer. But arguments of that sort are not the real stuff of the debate. One side finds bribery prima facie offensive and refuses to use it, whatever the consequences; the other thinks it totally entrenched, presenting an inescapable hurdle for those who wish to operate in certain foreign markets.[18] Any "rational" discussion of the use of bribes as a risk-insuring device is therefore likely to be offensive to one side of the debate and unsatisfying to the other. It is almost inescapable, too, that such a discussion will be seen as an apologia for the practice.

There is perhaps one point worth making nevertheless. The problem of bribery is either a smaller one or a bigger one than is ordinarily described. In the interest of reducing their risk in various developing countries, foreign investors are often obliged to make various payments that are not labeled as bribes. Influential local figures are commonly offered blocks of stock in what is then dubbed a joint venture, at prices well below their reasonable value. Local government officials are appointed to directorships in the enterprise, with appropriate emoluments. Ironically, such measures are often applauded as a sign of the foreign investor's responsiveness to local sensibilities. In this shadowy area of risk avoidance, the line between international chicanery and local adaptation will never be clearly drawn.

The analytical challenge

The avoidance of risk is a quintessential element in the strategy of foreign investors. As a rule, the decision to invest is motivated by a desire to reduce risks of various sorts: the risk of government restrictions on foreign imports, the relative unenforceability of the investor's rights under law or contract, and above all, the risk of preemptive action on the part of a competitor. Risk avoidance also affects the form of the investment; some forms of joint venture help the investor with limited resources to diversify more widely, whereas other forms of joint venture are thought to reduce political risk. On the other hand, even as a direct investment reduces one set of risks, it exposes the investor to another set, including the risk of expropriation. Accordingly, firms often attempt to establish a firm link with foreign markets or foreign sources of materials by long-term arrangements short of investment, but these too produce uncertain results.

The firms involved in the making of these complex judgments come predominantly from industries that are oligopolistic in structure. Because their risks are those that arise in the never-never land of oligopoly, where individual firms can affect prices and the actions of rival firms are interdependent, the analytical power of our microeconomic concepts proves somewhat limited. Those risks are often more easily analyzed in game-theoretic terms than in the familiar paradigms of systematic and random variance. To add to the difficulties, foreign direct investors are not usually investors in the usual sense; a critical portion of their investments commonly takes an intangible form, entailing assets that have no ready market price. Even the cost of such assets offers little help; such assets as technology or access to markets are provided at near-zero marginal cost.

As a result, the role that risk plays in international direct investment cannot be captured by minor addenda to the principles of finance, such as calculating the appropriate risk adjustment for a target rate of return or computing the appropriate price to be paid for a hedge. Foreign direct investors will resort to a series of stratagems for reducing the uncertainty of risk. Faced with that fact, this chapter has discussed, for want of a better term, the "organizational and institutional" responses of such investors to risk. But it is only a matter of time before the economics profession will formalize those responses in ways that incorporate them within the discipline. Indeed, that process is already well under way.

Notes

[1]See Williamson (1975, pp. 85–131,), Bernhardt (1977, pp. 213, 215), Porter (1980, pp. 306–7), and Scherer (1980, pp. 78, 89–91, 302–4). For a survey of recent literature on the incentives for vertical integration, see Kaserman (1978, pp. 483–510); also Jensen, Kehrberg, and Thomas (1962, pp. 378–79, 384).

[2]On the economics of backward integration in the raw materials industries, see for instance, Gort (1962, ch. 6) and Teece (1976, pp. 105, 115–18).

[3]For descriptions of the international oil industry, especially in relation to the issue of vertical integration, see Adelman (1972, pp. 318–19), Cooper and Gaskel (1976, pp. 72–74, 188), Teece (1976, pp. 83–89, 116–17), Mansvelt Beck and Wiig (1977), and Levy (1982). For the nonferrous metals, Charles River Associates, Inc. (1970, pp. 51–57), Bosson and Varon (1977, pp. 46–47), Duke et al. (1977), Banks (1979, pp. 21, 27, 45), Mikesell (1979a, pp. 108–9), and Goohs (1980).

[4]For a basic statement of this problem, see Caves (1977, pp. 43–45), Porter (1980, pp. 308, 317), and Scherer (1980, pp. 90–91).

[5]For an effort to demonstrate in theoretical terms that equilibrium exists only at the extremes of full integration or full nonintegration, see Green (1974).

[6]On "buy-at-home" policies as a nontariff barrier to international trade, see Curtis and Vastine (1971, pp. 202–4), and Cline, Kawarabe, Kronojo, and Williams (1978, pp. 189–94). On the attempts of European governments to set up and protect national champions in the aerospace and computer industries, see Hochmuth (1974, pp. 145–70) and Jéquier (1974, pp. 195–255). On the restrictions of developing countries, see Robinson (1976, pp. 169–238).

[7]For a discussion of the factors in high-technology industries, such as computers, tending toward vertical integration, see Katz and Philipps (in press). An econometric demonstration that firms in high-technology industries favor subsidiaries over independent licensees to a greater degree than in other industries is presented in Davidson and McFetridge (1981); the analysis is based on data presented in Vernon and Davidson (1979).

[8]See, for instance, Cyert and March (1963, ch. 6) and Cyert, Dill, and March (1970, pp. 87–88, 94–95, 107). The effort going into search can be considered a significant investment by the firm, as discussed generally in Arrow (1974, pp. 39–43).

[9]The perceptions of prospective lenders in such oligopolistic situations are described in Stiglitz and Weiss (1981, pp. 393–411). These perceptions tend to favor follow-the-leader investors by increasing their ability to borrow.

[10]The leading work on this point is Knickerbocker (1973). See also Aharoni (1966, pp. 55, 65–66) and Gray (1972, pp. 77, 96–98).

[11]Koninklijke Nederlandsche Petroleum Maatschappij (1950, p. 18), *Forbes* (1964, pp. 40–41), Graham (1974, pp. 33–34, 75), Michalet and Delapierre (1975, p. 44). But rival explanations are also offered to explain the cross investment phenomenon; see, for instance, Franko (1976, pp. 166–72).

[12]For illustrations, see Moran (1974, pp. 110–36), Thunell (1977, p. 99), Krasner (1978, p. 117), Radetzki and Zorn (1980, p. 186); also Zorn (1980, pp. 225–26).

[13]Pressures of this sort are usually applied informally by administrative means and so are difficult to document. But see Turner (1973, p. 101). For data on the trend to greater concentration of automobile producers in Latin American countries, see Jenkins (1977, pp. 145–50).

[14]Indicative of the more limited opportunities of the raw materials firms are data in Vernon (1971, pp. 39, 62).

[15]The subject is dealt with in Vernon (1979, pp. 7–15) and Aharoni (1981, pp. 184–93).

[16]For detailed data see Vaupel and Curhan (1973, pp. 309–19).

[17]See, for example, Mikesell (1979b, pp. 52, 56–57). OPEC members' purchases of petroleum management services are generally at a price approaching the return on an equivalent direct foreign investment by the oil companies; see Eiteman and Stonehill (1979, p. 242).

[18]For some of the more serious explorations of this subject see Kobrin (1976, pp. 105–11), U.S. Securities and Exchange Commission (1976), U.S. Senate (1976), Jacoby et al. (1977, pp. 125–45), Kugel and Gruenberg (1977, pp. 113–24), Kennedy and Simon (1978, pp. 1–5, 118–20).

References

Abegglen, J. C. (ed.). *Business Strategies for Japan* (Tokyo: Sophia University, 1970).

Abernathy, W. J., and Kenneth Wayne. *The Bottom of the Learning Curve: The Dilemma of Innovation and Productivity* (Boston: Division of Research, Graduate School of Business Administration, Harvard University, 1974).

Adelman, M. A. *The World Petroleum Industry* (Baltimore, Md.: Johns Hopkins University Press, 1972).

Aharoni, Yair. *The Foreign Investment Decision Process* (Boston: Division of Research, Graduate School of Business Administration, Harvard University, 1966).

——— "Managerial Discretion," in Raymond Vernon and Yair Aharoni (eds.), *State-Owned Enterprise in the Western Economies* (London: Croom Helmn, 1981).

Arrow, K. J. *The Limits of Organization* (New York: Norton, 1974).

Banks, F. E. *Bauxite and Aluminum: An Introduction to the Economics of Nonfuel Minerals* (Lexington, Mass.: Lexington Books, 1979).

Baranson, Jack. *Automotive Industries in Developing Countries* (Baltimore, Md.: Johns Hopkins University Press, 1969).

Barlow, E. R., and I. T. Wender. *Foreign Investment and Taxation* (Englewood Cliffs, N.J.: Prentice-Hall, 1955).

Bennett, David, and K. E. Sharpe. "Transnational Corporations and the Political Economy of Export Promotion: The Case of the Mexican Automobile Industry." *International Organization*, vol. 33, no. 2, Spring 1979, pp. 177–201.

Bernhardt, I. "Vertical Integration and Demand Variability," *Journal of Industrial Economics*, vol. 25, no. 3, March 1977, pp. 213–29.

Bosson, Rex, and Bension Varon. *The Mining Industry and the Developing Countries* (New York: Oxford University Press, 1977).

Bostock, Mark, and Charles Harvey (eds.). *Economic Independence and Zambian Copper: A Case Study of Foreign Investment* (New York: Praeger, 1972).

Bradley, David. "Managing Against Expropriation." *Harvard Business Review,* July–August 1977, pp. 75–83.

Brock, G. W. *The U.S. Computer Industry* (Cambridge, Mass.: Ballinger, 1975).

Buckley, P. J., and M. Casson. *The Future of Multinational Enterprise* (New York: Holmes and Meier Publishers, Inc., 1976).

Business Week. "The Reindustrialization of America." June 30, 1980, pp. 55–146.

Casson, M. *Alternatives to the Multinational Enterprise* (London: Macmillan Press, 1979).

Caves, R.E. "Uncertainty, Market Structure and Performance: Galbraith as Conventional Wisdom," in J. W. Markham and G. F. Papenek (eds.), *Industrial Organization and Economic Development* (Boston: Houghton Mifflin, 1970).

——— "Industrial Organization," in J. M. Dunning (ed.), *Economic Analysis and the Multinational Enterprise* (New York: Praeger, 1973).

——— *American Industry: Structure, Conduct, Performance* (Englewood Cliffs, N.J.: Prentice-Hall, 1977).

Charles River Associates, Inc. "Economic Analysis of the Copper Industry." Prepared for the General Services Administration, March 1970.

Cline, W. R., Noboru Kawarabe, T. O. M. Kronojo, and Thomas Williams. *Trade Negotiations in the Tokyo Round: A Quantitative Assessment* (Washington, D.C.: The Brookings Institution, 1978).

Commission of the European Communities. *Report by the Commission on the Behavior of the Oil Companies in the Community during the Period from October 1973 to March 1974*. EEC Studies on Competition-Approximation of Legislation, no. 26 (Brussels: European Economic Communities, December 1975).

Conley, Patrick. "Experience Curves as a Planning Tool," in R. R. Rothberg (ed.), *Corporate Strategy and Product Innovation* (New York: Free Press, 1981).

Cooper, B., and T. F. Gaskell. *The Adventure of North Sea Oil* (London: Heinemann, 1976).

Curhan, J. P., W. H. Davidson, and Rajan Suri. *Tracing the Multinationals: A Source Book on U.S.-Based Enterprises* (Cambridge, Mass.: Ballinger, 1977).

Curtis, T. B., and J. R. Vastine, Jr. *The Kennedy Round and the Future of American Trade* (New York: Praeger, 1971).

Cyert, R. M., W. R. Dill, and J. G. March. "The Role of Expectations in Business Decision Making," in L. A. Welsch and R. M. Cyert (eds.), *Management Decision Making* (London: Penguin Books, 1970).

Cyert, R. M., and J. C. March. *A Behavioral Theory of the Firm* (Englewood Cliffs, N.J.: Prentice-Hall, 1963).

Davidson, W. H. "Patterns of Factor-Saving Innovation in the Industrialized World." *European Economic Review*, vol. 8, no. 3, October 1976, pp. 207–17.

Davidson, W. H., and D. G. McFetridge. "International Technology Transactions and the Theory of the Firm." Unpublished, Amos Tuck School, Dartmouth College, 1981.

Dubin, Michael. "Foreign Acquisitions and the Spread of the Multinational Firm." Unpublished DBA thesis, Harvard School of Business Administration, 1976.

Duke, R. M., R. L. Johnson, H. Mueller, P. D. Quaffs, C. T. Roush, Jr., and D. G. Tarr. *Staff Report on the United States Steel Industry and International Rivals*. Bureau of Economics, Federal Trade Commission, Washington, D.C., November 1977.

Eiteman, D. K., and A. I Stonehill. *Multinational Business Finance* (2nd ed.) (Reading, Mass.: Addison-Wesley, 1979).

Fabrikant, Robert. *Oil Discovery and Technical Change in Southeast Asia: Legal Aspects of Production-Sharing Contracts in the Indonesian Petroleum Industry* (Singapore: Institute of Southeast Asian Studies, 1973).

Fagre, Nathan, and L. T. Wells, Jr. "Bargaining Power of Multinationals and Host Governments." *Journal of International Business Studies,* in press.

Forbes. "The Game that Two Could Play." Vol. 94, no. 11, December 1, 1964, pp. 40–41.

Frank, Isaiah. *Foreign Enterprise in Developing Countries* (Baltimore, Md.: Johns Hopkins University Press, 1980).

Franko, L. G. *The European Multinationals, European Business Strategies in the United States* (Geneva: Business International, 1971).

The European Multinationals (Stamford, Conn.: Greylock Publishers, 1976).

Joint Venture Survival in Multinational Corporation (New York: Praeger, 1977).

Freeman, Christopher. *The Economics of Industrial Innovation* (London: Penguin Books, 1974).

Ghadar, Fariborz. *The Evolution of* OPEC *Strategy* (Lexington, Mass.: Lexington Books, 1977).

Goohs, C. A. "United States Taxation Policies and the Iron Ore Operations of the United States Steel Industry." Unpublished, J. F. Kennedy School, Cambridge, Mass., Spring 1980.

Gort, Michael. *Diversification and Integration in American Industry* (Princeton, N.J.: Princeton University Press, 1962).

Graham, E. M. "Oligopolistic Imitation and European Direct Investment in the United States." Unpublished DBA thesis, Harvard School of Business Administration, 1974.

Gray, H. P. *The Economics of Business Investment Abroad* (New York: Crane, Russak and Co., 1972).

Green, J. R. "Vertical Integration and the Assurance of Markets." Harvard Institute of Economic Research, Discussion Paper 383, October 1974.

Habakkuk, H. J. *American and British Technology in the Nineteenth Century* (Cambridge: Cambridge University Press, 1962).

Hartley, Keith. "The Learning Curve and its Application to the Aircraft Industry." *Journal of Industrial Economics,* vol. 13, no. 2, March 1965, pp. 122–28.

Heslop, Alan (ed.). *The World Capital Shortage* (Indianapolis: Bobbs-Merrill, 1977).

Hochmuth, M. S. "Aerospace," in Raymond Vernon (ed.), *Big Business and the State* (Cambridge, Mass.: Harvard University Press, 1974).

Hogberg, Bengt. *Interfirm Cooperation and Strategic Development* (Ghoteborg: b BAS ek. fhoren, 1977).

Horowitz, Lester. "Patents and World Trade." *Journal of World Trade Law,* vol. 4, no. 4, July–August 1970, pp. 538–47.

Hymer, Stephen, and Robert Rowthorn, "Multinational Corporations and International Oligopoly: The Non-American Challenge," in C. P. Kindleberger (ed.), *The International Corporation: A Symposium* (Cambridge, Mass.: MIT Press, 1970).

Jacoby, N. H. *Multinational Oil* (New York: Macmillan, 1974).

Jacoby, N. H., Peter Nehemkis, and Richard Eells. *Bribery and Extortion in World Business: A Study of Corporate Political Payments Abroad* (New York: Macmillan, 1977).

Jenkins, R. O. *Dependent Industrialization in Latin America: The Automobile Industry in Argentina, Chile, and Mexico* (New York: Praeger, 1977).

Jensen, H. R., E. W. Kehrberg, and D. W. Thomas. "Integration as an Adjustment to Risk and Uncertainty," *Southern Economics Journal,* vol. 28, no. 4 April 1962, pp. 378–84.

Jéquier, Nicolas. "Computer," in Raymond Vernon (ed.), *Big Business and the State* (Cambridge, Mass.: Harvard University Press, 1974).

Jodice, D. A. "Sources of Change in Third World Regimes for Foreign Direct Investment, 1968–1976." *International Organization,* vol. 34, no. 2, Spring 1980, pp. 177–206.

Kaserman, D. L. "Theories of Vertical Integration: Implications for Antitrust Policy." *The Antitrust Bulletin,* vol. 23, no. 3, Fall 1978, pp. 483–510.

Katz, B. G., and Almarin Phillips. "Government, Technological Opportunities, and the Emergence of the Computer Industry," in Herbert Giersch (ed.), *Emerging Technology* (Kiel: Institute of World Economics, in press).

Kennedy, Tom, and C. E. Simon. *An Examination of Questionable Payments and Practices* (New York: Praeger, 1978).

Knickerbocker, F. T. *Oligopolistic Reaction and Multinational Enterprise* (Boston: Division of Research, Graduate School of Business Administration, Harvard University, 1973).

Kobrin, S. J. "Morality, Political Power and Illegal Payments." *Columbia Journal of World Business*, vol. 11, no. 4, Winter 1976, pp. 105–10.

"Foreign Enterprise and Forced Divestment in LDCs." *International Organization*, vol. 34, no. 1, Winter 1980, pp. 65–88.

Koninklijke Nederlandsche Petroleum Maatschappij, N. W. *The Royal Dutch Petroleum Company 1890–1950* (The Hague, 1950).

Krasner, S. D. *Defending the National Interest* (Princeton, N.J.: Princeton University Press, 1978).

Kugel, Yerachmiel, and G. W. Gruenberg. "Criteria and Guidelines for Decision Making: The Special Case of International Payoffs." *Columbia Journal of World Business*, vol. 12, no. 3, Fall 1977, pp. 113–23.

Lall, Sanjaya. "Monopolistic Advantages and Foreign Involvement by U.S. Manufacturing Industry." *Oxford Economic Papers*, vol. 32, no. 1, March 1980, pp. 102–22.

Levy, Brian. "World Oil Marketing in Transition." *International Organization*, vol. 36, no. 1, Winter 1982, pp. 113–33.

Maier, H. G. "International Patent Conventions and Access to Foreign Technology." *Journal of International Law and Economics*, vol. 4, no. 2, Fall 1969, pp. 207–31.

Mansvelt Beck, F. W., and K. M. Wiig. *The Economics of Offshore Oil and Gas Supplies* (Lexington, Mass.: Lexington Books, 1977).

Measday, W. S. "The Pharmaceutical Industry," in Walter Adams (ed.), *The Structure of American Industry* (New York: Macmillan, 1977).

Michalet, C. A., and Michel Delapierre. *The Multinationalization of French Firms* (Chicago: Academy of International Business, 1975).

Mikesell, R. F. *The World Copper Industry: Structure and Economic Analysis* (Baltimore, Md.: Johns Hopkins University Press, 1979a).

New Patterns of World Mineral Development (New York: British–North American Committee, 1979b).

Moran, T. H. *Multinational Companies and the Politics of Dependence: Copper in Chile* (Princeton, N.J.: Princeton University Press, 1974).

Naryenya-Takirambudde, Peter. *Technology Transfer and International Law* (New York: Praeger, 1977).

New York Times. "Ford Regroups for the Minicar Battle." December 4, 1975, pp. 1, 9.

Organization for Economic Cooperation and Development (OECD). *Restrictive Business Practices of Multinational Enterprises,* Report to the Committee of Experts on Restrictive Business Practices (Paris, 1977a).

Transfer of Technology by Multinational Corporations (Paris, 1977b).

Ozawa, Terutomo. *Japan's Technological Challenge to the West, 1950–1974: Motivation and Accomplishment* (Cambridge, Mass.: MIT Press, 1974).

Parker, J. E. S. *The Economics of Innovation,* 2nd ed. (New York: Longman, 1978).

Penrose, E. T. "International Patenting and the Less-Developed Countries." *Economic Journal*, vol. 83, no. 331, September 1973, pp. 768–86.

Pfeffer, Jeffrey, and Philip Nowek. "Patterns of Joint Venture Activity: Implications for Antitrust Policy." *The Antitrust Bulletin,* vol. 21, no. 2, Summer 1976, pp. 315–39.

Porter, M. E. *Competitive Strategy: Techniques for Analyzing Industries and Competitors* (New York: Free Press, 1980).

Radetzki, Marion, and Stephen Zorn. *Financing Mining Projects in Developing Countries* (London: Mining Journal Books, 1979).

"Foreign Finance for LDC Mining Projects," in Sandro Sideri and Sheridan Johns (eds.), *Mining for Development in the Third World: Multinational Corporations, State Enterprises and the International Economy* (New York: Pergamon Press, 1980).

Robinson, R. D. *National Control of Foreign Business Entry: A Survey of Fifteen Countries* (New York: Praeger, 1976).

Ronstadt, R. C. *Research and Development Abroad by U.S. Multinationals* (New York: Praeger, 1977).

Rosenberg, Nathan. "The Direction of Technological Change: Inducement Mechanisms and Focussing Devices." *Economic Development and Cultural Change*, vol. 18, no. 1, pt. 1, October 1969, pp. 1–24.

Perspectives on Technology (Cambridge: Cambridge University Press, 1976).

Samuelsson, H. F. "National Scientific and Technological Potential and the Activities of Multinational Corporations: The Case of Sweden." Mimeographed. Report to the OECD Committee for Scientific and Technological Policy, 1974.

Scherer, F. M. "Antitrust and Patent Policy." Mimeographed. Seminar on Technological Innovation, sponsored by U.S. National Science Foundation and the Government of the Federal Republic of Germany, Bonn, April 1976.

Industrial Market Structure and Economic Performance (Skokie, Ill.: Rand McNally, 1980).

Smith, D. M., and L. T. Wells, Jr. *Negotiating Third World Mineral Agreements: Promises as Prologue* (Cambridge, Mass.: Ballinger, 1976).

Stigler, G. J. "Imperfections in the Capital Market." *Journal of Political Economy*, vol. 75, no. 3, June 1967, pp. 287–92.

Stiglitz, J. E., and Andrew Weiss. "Credit Rationing in Markets with Imperfect Information." *American Economic Review*, vol. 71, no. 3, June 1981, pp. 393–409.

Stopford, J. M., and L. T. Wells, Jr. *Managing the Multinational* (New York: Basic Books, 1972).

Stuckey, J. A. "Vertical Integration and Joint Ventures in the International Aluminum Industry." Unpublished doctoral thesis, Harvard University, 1981.

Sundelson, J. W. "U.S. Automotive Investments Abroad," in C. P. Kindleberger (ed.), *The International Corporation* (Cambridge, Mass.: MIT Press, 1970).

Teece, D. J. "Vertical Integration in the U.S. Oil Industry," in E. J. Mitchell (ed.), *Vertical Integration in the Oil Industry* (Washington, D.C.: American Enterprise Institute, 1976).

Thunell, L. H. *Political Risks in International Business: Investment Behavior of Multinational Corporations* (New York: Praeger, 1977).

Tomlinson, J. W. C. *The Joint Venture in International Business* (Cambridge, Mass.: MIT Press, 1970).

Turner, Louis. *Multinational Companies and the Third World* (New York: Hill and Wang, 1973).

Turner, Louis, and J. M. Bedore. *Middle East Industrialization: A Study of Saudi and Iranian Downstream Investments* (Westnead, Farmborough, Hants, UK: Saxon House, 1979).

UNCTAD. *The Role of Trade Marks in Developing Countries* (New York: United Nations, 1979).

United Nations Economic and Social Council, Commission on Transnational Corporations. *Transnational Corporations in World Development: A Reexamination* (New York: United Nations, 1978).

U.S. Department of Commerce, Bureau of Economic Analysis. *U.S. Direct Investment Abroad, 1977* (Washington, D.C.: Government Printing Office, 1981).

U.S. Federal Trade Commission. *The International Petroleum Cartel* (Washington, D.C.: Government Printing Office, 1952).

U.S. Securities and Exchange Commission. *Report on Questionable and Illegal Corporate Payments and Practices* (Washington, D.C.: Government Printing Office, May 12, 1976).

U.S. Senate Committee on Banking, Housing and Urban Affairs. "Prohibiting Bribes to Foreign Officials." *Committee Hearings* (Washington, D.C.: Committee Print, May 18, 1976).

Vaupel, J. W., and J. P. Curhan. *The World's Multinational Enterprises: A Source Book of Tables* (Boston: Division of Research, Graduate School of Business Administration, Harvard University, 1973).

Vernon, Raymond. *Sovereignty at Bay* (New York: Basic Books, 1971).

Storm over the Multinationals (Cambridge, Mass.: Harvard University Press, 1977).

"The International Aspects of State-Owned Enterprises." *Journal of International Business Studies,* Winter 1979, pp. 7–15.

"Gone are the Cash Cows of Yesteryear." *Harvard Business Review,* November–December 1980, pp. 150–55.

Vernon, Raymond, and W. H. Davidson. "Foreign Production of Technology-Intensive Products by U.S.-Based Multinational Enterprises." Report to the National Science Foundation, no. PB 80 148638, January 1979.

Williamson, O. E. *Markets and Hierarchies: Analysis and Antitrust Implications* (New York: Free Press, 1975).

Zorn, Stephen. "Recent Trends in LDC Mining Agreements," in Sandro Sideri and Sheridan Johns (eds.), *Mining for Development in the Third World: Multinational Corporations, State Enterprises and the International Economy* (Elmsford, N.Y.: Pergamon Press, 1980).

5

Codes on transnationals: Ingredients for an effective international regime

In recent years, various international bodies have wrestled with the problem of finding appropriate formulas for defining the position of transnational corporations. Some of these efforts have led to the formulation and enactment of codes, such as the well-known OECD guidelines, covering various aspects of the operations of transnational corporations. Other projects targeted at these corporations have been developed in various organs of the United Nations, including the Centre on Transnational Corporations, UNCTAD, and the General Assembly; these have covered such diverse subjects as labor relations, technology transfers, restrictive business practices, illicit payments, the marketing of breast-milk substitutes, and accounting and reporting.

In addition to the codes and proposed codes considered in various international bodies, governments have entered into numerous bilateral treaties that touch on the rights and obligations of foreign direct investors. One compilation prepared by the OECD indicates that two hundred bilateral investment treaties had been signed as of January 1981, of which eighty-nine had been signed or ratified after 1973. Germany and Switzerland were far ahead in such new efforts to define investors' rights through bilateral agreements, but other investing countries also were involved.

With the striking expansion in the operations of transnational corporations during the past few decades, it is clear that some clarification of the rights and obligations of such corporations is needed. Any other conclusion, in fact, would have been quite surprising. Where their own national enterprises are concerned, practically every government has found it desirable to lay down some requirements governing business behavior; such requirements, as a rule, have covered an extensive and diverse set of subjects, including disclosure practices, tax practices, competitive practices, labor practices, and so on. However, these national regulatory regimes cannot be expected to provide an adequate system of oversight for foreign-owned enterprises, especially if they are units of a transnational corporation. For one thing, any such corporation is much more than the sum of its constituent

Presented at the Seventh World Congress of the International Economic Association, Madrid, Spain, September 1983; reprinted with permission of the International Economic Association.

affiliates; individual governments overseeing the activities of one of the affiliates are generally in a poor position effectively to deal with problems that relate to the system as a whole. Besides, as we shall presently see, the national regimes of different governments frequently make contradictory demands on a given transnational corporation; the corporation that responds to the requirements of one country may be required to evade the demands of another.

So far, the numerous efforts to develop a multinational regime with a capability for effective oversight have proceeded at a glacial pace.[1] The glacial character of the movement has been due to a number of factors. One of these is the great diversity with which different countries define the relationship between government and business; that diversity creates fundamental differences between governments as each seeks to find a framework for the transnational corporation that is compatible with its own national system. A second factor has been the worry of transnational corporations—a worry that is not without foundation—that any agreements regarding transnational corporations would be used as a weapon to punish and restrain. Still another factor has been the recognition of some governments that, in attempting to develop an international regime, they might be forced to accept some restraints on their own behavior, such as restraints on their efforts to extract benefits from the operations of the transnational corporation.

Factors such as these could prove controlling, limiting international action mainly to ineffectual hortatory declarations; indeed, that is a reasonable reading of the evidence to date. But there are slight signs that are less pessimistic in their implications, enough to justify an exploratory consideration of the nature of some of the impediments and of possible responses.

The struggle between concepts

Some difficult conceptual problems stand in the way of developing a multinational system of control over transnational corporations.

Rival concepts

In the national regulations relating to transnational corporations and in the international codes proposed for their control, two different concepts of the transnational corporation are found struggling with one another. One concept sees the transnational corporation as being composed of a number of separate enterprises, each independent unit endowed with its own resources and each potentially capable of responding to the obligations that the sovereign state imposes. The other concept is built on the assumption that the affiliates of a transnational corporation are linked by strong bonds, often responding to a common strategy and having access to a common pool of resources; and that concept leads governments which harbor a unit of a transnational corporation to think of ways of extracting benefits from the rest of the system that lies outside of their jurisdiction.[2]

In framing their national relations, most countries move from one concept to the other as they perceive their interests. For example, the so-called Calvo doctrine or something like it is embedded in national regulatory policies of many developing countries toward foreign-owned subsidiaries. That doctrine takes off from the proposition that each such subsidiary is indisputably a national subject of the government in whose jurisdiction it sits, and that if it appeals to a foreign government for protection it thereby forfeits all rights and remedies under local law. At the same time, however, governments adhering to the Calvo doctrine have been known to lay down numerous requirements that try to benefit from the links that relate the foreign-owned subsidiary to the transnational network. They have demanded that other subsidiaries of a multinational enterprise assume the debt of a bankrupt sister subsidiary;[3] that the foreign parent sell off portions of its equity to national stockholders;[4] that the foreign parent obtain prior permission for the reinvestment of profits of the subsidiary;[5] that the parent charge the subsidiary less than the going royalty rate on its technology;[6] and that the foreign parent arrange to increase the subsidiary's exports to affiliated units in other countries.[7]

The schizoid quality of governmental policy appears not only in the developing countries but in the mature industrialized countries as well. For instance, on the one hand, the U.S. government has resisted the view that a U.S. parent ought to be compelled to assume the debt of a bankrupt subsidiary located in Belgium, insisting that a U.S. parent had limited responsibility for the undertakings of its foreign subsidiary;[8] at the same time, however, the U.S. government has acted as if the subsidiaries of U.S. firms in foreign countries were subject to the strategic export controls imposed by the U.S. government.[9] The French government meanwhile has volubly resisted the U.S. claim of jurisdiction over U.S.-owned subsidiaries in France while at the same time taking an active hand in shaping the investment activities of French-owned subsidiaries in the United States.[10]

To be sure, one could conceive of a set of governmental policies that systematically dealt with the transnational corporation as if it were an integrated unit for some stated purposes and a cluster of independent units for other purposes. National laws regarding the attributes of enterprises are capable of making numerous fine distinctions. German law, for instance, explicitly recognizes that a group of corporations may be related in such a way as to share joint responsibilities among them in some respects but not in others; French law, as well as that of other continental countries, assigns weight to the geographical "seat" of a corporation in determining whether it is entitled to the rights of a national; the U.S. courts and U.S. statutes sometimes "pierce the corporate veil" in order to place obligations on the parent for some of the acts of a subsidiary.[11] Conceivably a common approach could be found that kept the points of conflict within bounds.

To develop that common approach, it will be necessary for governments

to reconcile some of the policies that most of them pursue. When governments think of an appropriate regime for "their" transnational corporations,
most tend to look for principles that will enlarge the rights of those corporations in foreign countries without impairing the responsibilities of such corporations to the home government. However, when governments (often the
same governments) are thinking of an appropriate regime for the foreign-
owned subsidiaries that lie within their own jurisdictions, they commonly
look for principles that will minimize the influence of foreign governments
and foreign parents. Finding mutually consistent principles on these points is
the critical challenge.

The conceptual bases of agreements

We observed earlier, however, that some agreements do exist purporting
to govern the international activities of transnational corporations, and that
others are in process of being negotiated. Can these be thought of as the
nucleus of a global regime?

One set of seemingly successful agreements is the network of bilateral
tax treaties that the OECD has sponsored among its member countries. The
success of the OECD in this specialized area is instructive.

In this case, the principal parties saw the problem as sufficiently acute to
justify real innovations. A number of countries including the United States
had been engaged in trying to extract from the transnational networks all the
tax revenues to which they thought themselves entitled. To that end, each
government had felt free to apply its own rules in determining which items of
income or expenditure of the transnational network fell within its taxing
jurisdiction, as well as in determining whether the network had appropriately priced a given transaction to which a unit in its jurisdiction was a party; the
answers to such questions, it is evident, would directly affect the size of the
taxable profits on which a government could levy. With many countries
playing the same game, the enterprises and the governments concerned soon
realized that in this case anarchy could be destructive for all parties. Inasmuch as any individual case of conflict commonly involved only a pair of
countries, bilateral agreements that had been tailored around some general
set of principles and that incorporated some means of settling disputes over
individual cases seemed adequate for dealing with most problems.

In addition to these tax treaties, there has been the recent proliferation
of bilateral agreements relating to foreign investors that were mentioned
earlier, agreements referred to generically as treaties of investment or treaties of establishment. Experience with this new wave of treaties is still limited; but in this case, unlike the case of the tax treaties, history does not offer
much encouragement that they will contribute to the development of a stable
regime.

The reasons for that judgment are obvious. By and large, governments of
developing countries that sign such agreements usually have a pressing immediate objective; they hope to send a strong signal to the international

business world that foreign capital and technology are welcome. Accordingly, such agreements ordinarily are tipped toward providing extensive guarantees from the host country to the prospective investing firm.[12] Characteristically, for instance, such treaties provide that once a foreign-owned subsidiary has been established in a host country, it will be entitled to the same treatment as a nationally-owned enterprise; that if the host country grants more favorable treatment to enterprises owned by investors from another foreign country, the same favorable treatment will be extended to enterprises of the treaty partner. Some governments also seek to ensure that if the subsidiary is entitled to still better treatment under the terms of a contract with the host government, the contractual terms will prevail; and that if established principles of international law set even a higher standard of treatment of the foreign-owned enterprise, those principles will be controlling.

Endowed with this extraordinary bundle of treaty rights in the host country, the subsidiary of the transnational corporation still retains its links to the home country. Such treaties do not restrain the home government from supporting the subsidiary's causes in the host country or from issuing commands to the subsidiary via the parent.

Treaties such as these, despite their patently unbalanced character, are not altogether useless. The explicit provisions for arbitration in the event of disputes can sometimes prove useful to the parties. But history suggests that the treaties are too unbalanced to provide the basis for a durable regime; the rights and obligations are so obviously loaded against the host country as to be a target for any dissenting political force in the country.

The statements of principles negotiated in 1976 among OECD members are somewhat less lopsided in their emphasis, probably reflecting the ambivalence of countries that are simultaneously the home government for some transnational corporations and the host government for others.[13] When viewed as a small first step on the part of governments in a prolonged process of mutual education, these OECD agreements may well have some value. But they are still far from representing an effective regime for the operations of transnational corporations, being recognized by all the parties as largely hortatory.

Moreover, the agreements neglect some of the most difficult issues relating to the operations of such corporations. They fail to deal, for instance, with the conflicts created by so-called performance requirements, such as the efforts of many countries unilaterally to force the local subsidiaries of transnational corporations to produce more, export more, and import less at the expense of the rest of the transnational network. Also unresolved are the problems raised by unilateral measures, such as those of the United States, aimed at securing the adherence of the overseas subsidiaries of U.S. parent firms to U.S. security export restrictions, as well as the less transparent efforts of the French and Japanese governments to influence the investment patterns of the overseas subsidiaries of their firms. Moreover, some major issues that have not been altogether avoided have been deliberately fudged. Illustrations of such egregious fudging is the admonition in the code that transnational corporations should abstain from involvement in local political activities to the extent that such involvement is "improper," and the further admonition that transnational corporations should allow each of their component entities the freedom to develop its own activities to the extent that such freedom is "consistent with the need for specialization and sound commercial practice."

The various U.N.-sponsored projects for the control of transnational corporations have been of even less value in helping to create an international regime for transnational corporations. To be sure, most of these proposals have been realistic in one important respect: They have aimed at the formulation of general principles rather than hard agreements, in the hope that those principles would eventually be incorporated in bilateral, regional, or other less-than-global instrumentalities.[14] The modesty of the objectives, however, has also had its drawbacks, for it has allowed governments the luxury of using the negotiations as a platform for pushing rival ideologies rather than for developing workable systems of oversight. In the mid-1970s, for instance, it was common for developing countries to distinguish sharply between the possession of natural resources and the possession of technology: A nation's natural resources were to be regarded as inalienable, representing a patrimony that foreign-owned enterprises were barred from controlling—but a nation's *technology* was to be viewed as the common heritage of mankind, which therefore could not appropriately be denied to other countries. That unhelpful set of propositions was characteristically countered by equally unproductive observations from some of the industrialized countries on the virtues of free competitive enterprise. Because the negotiations were aimed at general principles rather than at operating provisions, developing countries also saw little risk in negotiating *en bloc* and casting themselves exclusively in the role of host countries, overlooking the fact that some of them have now spawned transnational corporations of their own.[15]

With wide differences of view and deepseated inconsistencies in the various elements making up the position of many governments, the prospects for effective agreements that would produce a tolerable regime for transnational corporations do not seem bright. Yet there are very few governments that actually want to prevent the existence of such enterprises; most see themselves as engaged in an effort to increase the benefits and reduce the costs for their national economies that they associate with the operations of the enterprises. As long as that remains the case, agreements are still possible—especially if the principal parties eventually conclude that the very existence of the enterprises is being imperilled by the absence of an international regime.

Structuring effective agreements

A search for principles

As noted earlier, the gaps between national norms on the subject of business–government relations are overwhelming. And where transnational corporations are concerned, the gaps have been widened further by the tendency of governments in each instance to invoke the general concept that seems to suit its national interests best.

If governments eventually tackle the problems seriously, they are likely to find it necessary to make certain critical distinctions among various classes of rights and obligations. In any workable regime, for instance, some rights and obligations would inure to the transnational network as a whole, while others would be directed to the individual units of the transnational network. Among the provisions applicable to the network as a whole, for instance, would be requirements to report various specified types of information relating to the network as well as a means for dealing with cases in which the network is confronted with mutually contradictory commands from two sovereign states. Another set of distinctions would reflect the dual role of the parent firm; its rights and obligations as parent manager could usefully be distinguished from its rights and obligations as a foreign property owner. Distinctions such as these will prove helpful in addressing some of the functional fields that demand attention in the construction of any workable regime. Of the various functional fields which need addressing, that relating to political activity seems one of the most pressing.

Political activity

Defining the political rights and obligations of the affiliates of a transnational corporation is a subject of enormous sensitivity; although little discussed, it colors the general approach of many governments to the transnational corporation and affects their handling of many more technical aspects of such corporations' operations. Understandably, as long as those affiliates seem subject to the commands of the parent and of the government of the country in which the parent is located, other governments will feel uneasy about allowing such affiliates to engage in domestic politics without restraint. (Parent governments too occasionally feel uneasy about the possibility that a foreign subsidiary might be acting as a conduit through which political pressures are being exerted on the parent.)

Concerned over the possibilities associated with political activity, governments could conceivably build their agreements on the principle that for such purposes any subsidiary unit of a transnational corporation was to be treated as a foreign entity. From that principle, two corollaries would flow: that its domestic political activities should be limited to those appropriate for foreigners; and that, as a foreigner, it should have the rights that foreigners normally have to solicit the support of their own governments.

Barring the local affiliates of a transnational corporation from participating in the national debate over some important groups of issues, however, may be a distasteful choice for some countries, especially for countries whose system of governance is that of a participatory democracy. One could picture a group of governments, brought together by the OECD or by a regional organization, that took a very different tack with respect to the political activity of any unit of a transnational corporation. The group might agree, for instance, that each unit should be looked upon in the first instance as a national of the country in which it was located. That principle, however, would be linked to its obvious corollary: Government signatories might agree not to attempt to influence the political behavior of an entity outside their respective jurisdiction, whether by direct pressure on that entity or by punishing or rewarding an affiliate of the entity that was in its own jurisdiction. If that principle were adopted in unqualified form, it would for instance bar U.S. efforts or similar efforts by other countries to extend the country's security export controls to foreign subsidiaries as well as the attempts of governments to impose blacklists on the affiliates of transnational corporations outside their jurisdiction. In accordance with the same principle, foreign governments, including notably the governments of parents, would be expected not to provide direct diplomatic support to foreign subsidiaries. In this limited area, therefore, the concept of separateness of the affiliate of the transnational corporation would dominate over the concept of the network's unitary character.

Subsidiaries as property

Obviously, a radical political principle of the sort just described could not be negotiated in isolation. Any system of international agreements would have to provide at the same time for the rights and obligations of foreigners as property owners. This is a well-ploughed area of international law, extending back into history and developed more recently under the stimulus of the numerous expropriations of foreign-owned property that have taken place since World War II.

Until the 1970s, the standards that governments generated for dealing with the rights of foreigners as property owners were reasonably clear. In general, no government was barred from taking over the assets or the equity of a foreign-owned enterprise for public purposes broadly defined; but the property owner was seen as entitled to receive prompt and adequate compensation.[16] In the 1970s, however, various U.N. declarations began conspicuously to omit references to foreigners' rights of compensation.

It is hard to envisage any freely negotiated intergovernmental regime for transnational corporations that did not include recognition of the rights of foreign parent firms as property owners, more especially, the right to some form of compensation for the impairment of the value of their property. Indeed such a regime probably would be expected to provide for at least two problems that have been the source of considerable acrimony in the past: measures by governments directed especially at foreign-owned property, short of expropriation, that materially impaired the value of the property; and methods of assessing the amount of compensation due to the foreign owners.

Because the issues in this field have been so well ploughed, the alternatives are already fairly well understood and well developed.[17] Provisions that simply require consultation between governments on such disputed issues are not much use. Various mechanisms are available for arbitration and evaluation, including notably the International Centre for the Settlement of Investment Disputes. Many governments would want strong assurances that some such mechanism would be employed in any comprehensive regime for transnational enterprises.

In the past, many developing countries—especially countries in Latin America—have refused to accept the principle of compulsory arbitration, insisting that all aspects of expropriation should be handled under domestic law. It may be, therefore, that such resistance would prove the stumbling block to the development of any effective regime. On the other hand, if other aspects of a comprehensive regime appeared sufficiently attractive to developing countries, such as the restraints imposed on the political activity of the transnational units and adequate disclosure provisions for the transnational networks as a whole, those countries may conceivably be prepared to consider some effective method of protecting the property rights of foreigners.

Other functional fields

Establishing the rights and obligations of transnational corporations will require governments to develop a variety of agreements and institutions, each tailored to its own functional field. Each such agreement will presumably lay out principles and procedures that are applicable to the particular field. One problem that many of these functional fields will share, however, is how to draw the line between national jurisdictions, so that the transnational network is not confronted with conflicting obligations imposed by two different states.

On this issue, the network of bilateral tax treaties suggests an obvious set of principles. The diversity among governmental policies toward enterprises in their respective jurisdictions is wide and promises to remain so. The function of international agreements should be seen as largely to bridge those differences where they generate conflict. Based on that principle, each signatory government would normally be free to lay down rules for action within its own jurisdiction. If the foreign parent of an enterprise could sustain the case that it was being discriminated against because of foreign ownership, then it would have a basis for claiming compensation. If the measures adversely affected' other signatory governments by their reverberations through the transnational network, then signatories would be under an obligation to modify their national actions in order to conform with the specified principles and with the outcome of specified procedures in the agreement; but the principles and procedures would be fashioned separately for each functional area, according to its needs. That approach, for instance, could readily be applied to policies in the field of restrictive business practices and of performance requirements.[18]

In the end, however, one must concede—albeit reluctantly—that most governments and most transnational corporations have not yet reached the point at which they are prepared to confront the hard issues associated with creating a stable regime for transnational corporations. Now and then, small groups of likeminded countries may be persuaded to confront some of the issues. But a long period of experimentation and travail will be needed before anything like a comprehensive international regime for transnational corporations takes shape.

Notes

[1]For recent summaries of the state of such projects, see Norbert Horn (ed.), *Legal Problems of Codes of Conduct for Multinational Enterprises: Studies in Transnational Economic Law*, Vol. 1 (Deventer, The Netherlands: Kluwer, 1980); "Symposium: Codes of Conduct for Transnational Corporations," *American University Law Review*, vol. 30, no. 4, Summer 1981, pp. 903–1048; *CTC Reporter*, Centre on Transnational Corporations, New York, no. 12, Summer 1982. In process is a work coedited by Gary C. Hufbauer and Seymour J. Rubin under the auspices of the American Society of International Law.

[2]For a useful discussion of the rival concepts, see Norbert Horn, "Codes of Conduct for Multinational Enterprises," in Horn (ed.), *Legal Problems of Codes of Conduct*, pp. 63–69.

[3]Michael Gordon, "Argentine Jurisprudence: The Parke Davis and Deltec Cases," *Lawyers of the Americas*, vol. 12, Summer 1980, pp. 320–45.

[4]Lloyd Pike, "The Andean Foreign Investment Code: An Overview," *Georgia Journal of International and Comparative Law*, vol. 7, no. 2 (1977), pp. 160–61; and David Morawetz, *The Andean Group: A Case Study in Economic Integration among Developing Countries* (Cambridge, MA: MIT Press, 1974), pp. 46–47.

[5]"The Andean Foreign Investment Code: An Overview," pp. 663–67.

[6]Frank E. Nattier, "Limitations on Marketing Foreign Technology in Brazil," *International Lawyer*, vol. 11, Summer 1977, pp. 442–43; and Alan L. Hyde and Gaston Ramirez de la Corte, "Mexico's New Transfer of Technology and Foreign Investment Laws—To What Extent Have the Rules Changed?" *International Lawyer*, vol. 10, Spring 1976, p. 236.

[7]U.S. Department of Commerce, International Trade Administration, *The Use of Investment Incentives and Performance Requirements by Foreign Governments* (Washington, DC: Government Printing Office, 1981), pp. 7–11.

[8]R. Blanpain, *The Badger Case and the OECD Guidelines for Multinational Enterprises* (Deventer, The Netherlands: Kluwer, 1977).

[9]"When the Pipeline Row is Over," *The Economist*, October 30, 1982, pp. 16–19.

[10]"Dirigisme Waxes and Wanes in Socialist France," *The Economist*, November 27, 1982, p. 78.

[11]For a country-by-country summary of some of the complexities among OECD countries, see *International Investment in Multinational Enterprises: Responsibility of Parent Companies for their Subsidiaries*, OECD, Paris, 1980.

[12]Official summaries of the policies of Germany, Belgium, Japan, Switzerland, and the United Kingdom appear in OECD Document DAF/81.40, distributed to delegates to the Committee on International Investment and Multinational Enterprises, November 13, 1981. The U.S. government in 1982 reactivated its program of such treaties, which had been dormant for about twenty years, by negotiating an agreement with Egypt on similar lines.

[13]*Declaration by the Governments of OECD Member Countries* and *Decisions of the OECD Council on Guidelines for Multinational Enterprises, National Treatment, International Investment Incentives and Disincentives, Consultation Procedures*, Organization for Economic Cooperation and Development (OECD), Paris, 1976.

[14]This aspect of the U.N. codes is explored in S. J. Rubin, "Transnational Corporations and International Codes of Conduct: A Study of the Relationship between International Legal Cooperation and Economic Development," *American University Law Review*, vol. 30, no. 4, Summer 1981, pp. 903–21.

[15]In Latin America, for instance, the foreign subsidiaries of transnational corporations headquartered in other Latin American countries are referred to ambiguously as "empresas conjuntas," not as units of transnational corporations. For a description of the development of transnational corporations headquartered in developing countries, see L. T. Wells, Jr., *Third World Multinationals* (Cambridge, MA: MIT Press, 1983).

[16]H. J. Steiner and D. F. Vagts, *Transnational Legal Problems: Materials and Text* (2d. edition) (Mineola, NY: Foundation Press, 1976), pp. 431–32.

[17]Rudolf Dolzer, "New Foundations of the Law of Expropriation of Alien Property," *American Journal of International Law*, vol. 75, no. 3, July 1981, pp. 553–89.

[18]An authoritative and perceptive analysis of jurisdictional conflict coupled with proposals of a more evolutionary kind than those proposed here is found in Douglas E. Rosenthal and William M. Knighton, *National Laws and International Commerce: The Problem of Extraterritoriality*, Chatham House Papers 17 (London: Routledge and Kejan Paul, 1982).

Part 3

The State-Owned Enterprise

6
The international aspects of state-owned enterprises

Introduction

Those of us who are concerned with the problems of international business need very little reminding of the importance of state-owned enterprises operating outside of socialist economies. In oil, enterprises such as the National Iranian Oil Company and the British National Oil Company play a prominent role; in agricultural products, one finds entities such as the Canadian Wheat Board and the Japanese Food Agency; and in the high-technology field, firms such as Rolls Royce and Aerospatiale. The prominence of these institutions in international business offers two challenges: to identify and master the problems in international business management that are distinctive to such state-owned enterprises and to envisage the changes in existing international business practices that such enterprises are likely to produce.

The emerging patterns

Origins and motives

State-owned enterprises, it is safe to assume, have existed for as long as the states themselves. Joseph's grain speculations in Egypt were certainly not the first of these undertakings—and quite obviously not the last.

Thirty years ago, however, if one were undertaking an inventory of state-owned enterprises outside the communist countries, most of these would have fallen into the category of public utilities. In a few countries, including Mexico and Italy, such enterprises were more pervasive. And in a few other countries, including Britain and New Zealand, some state-owned marketing boards were in operation—legacies of the Great Depression or of World War II. But the role of state-owned enterprises in international markets was on the whole quite secondary.[1]

Today, the picture is somewhat changed. State-owned enterprises are found in a wide range of industries both in the advanced industrialized

Reprinted with permission of the publisher from *Journal of International Business Studies*, Winter 1979.

countries and in the developing nations.[2] State-owned trading firms, charged with the international purchase or sale of some specified product for a given country, have proliferated.[3] Although private enterprises still predominate in the production and foreign trade of the market economies, the state-owned segment occupies a dominant role in many key areas.

Governments have acquired the ownership of enterprises under all sorts of circumstances and with a wide variety of motives. In many cases, the original motives for establishing a state-owned enterprise have had little to do with its subsequent operations; the activities of Renault and Ente Nazionale Indrocarburi, for instance, have been quite unrelated to the original reasons for the nationalization of these organizations. Nevertheless, the strategies of state-owned enterprises have not been wholly unrelated to the circumstances of their birth. It is relevant, therefore, to review some of the circumstances under which state-owned trading and state-owned producing enterprises have been brought into existence.

State-owned enterprises have been employed to levy taxes by selling at high monopoly prices (as in the case of the French and Italian tobacco and alcohol monopolies) or by buying at low monopsony prices (as in the case of Ghanaian cocoa). They have also been used to dispense subsidies through sales at reduced prices (as in the case of Mexico's CONASUPO). In many of these cases, the functions might just as well have been performed by a government ministry through a system of direct taxes or subsidies, but enterprises have been assigned the task simply as a matter of accident or of administrative convenience.

The fiscal function, in practice, proves to be almost indistinguishable from still another function commonly performed by governments in respect to agriculture—namely, the reduction in the risk that agricultural producers confront by virtue of highly unstable prices. By taxing in bonanza years and paying subsidies in lean years, state-owned enterprises are in a position to reduce the risks that agricultural producers normally confront.

In all such instances, of course, the financial statements of the enterprises must be interpreted with care. Large profits may reflect nothing more than the taxing capability of the state, implemented by the grant of a monopoly to the state-owned enterprise, whereas large losses may conceivably be the expression of a conscious policy of grants from the public purse to some part of the national population. Where losses do occur, it is not easy for an outsider to distinguish between those that represent a planned policy of income redistribution and those that are rationalized after the fact in such terms.

The enterprise as national champion

Governments have also taken to creating state-owned enterprises as a means of developing or maintaining an industry that the private sector seems unwilling to enter or unable to defend. Sometimes these enterprises are created because no private investor, local or foreign, is prepared to set up the wanted facilities. At other times, the objective in creating the state-owned firm is to ensure that the national industry will not be dominated by foreign-owned enterprises.[4] In both the advanced and the developing countries, one encounters numerous illustrations of both motivations—for instance, Brazil's principal iron ore producer, Companhia Vale do Rio Doce, and Venezuela's Sidor at different stages in their history exhibited one or another of these motivations. Aerospatiale in France and Rolls Royce in Britain, mentioned earlier, would fall in the same general category. In any case, the governments' ability to assume very large risks and their ability to provide capital on favorable terms were factors that made it possible to launch or to maintain such enterprises.

The enterprise as mobilizer of national monopoly and monopsony power

Textbooks on international trade are filled with demonstrations of the fact that governments can improve their terms of trade by applying an appropriate tariff on imports or a tax on exports. Instead of attempting to produce that result through the relatively clumsy device of taxes or tariffs, however, governments in some countries—mainly developing countries—are trying to achieve the same objective through state-trading entities.[5] The export marketing boards in developing countries—such as, those that control the exports of Ghanaian cocoa and Colombian coffee—are charged in part with achieving that result. So, too, are the national oil companies of most oil exporting countries, such as Pertamina and NIOC.

It is worth noting, however, that arrangements for the mobilizing of monopoly or monopsony power are not confined to state-trading entities. Privately owned enterprises are organized also in some industries to exploit their potential market power: on the export side, the Webb–Pomerene associations of the United States, for instance; and on the import side, the buying agents in the Japanese coal trade and the German iron ore trade. Private arrangements of this sort, however, are typically wrapped in greater secrecy than their state-sponsored counterparts; so it is not clear what the relative propensities of the public and the private sectors may be in developing such arrangements.

The enterprise as official agent in bilateral trade arrangements

State-owned enterprises are particularly useful for countries, such as Brazil, that have entered into bilateral trade agreements with other countries designed to keep their two-way trade flows in balance. One object of such agreements is to ensure that neither party will have to pay foreign currency to the other in settlement of its transactions. In practice, that outcome generally requires a certain amount of management when one partner or the other proves to be the more effective seller. When imbalance exists, a country with a large contingent of state-owned enterprises, such as Sri Lanka or India, is in a position to right the imbalance by commanding such enterprises to buy their foreign requirements from the other trading partner, irrespective of commercial considerations. Actions of this sort are generally as darkly guarded as measures in the field of private restrictive practices; so once again, we are treading in largely unknown territory.

The enterprise as agent of industrial policy

Industrial policy itself covers a wide range of national objectives. State-owned enterprises in this category, therefore, are targeted at a heterogeneous set of goals. Perhaps the most familiar is the desire of governments to develop a lagging section of the country. In Italy, Britain, and France, among other countries, state-owned enterprises have often been commanded to take on the special costs of setting up and operating a plant in a backward area.[6]

Another familiar purpose of industrial policy has been to prevent senescent industries, such as shipbuilding and steel in some of the advanced industrialized countries, from folding up—or from folding up too rapidly—under the pressure of foreign competition. In this sort of function, state-owned enterprises have played an important role, acting as a conduit from the public treasury to support the troubled enterprise.[7]

In the field of industrial policies the line between managing structural changes and managing cyclical changes can be very thin. Predictably, state-owned enterprises have been used for both. In Britain, Italy, and Mexico, among many others, state-owned enterprises have refrained from laying off their redundant workforce in periods of declining demand.[8]

Finally, state-owned enterprises are often called upon in some countries to exercise special constraints in raising prices.[9] How well they do in response to such exhortations has not been widely tested. The nearly universal losses of state-owned bus companies and railroads suggest that these public pressures may have some effect, thereby redistributing income somewhat in the countries where they operate. But whether the same effect can be discerned in enterprises that produce internationally traded goods is less clear.

A multiplicity of goals

State-owned enterprises, then, are born in ambiguity, an ambiguity to which their managers must be constantly responsive. Governments that have chosen to create such enterprises presumably expect something distinctive from their performance—something more than could be achieved by the promulgation of a tax or a tariff or a price regulation. That added something is presumably to be provided by the fact that the enterprise, although owned by the government, is a separate unit, distinct from the government and subject to a separate management; yet, at the same time, the enterprise must respond to a set of signals from government to which private managers would presumably be less alert—signals that relate not to profit but to other goals associated with the well-being of the nation.

In some circumstances, the multiplicity of goals would conceivably be manageable. If, for example, specific trade-off functions were laid down among competing goals, the manager might still be able to construct a strategy that was optimal when measured against the mandate of the firm. But governments are characteristically composed of a coalition of forces, each of which places rather different weights on conflicting goals. One ministry, therefore, may stress inflation goals, another employment goals, another budgetary goals; one politician will favor his area of the country, another politician his. And any of these elements in the coalition could easily have some voice in determining the rewards and punishments meted out to the manager.[10]

The role of the manager is complicated by another dimension. The tenure of ministers in most governments is short—shorter in many cases than the tenure of professional managers in state-owned enterprises. By responding faithfully to the goals of one administration, therefore, the manager will not necessarily contribute to his career goals; the preoccupation of one administration to achieve budgetary balance, for instance, could easily be succeeded by the preoccupation of the next administration to maintain employment.

How managers live with the problem of responding to the conflicting and mercurial goals of government is a subject that has barely been researched in any systematic way. But the outlines of a set of generalizations are suggested even by the unstructured evidence.

A process of unceasing bargaining appears to be going on between most state-owned enterprises and the government bureaus, ministers, and politicians to which the enterprises are presumed responsive. As noted earlier, the government side is in a position to offer a variety of benefits. It can provide subsidized capital, underwrite unusual risk, provide protection from imports, forgive direct and indirect taxes, and offer exemption from government regulations. In return, state-owned enterprises can take on high-risk projects, hire unwanted labor, place plants in backward areas, hold down prices and profits, and tax some selected classes of customers while subsidizing others. To be sure, using the same ingredients, governments have been known to make bargains with private enterprises as well,[11] but the evidence seems to point to the general conclusion that the special relationships between state-owned enterprises and governments based upon such bargains are more extensive and intensive than those made with private enterprises. In some countries and some periods, as in Sweden today, the distinction may be slight; but in other times and places, the distinction is quite strong.

A second broad generalization is also suggested by the evidence. Managers of state-owned enterprises commonly try to increase their independence from the government apparatus, a tendency variously described as a desire for autonomy or discretion or increased bargaining power.[12] The underlying motives for this widely observed phenomenon are unclear. Perhaps managers feel more secure about their future if they are less reliant on government; perhaps they feel also that greater independence offers greater scope for self-expression and leadership. Whatever the reasons may be, managers are engaged typically in maneuvers that seem aimed at making them more independent of governmental decisions. Maneuvers of this kind include efforts to develop a cash flow that is independent of the control of their supervising ministries, as well as efforts to link up with foreign partners who are capable of providing resources that lie beyond national controls.

The manager's search for independence from government may appear to entail certain personal risks at times. But from the viewpoint of the firm as a whole, it represents a low-risk strategy. According to the record, state-owned enterprises that get into trouble as a result of an independent strategy are rarely allowed to founder; when the help of the government is needed again, that help is usually forthcoming. Numerous cases that support this generalization are to be found both in Europe and the developing world.

Juggling multiple objectives, negotiating for special support, grouping for increased autonomy, managers of state-owned enterprises operate under conditions that differ somewhat from those of their private counterparts. To be sure, none of these problems is unknown to the private sector; but their incidence seems on the whole less weighty. Exactly how these differences affect the behavior of the manager of the state-owned enterprise, however, is a subject that is not yet well delineated. This is a rich field for study by students of international business.

Some international implications

Even without the requisite study of managerial behavior, however, it is possible to hypothesize where some of the international implications may lie.

The propensity to use domestic inputs

The domestic political process of most countries generally pushes government buyers toward a policy of buy-at-home—and even to a more restrictive variant, buy-at-home-only-from-local-enterprise.[13] Government-owned enterprises, we can assume, are more vulnerable to the domestic political process than are privately owned enterprises. That vulnerability would be especially great where the item being purchased consists of a steady flow of a standardized product over a sustained period—such as, an intermediate chemical; where, in addition, the only handicap of the domestic source is its relatively high price; and where the state-owned enterprise produces mainly for the local market. The expectation that the state enterprise will favor national sources would apply not only to state-owned enterprises engaged in production but also to state entities engaged primarily in trading.

It may be, however, that state-owned enterprises have more freedom in some circumstances to draw on foreign products than do private firms similarly situated. For instance, in a country that imposes licensing controls on imports, state-owned enterprises working inside the governmental system may be in a favored position to secure authorization for the importation of foreign machinery.

In the end, therefore, we may find systematic patterns of behavior on the part of state-owned enterprises that range from less use of foreign inputs in some specified circumstances to greater use of foreign inputs in others.

The propensity to export

It goes without saying that state-owned enterprises will be exhorted by their governments to increase exports, and it is reasonable to assume that their disposition to respond to such pressures will be fairly high. But whether they will actually succeed in exporting at a higher rate than private firms is a more complex question.[14]

In the case of products that are undifferentiated by firm source, where the critical question to the buyer is one of price, it may be that state-owned enterprises are operating under a certain advantage. Their presumed ability to receive subsidized inputs, such as capital, and their reported capacity for covering unplanned deficits from public sources should render them more ready than their private competitors to reduce prices as a way of increasing exports.

The tendency to reduce prices may in fact be strengthened by another factor. The objective of governments in exhorting state-owned enterprises to increase exports will usually be to increase jobs or foreign exchange earnings rather than to maximize the firm's profits. It can be demonstrated that the firm which hopes to maximize jobs or gross revenues will tend to charge a lower price for its product than the firm which is maximizing profits.

The disposition of the state-owned enterprises to reduce prices, it would seem, will be enhanced even further in periods of declining demand. At such times, state-owned enterprises will be under particularly strong pressure to maintain employment and foreign exchange earnings. With the labor bill seen as a fixed cost and with cash flows assured, managers would find it hard to resist the temptation to cut prices.

Nevertheless, the ability of state-owned enterprises to achieve their export objectives through price reductions may well prove to have some important limits. The case of Venezuela's iron ore policy illustrates one such limitation. Venezuela represents one of that special subset of developing countries which seems to have adequate foreign exchange earnings for the present and which is concerned with protecting its domestic resources for long-term national use. In those circumstances, the state-owned enterprise may well be instructed to hold back its sales to foreign markets to a degree that would not be matched by a private enterprise. Moreover, political factors will sometimes play a part in such cases, stifling the urge to cut prices; the unwillingness to upset other sellers, especially other sellers from developing countries, may act as the added brake.

Apart from that special type of case, there is the more familiar case encountered in many oligopolistic markets which leads to price restraint. The price reductions of one seller may be matched by the price reductions of another, in a process that benefits none of the producers. Where that possibility exists, the established leaders in the market are generally loath to start the price-cutting process. To be sure, new state-owned firms in developing countries may not always be concerned about this sort of risk; lacking an established position in the market, some may see the advantages of price-cutting as exceeding the risks. Eventually, however, the risks of competitive price-cutting are appreciated by state-trading firms as they develop a market position and a background of experience; witness the restrained price policies of the Soviet Union in oil, aluminum, and diamonds.[15]

Another constraint on the exports of state-owned enterprises may be found arising from a different source; namely, from an indisposition to make any very elaborate commitments to the requirements of foreign markets. Here and there, one sees concrete manifestations of such a tendency, as parliaments and ministries complain over some investment in a foreign market by one of their state-owned enterprises. That tendency, if it actually exists, would be expected to manifest itself in a number of different ways: first, in a reluctance to invest much in creating a permanent presence abroad, especially if it entails the sinking of real resources; second, in an indisposition to tailor products to the need of the individual foreign markets. If those tendencies in fact exist, state-owned enterprises may prove to be handicapped in the marketing of a wide range of goods.

Links among state-owned enterprises

It seems reasonable to anticipate that state-owned enterprises will tend to be drawn to one another in the conduct of their international business, preferring such links to those with private enterprises. One reason for this expectation is self-evident: Governments that find it convenient to do business with one another are likely to designate their respective state-owned enterprises to act for them in the execution of their contemplated deals: swaps of oil for technology, for instance, have brought the state-owned enterprises of Europe into various partnerships with those of the Middle East.[16]

In addition, however, state-owned enterprises may be brought together by a common tendency to prefer commercial arrangements that are longer in duration than those desired by private enterprises. The reasons for that expectation are conjectural. But one possibility is that state-owned enterprises, especially those that serve their own national markets, feel a greater sense of assurance and security about their place in the domestic market than do their private counterparts and hence, a greater willingness to tie up their sources of materials for the long pull. Another possibility is that state-owned enterprises in general have fewer fears of long-term commitments than do private enterprises simply because their downside risks are lower. If such a commitment eventually proves to be a handicap to competition, the state-owned enterprise need not worry about the possibility of bankruptcy; either it will be relieved of its obligations through government intervention or it will be bailed out of its difficulties by government subsidies. Meanwhile, some of its planning uncertainties will have been reduced by the presence of a long-term agreement.

The disposition of state-owned enterprises to accept long-term commitments plus the semi-official cast placed upon the business activities of such firms suggest that they may especially be disposed to enter into regulatory international agreements, drawing on the patterns of the private cartels of pre-World War II and the official commodity agreements of the postwar period. That expectation is even more plausible if it should turn out that state-owned enterprises were indisposed to created overseas subsidiaries. Overseas subsidiaries are commonly used by private enterprises to create vertically integrated structures which buffer the participants from the risks of the market. If that strategy is not quite so available to state-owned enterprises, they may be more strongly disposed to turn to other arrangements to reduce their market risks, including the cartel and the commodity agreement.

Links with multinational enterprises

Despite the special strengths of state-owned enterprises, such enterprises may still find themselves operating at a disadvantage as compared with their private multinational competitors.

The disadvantage is likely to be most in evidence in those industries in which wide geographical spread bestows special advantages on the firm. On the assumption that state-owned enterprises will find it difficult to invest widely abroad, such enterprises may be unable to capture all the potential advantages that exist in such situations; for example, it is easy to contemplate that private enterprises will retain some considerable advantage in the global distribution—though not necessarily the production—of oil and minerals. State-owned enterprises that are created through the nationalization of private companies commonly retain such companies as distributors of their product. In Venezuela, for instance, state-owned iron ore is distributed in part by U.S. Steel; in Guyana, state-owned bauxite by Alcan; and in most of the Middle East, state-owned crude oil by multinational oil enterprises.

A second situation in which private enterprises may succeed in maintaining some advantage over state-owned enterprises is in some of the high technology fields, especially in those cases in which economies of scale are important yet flexibility must be maintained. Situations of this sort are sometimes encountered when enterprises are engaged in a large-scale development program on a technological frontier. State-owned enterprises—and a fortiori, consortia of state-owned enterprises—have often been hampered by excessive rigidity in such situations.

In such cases, state-owned enterprises will find it useful at times to enter into partnerships with private multinational enterprises.[17] State-owned enterprises are likely to have two reasons to enter into such partnerships: (1) in order to ensure that their performance is equal to that of the multinational enterprises with which they compete in world markets, whether in the distribution of goods or in the application of advanced technologies; and (2) in order to increase their autonomy in relations with their home governments.

Illustrations of partnerships between state-owned enterprises and multinational enterprises are already quite common. These are embodied in licensing agreements, joint ventures, and management contracts which often assign to the private multinational partner a considerable role in the operation of the facilities of the state-owned enterprise. In some cases, the foreign partner is the source of important technology; in other cases, the foreign partner is the marketing agent.

From the viewpoint of the privately owned multinational enterprises, of course, partnerships of this sort are second-best solutions. The preferred solution would usually be a vertically integrated, closely controlled structure, if that were possible. But on the principle that half a loaf is better than none, one can anticipate that privately owned multinational enterprises will continue to enter into such arrangements.

My present guess, therefore, is that the substantial growth of state-owned enterprises might inhibit the expansion of multinational enterprises; but that multinational enterprises would adapt to some extent by a change in role. As a result, there may be room for substantial cooperative activity between the two groups of enterprise.

Conclusion

What is uncertain about such projections, however, are the relative weights of the various tendencies described. On the one hand, state-owned enterprises may not develop in sufficient number to make any of these hypotheses terribly important. On the other hand, they may develop in such overwhelming numbers that the multinational enterprise finds it difficult to survive and prosper. Getting a keener sense of the relative weights of these various tendencies should be one of the important objectives for future research in this field.

Notes

[1]See Stuart Holland, "Europe's New State Enterprises," in Raymond Vernon, ed., *Big Business and the State* (Cambridge, MA: Harvard University Press, 1974), pp. 25–26 for a discussion of the nature of European state enterprises prior to 1950; for the evolution of state firms in Britain, see Richard Pryke, *Public Enterprise in Practice—The British Experience of Nationalization After Two Decades* (London: MacGibbon & Kee, 1971), pp. 10–12.

[2]Leroy P. Jones, *Public Enterprise and Economic Development: The Korean Case* (Seoul, Korea: Korea Development Institute, 1975). John B. Sheahan, "Public Enterprise in Developing Countries," in William Shepherd, ed., *Public Enterprise: Economic Analysis of Theory and Practice* (Lexington, MA: Lexington Books, 1976), p. 214 lists indicators of the relative importance of public enterprise in nine developing countries.

[3]M. M. Kostecki, "State Trading in Industrialized and Developing Countries," *Journal of World Trade Law,* May/June 1978, pp. 187–207, especially p. 205.

[4]Stuart Holland (See note 1), p. 31–32, treats much of the postwar growth of state enterprises in Europe as a response to the challenge of U.S. multinationals.

[5]M. M. Kostecki (see note 3), p. 207.

[6]See John B. Sheahan, "Experience with Public Enterprise in France and Italy," in William Shepherd, ed. (see note 2), pp. 158–160 for details of Italian state enterprise participation in development of the Italian South; see also M. V. Posner and S. J. Woolf, *Italian Public Enterprise* (Cambridge, MA: Harvard University Press, 1967), pp. 108–112.

[7]"The State in the Market," *The Economist,* Special Report, 30 December 1978, pp. 37–58. See especially pp. 48–49 for a discussion of state support for the ailing shipbuilding industry.

[8]Richard Pryke (see note 1) p. 99, notes that British state firms are loath to lay off labor.

[9]See for instance Robert Millward, "Price Restraint, Anti-Inflation Policy and Public and Private Industry in the U.K. 1949–1973," *Economic Journal,* June 1976.

[10]See Yair Aharoni, "The Public Sector as an Owner and Producer—The State-Owned Enterprise," ch. 9, in *Markets, Planning and Development—The Private and Public Sectors in Economic Development* (Cambridge, MA: Ballinger, 1977) for a discussion of the problems of controlling state firms.

[11]See Assar Lindbeck, *Swedish Economic Policy* (Berkeley, CA: University of California Press, 1974), p. 77 for a Swedish example; also Mario C. Ferrario, "Strategic Management in State Enterprises" (D.B.A. diss., Harvard Business School, 1978).

[12]Aharoni (see note 10), p. 275.

[13]For government pressures on state enterprise purchasing policies, see K. D. Walters and R. J. Monsen, "The Nationalized Firm: The Politicians' Free Lunch?" *Columbia Journal of World Business,* Spring 1977, p. 95. M. S. Hochmuth cites the pressure brought to bear on Lufthansa by the German government in order to get the airline to buy the A-300B airbus (in which the German government has a substantial stake) in "Aerospace," in Vernon (see note 1), p. 158.

[14]A. Besant and C. Raj, *Public Enterprise Investment Decisions in India* (Delhi, India: The Macmillan Co. of India Ltd., 1977), p. 137 gives details of the export promotion policies of some Indian state enterprises though they claim that foreign exchange outlays for operating expenses by such firms often exceed their earnings of foreign currency.

[15]"Probing the Club," *The Economist,* 23–29 September 1978, p. 97 gives details of cooperation between western aluminum producers and Soviet exporters.

[16]Louis Turner, *Oil Companies in the International System* (London: George Allen & Unwin, 1978), p. 180 notes bilateral agreements between OPEC countries and various European (and Japanese) governments.

[17]See Peter Evans, "Multinationals, State-Owned Corporations, and the Transformation of Imperialism: A Brazilian Case Study," *Economic Development and Cultural Change,* October 1977, especially pp. 54–56, for a discussion of how a tripartite arrangement among multinationals and domestic private and state capital provided the Brazilian petrochemical industry with access to international capital, management, and technology while retaining the advantages of domestic ownership.

7

State-owned enterprises in the world economy: The case of iron ore

RAYMOND VERNON AND BRIAN LEVY

Only two or three decades ago, international trade was overwhelmingly in the hands of private firms. Today, however, state-owned enterprises hold a strong position in most raw materials, as well as some manufactured products; and the prospects are that this position may grow.

This chapter examines an industry in which state-owned enterprises have greatly enlarged their role in recent years, the world iron-ore industry. The chapter points to a number of conclusions about the effects of state-owned enterprises in international markets. Some conclusions may prove unique for the iron-ore industry, but others promise to apply more widely.

In industries such as iron-ore mining, where the fixed costs are high and where participants are limited in number, individual firms characteristically place considerable emphasis upon strategies that are designed to reduce their market risks. Until the 1970s, large private enterprises in these industries commonly tried to reduce such risks by creating vertically integrated linkages between mine and mill—that is to say, by internalizing the market for iron ore.

When state-owned enterprises became a major factor in the industry in the 1970s, the strategy of linking mines to mills continued to be prevalent wherever both could be located within the same national territory, but vertical integration across national borders became less common. Instead, state-owned enterprises sought other ways to achieve stability in international markets. How successful have they been in reducing the risks and uncertainties of these markets? What has been their effect on the structure of the international market itself? To answer these questions it is necessary first to review some key aspects of the changing structure of the industry.

The research on which this chapter is based was financed in part by the Tinker Foundation, the Ford Foundation, and the Corporation Venezolana de Guayana, and was greatly assisted by the support of the Companhia Vale do Rio Doce. The field work of Janet Kelly Escobar in Venezuela and Brazil was of considerable importance to the authors, as was that of Ravi Ramamurti in India. Sam Citron and Richard Strasser also made substantial research contributions.

Reprinted with permission of the publisher from *Public Enterprise in Less-Developed Countries,* Leroy P. Jones (ed.), Cambridge, England: Cambridge University Press, 1982.

113

A profile of sources and markets

Changing trade patterns

The location of the world iron-ore industry has depended upon nature's accidents and man's discoveries, producing a fairly concentrated geographical pattern.[1] Nevertheless, the world production patterns for iron ore, shown in Table 1, exhibit some startling shifts over the past quarter century. Most notable has been the decline in the relative positions of the United States and France and the rise of those of the USSR, Australia, and Brazil.

Table 1. *World iron-ore production, 1950 and 1977*

Producing country	1950 Tons (thousands)	1950 Percent of total	1977 Tons (thousands)	1977 Percent of total
USSR	39,651	16.1	233,947	28.7
Australia	2,453	1.0	95,960	11.8
United States	98,932	40.5	80,718	9.9
Brazil	1,987	0.8	65,942	8.1
China	3,000	1.2	49,211	6.0
France	29,990	13.3	36,400	4.5
Canada	3,281	1.3	52,774	6.5
India	3,125	1.3	40,564	5.0
Liberia			26,082	3.2
Sweden	13,611	5.6	25,015	3.1
Venezuela			21,653	2.7
South Africa	1,189	0.4	15,255	1.9
Chile	2,950	1.2	10,039	1.2
Others	42,293	17.3	60,236	7.4
Total	244,469	100.0	813,996	100.0

Source: American Iron and Steel Institute, *Annual Statistical Report, 1977* (Washington, D.C., 1978), p. 90.

Behind these trends lie several important forces. First, the world's steel industry, the principal users of iron ore, has been shifting rapidly. Second, the traditional steel-producing economies have been exhausting their domestic supplies of usable iron ore. In 1977 the United States imported 32.3 percent of its iron-ore requirements as compared with 7.2 percent in 1950. Even more drastic changes in source were recorded in the principal European countries. Finally, the new producers of steel—notably including Japan— have been obliged to place far greater reliance on imported ore than the older producers.

Along with the depletion of the domestic sources, a decline in the cost of long-haul shipments of ore and other products added to the use of foreign ore sources. Back in 1953, there were no ore transport vessels with a capacity above 20,000 tons. By 1978, thirty-five ships had a capacity of more than

100,000 tons of ore.[2] The increase in the average size of the ore carrier fleet has led to a marked decline in costs. For instance, the overall costs per ton when shipping ore in a 120,000-ton carrier amount to about one-third of the costs of transporting ore in a 15,000-ton vessel.[3]

In the new patterns of iron-ore trade that emerged, a few country-to-country movements were of particular importance: Australia to Japan, a movement that accounted for more than 20 percent of the world's international trade in the product; Canada to the United States, accounting for about 9 percent; Brazil and India to Japan, each representing 6 percent or 7 percent; and Brazil to Germany, accounting for 3 percent or 4 percent.

Changing patterns of participation

The extraordinary shifts in the world's iron-ore markets have been accompanied by an equally dramatic shift in the participants in those markets.

Thirty years ago, most of the iron ore used by the steel companies of the world came from mines situated within their respective national territories. And most of these mines were linked to the steel mills by ownership or other close ties.

The intimate links between the mills and the mines were a consequence of the oligopolistic structure of both industries; in markets of this sort, transactions conducted on an arm's length basis between unrelated buyers and sellers tend to be fairly costly.[4] In the case of iron ore, these costs are increased by the fact that metal ores are not a totally standardized product, either chemically or physically. Finding the right ores—or, alternatively, adjusting to the wrong ores—can be costly. The receiver of ore has a high stake in the reliability of the shipper and vice versa.

A second reason for the tendency toward vertical integration has to do with the cost structure of both steel firms and iron-ore mines. Both bear high costs if demand falls off in the periods of downturn,[5] a fact that conduces each to try to capture its downstream customers. In fact, in periods of surplus, the unintegrated iron-ore producer is exposed to the risk that the steel mills will turn to their captive mines for their supplies, using the unintegrated mines as sellers of last resort.[6] On similar lines, the unintegrated steel mills are found worrying about periods of ore shortage, fearful lest the existing supplies will be delivered to their integrated rivals.

Even before World War I, the American steel industry was operating on a vertically integrated basis. And ever since then, the steel firms have directly controlled nearly 80 percent of their domestic ore sources.[7]

In Europe, meanwhile, with the exception of the iron-ore mines of Sweden, practically all mines have been captives of European steel companies.[8] The Swedish mines were nominally independent; but Sweden's pre-World War II dependence on the German market and the long history of cartelization in the steel industry of Europe suggest that the movements of Swedish ore were controlled by agreements in the downstream steel markets.[9]

Nevertheless, despite the apparent advantages of vertical integration in the iron and steel industry, nonintegrated mines captured considerable shares of the world market in the 1960s and 1970s. Behind the shift lay two principal factors: the emergence of Japan as a steel producer and the emergence of state-owned enterprises as producers of iron ore.

The swift rise in Japan's demands for iron ore began to be evident in the early 1960s at a time when the Japanese government was still loath to authorize direct investments abroad.[10] Nor were the Japanese steel companies themselves exposed at the time to all the stimuli that normally encourage vertical integration. For one thing, as long as they were competing inside the Japanese market they had nothing to fear from one another in terms of iron-ore supplies or iron-ore prices; all of them were joined together, under the leadership of the Ministry of International Trade and Industry, in joint purchase contracts with foreign iron-ore suppliers. In addition, Japan's restrictive import policies protected local steel producers from foreign competition.

In the absence of ownership, Japanese ore buyers during the 1950s and 1960s sought other ways of achieving stability in ore supplies. The Japanese offered long-term procurement contracts and loans to independent mining entrepreneurs, who used these contracts to raise additional capital.[11]

Despite the Japanese example, European and U.S. steel companies were consistent in displaying a preference for direct ownership of the mines. By 1970, Bethlehem, Republic, and U.S. Steel had taken direct ownership of mines in Chile, Liberia, and Venezuela; and by 1976, three-quarters of Canada's ore output was under the control of American steel firms or ore houses closely linked to these firms. By 1970, too, British, Italian, Belgian, and German steel producers had developed substantial ownership positions in the iron-ore mines of Mauritania, India, Liberia, Canada, and Brazil.[12]

But as Table 2 indicates, betwen 1964 and 1975 state-owned suppliers began to supplant captive mines as the major source of imported ore. Except for a few locations, the international vertically integrated structure set up by American and European steel companies did not endure. The new situation, as we shall shortly see, was acutely disturbing to some of the world's principal users of iron ore and generated various countermoves on their part.

The emergence of state-owned enterprises

Their enhanced position

Table 3 lists the principal state-owned enterprises that are active in the world iron-ore industry. Two tendencies are clear from the table: that state-owned enterprises have been appearing in the industry with increasing frequency, and that the nationalization of foreign holding companies has become increasingly common.

Table 2. *Percentage of imports by Japan, United States, and European Coal and Steel Community countries, by sources, 1950–77*

	1950	1964	1975	1977
Japan				
From independents				
Private	100.0	90.1	66.0	63.7
State owned		9.9	34.0	36.3
Total	100.0	100.0	100.0	100.0
United States				
From sources captive to				
U.S. steel firms	53.9	95.9	44.6	73.1
From independents	46.1	4.1	55.4	26.9
Private	37.7	1.4	2.4	1.5
State owned	8.4	2.7	53.0	25.4
Total	100.0	100.0	100.0	100.0
ECSC Countries				
From sources captive to				
ECSC steel firms	12.3	14.9	21.4	22.7
From sources captive to				
U.S. steel firms	0.9	14.9	9.9	11.1
From Swedish independents	57.8	38.0	15.1	13.2
From other independents	29.0	32.2	53.6	52.9
Private	28.4	22.4	21.2	17.5
State owned	0.6	9.8	32.4	35.4
Total	100.0	100.0	100.0	100.0

Source: United Nations, *Yearbook of International Trade Statistics, 1977* (New York, 1978), pp. 962–63; "1977 Iron Ore Shipments of Companies," *Skillings Mining Review 67,* No. 27 (July 8, 1978): 8–9; Walter C. Labys, *The Role of State Trading in Mineral Commodity Markets: Copper, Tin, Bauxite and Iron Ore,* paper presented at Conference on State Trading, April 1979 (Montreal: Ecole des Hautes Etudes Commerciales), p. 31a.

The expansion of the operations of state enterprises helped transform the international markets. State enterprises reduced the extent of vertical integration in the industry by preempting positions that private steel firms might eventually have controlled and by cutting back the scope of the private firms' existing positions; by the late 1970s, the state-owned suppliers accounted for almost 40 percent of internationally traded ore.

What can be said about the business behavior of these enterprises?[13] Our studies suggest that strong generalizations can be made about the factors that bring state-owned enterprises into existence. But once they are in existence, generalizations about their operating policies are considerably more difficult to make.

Table 3. **Principal state-owned ventures exporting iron ore, 1978**

Country	Name of establishment	Date established as state enterprise	Iron ore production, 1978 (in thousands of tons)
Brazil	Companhía Vale do Rio Doce (CVRD)	1942	50,574
Sweden	Luossavaara-Kiirunavaara AB (LKAB)	1907–57[a]	23,967
South Africa	South African Iron & Steel Industrial Corporation (ISCOR)	1928	19,796
Liberia	Lamco Joint Venture	1960[b]	10,572
	Bong Mining Company	1963[b]	7,387
India[c]	National Mineral Development Corporation (NMDC)	1958	6,909
	Mines and Metals Trading Corporation (MMTC)	1964	Export trading only
Venezuela	CVG Ferrominera Orinoco S.A.	1974	12,956
Chile	Compañía de Acero del Pacifico S.A. (CAP)	1971	6,935
Mauritania	Société Nationale Industrielle et Minière (SNIM)	1974	6,336
Peru	Empresa Minera del Peru	1975	4,854

[a]The Swedish government held 50 percent of the company's shares in 1907; in 1957 the government took over the company entirely.
[b]The Liberian government has not attempted to exercise any control over these projects, which are effectively controlled by foreign partners.
[c]Along with the export operations listed here, iron-ore mines captive to the state-owned steel companies mine about 12 million tons of ore annually.

Source: Walter C. Labys, *The Role of State Trading in Mineral Commodity Markets: Copper, Tin, Bauxite and Iron Ore* (Montreal: Ecole des Hautes Etudes Commerciales, Conference on State Trading, April 1979), p. 31a.; "1978 Iron Ore Shipments of Companies," *Skillings Mining Review* 68, No. 27 (July 7, 1979): 12–13.

Origins of the state-owned enterprises

The iron-ore mining industry is one of those sectors that governments usually prefer to have under national control. That desire, however, has not always led governments to set up state-owned enterprises. The decision seems to have turned on three factors: on the nature of the ideology prevailing in the country; on the financial and managerial strength of the country's private sector; and on the country's perception of its capacity to run the operations.

The ideological factor, for instance, seems to have been responsible for the fact that Australia and Canada continue to tolerate the existence of private foreign mining operations on a large scale; largely as a result, foreign mines still account for somewhat more than one-third of internationally traded iron ore. All the nationalizations since 1958, listed in Table 3, have taken place in developing countries.[14]

To be sure, even among developing countries, the decision to establish a state-owned enterprise is a highly selective one. Some industries in these countries have been targets for nationalization, whereas others have not. And where nationalizations have been widespread in a given industry, the timing of the decision has varied considerably in different countries.[15]

In the case of Brazil, the opportunity to recapture the national iron-ore industry from foreigners came with the special circumstances that accompanied World War II. An offer by the United States and the United Kingdom to provide capital and markets overcame some of the critical difficulties that often stand in the way of nationalization.

The military-backed Brazilian government that supported the creation of Companhía Vale do Rio Doce (CVRD) in 1942 had previously annulled the long-standing concession of an American entrepreneur to export iron ore, expressing its determination that the Brazilian mining and metallurgical industries were to be developed by Brazilians.[16] The decision to create a state-owned enterprise in steel was taken only after efforts had failed to establish a steel industry owned by private national interests. And once created, the state-owned steel industry continued to seek private local participation.[17]

Consistent with that spirit, local private mining firms have been allowed to carve out a niche for themselves alongside CVRD. And once Brazil overcame the fear of foreign domination, even foreign mining firms were allowed to develop a substantial position in the Brazilian ore industry.[18]

The South African case offers an interesting variant on Brazil. In this instance, the struggle for control was between the Dutch-speaking Afrikaners of the country and the dominant Anglophile businessmen who, though themselves South Africans, had strong ties to the foreign business community. From the 1920s, South African state-owned enterprises, as instruments of domestic industrialization, were used as a countervailing force to the power of the traditional private sector.[19]

The South African Iron and Steel Industrial Corporation (ISCOR), which has dominated South Africa's steel industry since its establishment in 1928, has been active in the iron-ore export business for less than a decade. In the early 1970s the government chose ISCOR over a private rival to develop vast, newly discovered ore resources, a project that entailed the building of a 500-mile railway line through deserted country. Although the railway line was eventually transferred to South African Railways, ISCOR's early control of the line set the seal on its advantage. In 1979 ISCOR sold 15 million tons of iron ore abroad. Meanwhile, one private firm, a pioneer in the export of iron ore, had already faded away; another private survivor was operating at a small portion of ISCOR's level.

In the cases of both Brazil and South Africa, nationalization was seen mainly as a step in the process of curbing foreign-owned enterprises and their allies in the local economy, not as a step on the road to socialism. Similar motivations were evident in the spate of nationalizations that occurred in the early 1970s in Chile, Mauritania, Peru, and Venezuela.[20] In India, by contrast, the official ideology that accompanied the emergence of state enterprises contained explicit socialist overtones.[21] How deep those convictions ran is a matter for debate. Private business generally continued to play a substantial role in the leading political parties;[22] high government officials at times continued to be drawn from the ranks of private business; and government officials sometimes transferred to the private sector.[23] And some major sectors of the economy were earmarked for continued participation by private enterprise.[24] Finally, the largest private Indian businesses have managed to grow rapidly since independence.[25]

However one may label Indian ideology, it nevertheless called for the close control of enterprise by a government bureaucracy. As subsequent events would demonstrate, that control could be achieved both by ownership and by regulation. The regime that came to control India's iron-ore mines reflected how narrow the gap between the two approaches could sometimes be.

The ideological nuances underlying the decision to establish a state-owned iron-ore enterprise have varied somewhat from country to country. But in all these countries, the propensity to nationalize seems to have been increased by the government's perception that the problems of managing the facilities and marketing the ore were shrinking.

The proposition that national capabilities help to determine the timing of nationalizations is an idea implicit in the concept of the obsolescing bargain.[26] Initially, according to the concept, governments may offer attractive terms to induce foreign firms to make an investment, aware of their own inability to take the project on. But as domestic capabilities to perform complex tasks improve, host governments use their muscle to extract a growing share of the investment's profits. Eventually host countries no longer feel any need to share profits with foreign investors and consider the strategy of owning the mining operations themselves.

The propensity to nationalize is growing over the course of time not only because governments see themselves as becoming more capable but also because they have increasing access to international markets that offer technology without equity strings.[27] In addition, governments are finding it easier to mobilize the financial resources needed for the take-over and operation of state-owned enterprises. In the late 1950s the World Bank refused to help India in the financing of its industrial sector on grounds that the funds were being used by nationalized industry.[28] Today, intergovernmental credit agencies lend readily to state-owned enterprises, although many are barred from lending to private firms.

Finally, one other special factor seems to have speeded the trend to nationalization. Encouraged by the extraordinary events in oil in the first half of the 1970s, many developing countries briefly entertained the expectation that all raw materials were moving into a period of scarcity. Such a period would liberate them from the final restraint that bound them to international companies, namely, the need for a reliable market. That expectation did not last very long—but long enough to stimulate the nationalization of foreign-owned ore mines in several developing countries.

In sum, then, the growth of the state-owned enterprise can be seen as one of the consequences of improved domestic capabilities in the developing countries, coupled with increased access to international capital and technical skills.

The new international environment

Despite the increased importance of state-owned enterprises in the world's iron-ore markets, certain key characteristics of those markets have remained unchanged. One of these is the high concentration of sellers and buyers. Table 4 demonstrates that although the identities of the principal exporters and importers have changed over the years, the degree of geographical concentration has remained very high on both sides of the market, and the actual buyers and sellers have remained very few in number. In 1975 the four largest importing entities accounted for 69 percent of the international iron-ore trade,[29] and the four largest ore-exporting firms accounted for at least 53 percent of the trade.[30]

Table 4. *Geographical concentration of world trade in iron ore, 1950, 1964, and 1975, in percent*

	1950	1964	1975
World exports: percentage accounted for by:			
Four largest exporting countries	62.6	50.3	65.3
Eight largest exporting countries	82.7	73.9	85.9
World imports: percentage accounted for by:			
Four largest importing countries	65.8	64.3	74.4
Eight largest importing countries	88.3	85.6	91.6

Source: Data for 1950 and 1964 are from Gerald Manners, *The Changing World Market for Iron Ore 1950–1980* (Baltimore: Johns Hopkins University Press, 1971), pp. 344, 348; and for 1975, from United Nations, *Yearbook of International Trade Statistics, 1977* (New York, 1978), pp. 502–3.

The persistence of this concentration has meant that any given seller of iron ore, unless strongly linked to some specific buyers, was exposed to a high degree of market risk. In their search for such linkages, state-owned enterprises have made considerable use of long-term contracts with foreign ore buyers. Some of these contracts have included firm commitments covering long periods of time that specify both the prices and the volume of the ore to be transferred.[31] Some have linked such commitments to other undertakings, such as a loan to the ore mine from a third party.[32] But others, though dubbed long-term, are less firm in nature: They may specify a range instead of a fixed figure for the volume of ore to be sold; they may specify a formula by which the price is periodically to be fixed; or they may simply provide that the price is to be renegotiated periodically.[33] Finally, some trading agreements are only tacit or implicit, representing a continuing relationship between traditional trading partners.

To be sure, firms with long-term contracts are less exposed to market fluctuation than those without such contracts. By 1978, both Germany and Britain had cut back entirely on purchases from the short-term market, which had accounted for about 20 percent of each country's ore needs in 1974; partly for that reason, both Venezuela and Peru, having canceled their earlier contractual ties upon nationalization, lost ground in Europe. By contrast, volumes traded under various contracts between British Steel and Canada's Carol Lake and various contracts of Brazil's CVRD and Mineracões Brasileiras Reunidas (MBR) mines resisted the declining trend of ore imports.

Despite these examples, however, experience over the past two decades points to the conclusion that the family of contracts described earlier provides nothing like the stability and predictability in sourcing that is ordinarily associated with ownership. Buyers commonly back away from their commitments when ore is in very easy supply, and the sellers do likewise when ore is in tight supply.[34]

For instance, U.S. Steel did not fulfill the purchase commitments, which it made to Venezuela's Ferrominera Orinoco, associated with the nationalization of its ore holdings in that country.[35] The Japanese now and then have taken delivery of less than the volumes for which they had contracted from Australia; moreover, prices have been adjusted more often and more drastically than was agreed in the supply contracts.[36] The Germans have found a way around a long-term deal with CVRD, under which they were to match their exports from a captive mine in Brazil ton for ton with exports through CVRD.[37]

Notwithstanding the equivocal nature of these so-called long-term contracts, they do of course have a certain utility for buyers and sellers. By reducing the needs of each continuously to search for new partners, they hold down transaction costs and limit the costs of technical adjustments that are associated with changes in the sources of ore. But they do very little to achieve another objective of the ore-exporting and ore-importing enterprises, that is, the reduction of uncertainties associated with changes in supply, demand, and price.

National politics and international integration

With long-term contracts proving to be no panacea to the problem of international integration, state-owned enterprises have had to search for other ways to deal with instability in international markets. Their responses to this instability have been very different from enterprise to enterprise. And these differences, in turn, stem in part from the distinctive history, the distinctive set of institutions, and the distinctive problems of the country in which each enterprise operates.

Brazil

Bazil's iron-ore industry, as we have already noted, was dominated by a state-owned enterprise for pragmatic, rather than ideological, reasons. Nevertheless, CVRD's operations have been distinctly different in some respects from the operations of a private enterprise. To begin with, the state-owned status of the firm has helped it to gain access to capital on a very large scale. With the help of such capital, CVRD has been the government's agent in the development of a vast infrastructure of railroads, roads, and ports, an infrastructure that has been placed at the service of other enterprises, foreign as well as national. Morcover, CVRD has placed extraordinary emphasis on the import substitution process, throwing as much business as possible to firms based in Brazil. In 1969 only 25 percent of CVRD's purchases were made in Brazil; but by 1975, more than 80 percent of CVRD's suppliers were Brazilian-based.[38]

CVRD's state-owned status also has had other effects on its operations. It has, for instance, been involved in various complex deals—government-to-government deals in some cases—involving large-scale two-way swaps of goods and services.[39]

CVRD's close ties to the Brazilian official establishment, however, have not prevented it from taking on many of the characteristics of an ebullient, autonomous private enterprise. In its early years, such tendencies were not much in evidence, inasmuch as CVRD had no substantial cash flows of its own. Once established, however, CVRD developed a considerable quantity of internally generated funds and independent borrowing capacity. Operating on the basis of a rich supply of ores and an efficient infrastructure, CVRD pushed aggressively into world markets, cutting prices as necessary to increase its market share.

More recently, CVRD has begun to develop arrangements that suggest it would like to stabilize the market conditions in which it operates. Thus far, its status as a state-owned enterprise has not prevented it from developing various strong linkages to foreign customers. It has recently constructed three ore processing plants in joint ventures with Italian, Japanese, and Spanish steel companies; it has concurred in the almost fourfold expansion of Ferteco Mineracao, the captive mine of a group of German steel companies, on the condition that the Germans increase their purchases from CVRD as well; and it has agreed to develop a new ore mine jointly with five Japanese steel firms.[40] For the 1980s, CVRD harbors huge expansion plans, which will almost surely require added links with foreign users.[41]

South Africa

In South Africa, as we observed earlier, the gulf between private and state-owned firms has been somewhat wider than in Brazil. The Iron and Steel Industrial Corporation (ISCOR), like CVRD, has received subsidized capital and special infrastructural support. In addition, though, ISCOR has had to contend with government-controlled prices for its steel products, as well as a government-prescribed product range. So far, ISCOR has not developed any strong links to foreign firms, although at one time the firm did seek without success to develop a downstream joint venture with some foreign steel firms.[42]

Venezuela

Unlike Brazil and South Africa, Venezuela has adopted the strategy of achieving stability by domestic integration. Venezuela's state-owned iron-ore undertaking, Ferrominera, has operated under strikingly different conditions from those of Brazil's CVRD or South Africa's ISCOR, reflecting the importance of differences in the domestic setting. For one thing, Venezuela's petroleum exports have relieved the country of the chronic balance-of-payment problems that other developing countries commonly confront. Accordingly, Venezuela has not placed the expansion of its exports very high on its agenda of national objectives. Oil exports have also given Venezuela an exchange rate that has prevented it from emulating Brazil by expanding its exports of manufactured goods.

Perhaps in part for these reasons, Venezuela has been in the lead in trying to persuade other developing countries of the undesirability of price cutting in raw-material exports; indeed, more than any other country, Venezuela was responsible for the creation of OPEC in 1960. In this same vein, Venezuela has looked on the further processing of its raw materials as desirable irrespective of the cost; and it has seen its iron-ore supplies as a resource to be husbanded for an indigenous steel industry that seems destined to be a high-cost producer.

When Ferrominera came into existence in 1975, therefore, it had no burning mandate to expand its output and exports. On the contrary, the company was regarded by government officials as the custodian of properties that would eventually be used to supply raw materials to Sidor, the state-owned steel company. At the same time, however, both Ferrominera and its erstwhile foreign owners saw advantages in maintaining some of their prenationalization ties and in exhibiting the appearance of continuing some of the earlier relationships.[43] Venezuela had no desire to frighten away foreign investors in other industries not ripe for nationalization; besides, the managers of Ferrominera itself wished to continue to sell some of their ore to the former owners, as well as to use the technical services, the marketing services, and the shipping facilities of U.S. Steel. For their part, U.S. Steel and Bethlehem Steel needed time to reconstitute their sources of supply and reduce their dependence on Ferrominera.

Fundamentally, however, Ferrominera has only been marking time until the day when Sidor's needs may be sufficient to absorb its output. Having lost some of its position in U.S. markets as a result of cutbacks in the purchases of its former U.S. owners, Ferrominera has made no apparent effort to fill the gap. Moreover, the company appears to have been yielding ground to Brazilian competition in European markets. But in light of its underlying mandate, none of these developments has appeared critical to the Venezuelan government.

India

India, like Venezuela, has tried to avoid the uncertainties of foreign markets by turning to domestic integration. Indian policy has long recognized that public and private enterprises might operate side by side in the national market.[44] Accordingly, the interagency Iron Ore Board, in which half a dozen ministries are represented, has applied its policies to all firms in the industry, private and public. Major investments and major trade practices, therefore, have been the subject of high government policy, beyond the control of the management of any single public or private enterprise.

To be sure, the power of the governmental policy board has been augmented by the fact that so much of India's iron-ore industry lies in the government's hands. Part of such ownership takes the form of captive mines attached to the state-owned steel plants of India;[45] the output of these captive mines accounts for about 40 percent of the nation's annual ore output and is used entirely for internal consumption. A separate state-owned entity, the National Mineral Development Corporation (NMDC), produces another 15 percent, most of which is exported by the Metals and Minerals Trading Corporation (MMTC), another state-owned enterprise. Small private firms, which mine about one-quarter of India's iron-ore output, have also been obliged to export their ore through MMTC, which arranges for access to an international market that might otherwise be unavailable. Only the large private miners of Goa are allowed to export their ore directly, in order not to disturb their long-standing links to buyers. But even in this case, their export arrangements are held on a short leash.

Despite its general policy, India has allowed a few long-term links to operate. It has tolerated, for instance, the continued exercise of Italian Finsider's right to 2 million tons annually of Goan ore production. And it forged a cooperative venture with an Iranian state-owned steel firm under which the Iranians would finance a new iron-ore project in return for a long-term claim on its ore.[46] But by and large, export goals have been set by government planners, and these sought to restrict exports of ore in favor of anticipated demands by the domestic steel industry.[47] Furthermore, though the privately owned Goan mining firms are allowed to ship their ore to Japan without the intervention of the MMTC, their contracts with Japanese buyers have been concluded under close state supervision; among other things, contracts in excess of a year or two in duration are prohibited.[48]

In sum, although the state-owned enterprises of different nations have operated under different degrees of supervision and have developed in different directions, they appear to have shared an interest in limiting their risks in foreign markets. Responding to that objective, some have diverted their iron-ore production in increasing proportions to their domestic markets. Those that continue to rely on international markets typically have sought security in various types of long-term arrangements with their customers—but so far with uncertain results.

Future contours of the international ore market

The public character of state-owned enterprises will no doubt have some influence on the contours of the world ore market. For instance, their public character may influence the structures that replace the ownership ties that once linked the mines and mills of different countries. Here our case studies offer tantalizing hints. In the case of India, for instance, the effect may be trivial; public and private enterprises alike may operate under the same tight governmental strictures. In the case of Brazil, however, the public character of CVRD may well create special inhibitions. We assume—though with little supporting evidence so far—that CVRD will not have the same freedom as a private enterprise to create vertical linkages across Brazil's borders. This assumption rests on the observation that when the managers of state-owned enterprises forge strong foreign linkages, it helps them to slip loose from governmental control. To maintain or restore this control, we expect government officials from time to time to restrict or even to dissolve such linkages. Because so many of the iron-ore producers are state owned, we expect to see an international market develop in which vertical integration across borders is considerably restrained.

Another generalization worth considering is that state-owned iron-ore producers will be less responsive than captive mines to both short-term and long-term changes in international ore demand. That possibility follows in part from our assumption that state-owned enterprises will be compelled to maintain less intimate ties to their foreign buyers. As a result, they may be in a poorer position to foresee a decline in foreign short-term or long-term demand; and even if such a change is foreseen, they may feel less certainty about the relationship of the projected change in their own future sales levels. Finally, in the event that demand actually declines, state-owned enterprises may be slower to adjust production levels than their private counterparts. In periods of declining demand, state-owned enterprises may see their labor costs as fixed and invariant and hence may see no reason to cut their production.

If demand should grow rapidly, rather than decline, there is also a possibility that state-owned enterprises may be less prepared than private enterprises for that development. Again, the state-owned enterprise may lack information or, possessing the information, may be uncertain as to whether it would share in the increase. That handicap, however, could be offset by the fact that some state-owned enterprises by reason of their public character have relatively easy access to the capital needed for expanding their facilities, a factor that could be important in a period of scarce capital and high interest rates.

The increased importance of state-owned enterprises in iron-ore production is also likely to encourage the trend toward vertical integration within national borders, thereby reducing the overall importance of international markets. That view is based on two expectations. First, state-owned mines such as those in Venezuela are more likely to serve their home steel industry as a matter of absolute priority than would be the case if they were privately owned. Second, in recognition of their increasing vulnerability, steel mills in foreign countries that have relied on foreign ores are likely to look for safer sources of ore. Steel mills in the United States are already following that strategy. In response to the erosion of international vertical integration, these firms have turned back to their higher-cost captive-ore sources in North America.[49] The willingness of U.S. mills to rely on relatively costly ores is increased by two factors: by the generous provisions of U.S. tax law, which permit the steel firms to charge a 15 percent depletion allowance in figuring the taxes on their mining operations, and by the prospect that the U.S. government may restrict the importation of steel from lower-cost sources, including those with access to cheaper ores.

To be sure, neither Japan nor Europe has the option of reverting to a policy of self-sufficiency for its iron ore; nor do many of the iron-ore exporting countries have the option of absorbing their ore production internally. Accordingly, an international market will continue to exist in which the state-owned enterprises will play a major role. One final set of questions to be considered, therefore, is whether the emergence of independent ore producers is likely to presage some OPEC-like agreement in the iron-ore industry. In particular, does the prevalence of state-owned enterprises among these independents make the emergence of a cartel more or less likely?

Here again, one is forced to speculate. Our view is that the existence of state-owned enterprises is more likely to constitute an impediment to such agreements than otherwise. As this review indicates, the various state-owned enterprises involved in the world ore market operate from strikingly different perspectives, pursuing a much more diverse set of goals than would be the case for a group of profit-seeking privately owned mines in an oligopolistic industry. In general, market participants who are motivated by diverse goals find it more difficult to coordinate their efforts than those with common goals.[50] As a result, the fact that so many iron-ore mining operations are state-owned may present an added obstacle to the formation of an effective cartel.[51]

As the role of state-owned enterprises increases, their governments may feel in somewhat better control of their respective national economies and somewhat better equipped to pursue national goals. But the growth of state-owned enterprises could also increase the uncertainties in the world iron-ore market, adding to the difficulties of the importers and exporters that continue to rely on that market. In global welfare terms, it is difficult to say whether the net contribution of the state-owned enterprises will be positive.

Notes

[1]See Gerald Manners, *The Changing World Market for Iron Ore, 1950–1980* (Baltimore: Johns Hopkins University Press, 1971).

[2]See Lloyd's Register of Shipping, *Statistical Tables* (London: Lloyd's Register of Shipping, 1978), p. 60.

[3]Between 1951 and 1965 the costs per ton of ship construction were cut in half, although they increased again thereafter. See Manners, *Changing World Market*, p. 175; and United Nations Conference on Trade and Development, *Review of Maritime Transport, 1976* (New York: United Nations, 1978), p. 26. By the 1970s the capital cost per ton of building a 120,000-ton vessel was less than 60 percent that of a 15,000-ton ship; and the operating costs per ton for the larger vessel were one-fourth those of the smaller ship. See R. O. Goss and C. D. Jones, "The Economics of Size in Dry Bulk Carriers," in *Advances in Maritime Economics*, ed. R. O. Goss (Cambridge: Univeristy Press, 1977), pp. 90–123.

[4]See, e.g., Oliver Williamson, "The Vertical Integration of Production: Market Failure Considerations," *American Economic Review* (May 1971), pp. 112–21; see also Peter Buckley and Mark Casson, *The Future of the Multinational Enterprise* (New York: Holmes & Meier, 1976).

[5]See F. M. Scherer, *Industrial Market Structure and Economic Performance* (Chicago: Rand McNally, 1970), pp. 192–95.

[6]See Raymon Vernon, "The Location of Economic Activity," in ed. John Dunning, *Economic Analysis and the Multinational Enterprise* (London: Allen & Unwin, 1974); see also F. T. Knickerbocker, *Oligopolistic Reaction and the Multinational Enterprise* (Boston: Graduate School of Business Administration, Harvard University, 1973).

[7]For details of U.S. controls, see R. B. Mancke, "Iron Ore and Steel: A Case Study of the Causes and Consequences of Vertical Integration," *Journal of Industrial Economics* 20, No. 3 (July 1972): 220–29; also Nancy Wardell, "United States Iron Ore Imports: Sourcing Strategies for U.S. Steel Companies" (D.B.A. thesis, Harvard University, 1977), Chap. 2. Much of the remaining 20 percent has been in the hands of four firms, apparently under the effective control of the U.S. steel producers. See House of Representatives, Committee on the Judiciary, *Report of the Federal Trade Commission on the Control of Iron Ore* (Washington, D.C.: U.S. Government Printing Office, 1952), p. 53.

[8]See G. D. Feldman, *Iron and Steel in the German Inflation, 1916–1923* (Princeton: Princeton University Press, 1977), esp. Chap. 4; International Metalworkers Federation, Iron and Steel Department, *The Largest Steel Companies in the Free World* (Steelworkers Conference, Vienna, 1959), pp. 36, 68; *Acieries Reunies de Burbach-Eich-Dudelange, Annual Report, 1975* (Luxembourg, 1976), p. 20; European Group for Financial Research, "The European Steel Industry: A Comparative Study of Twelve Companies," mimeographed (1960), p. 159.

[9]See A. F. Rickman, *Swedish Iron Ore* (London: Faber & Faber, 1939), pp. 156–64; see also Ervin Hexner, *International Cartels* (Chapel Hill: University of North Carolina Press, 1946), pp. 203–15.

[10]See R. B. McKern, *Multinational Enterprises and Natural Resources* (Sydney, Australia: McGraw-Hill, 1976), p. 57.

[11]For illustrations of such arrangements in India, see Committee on Public Undertakings (1972–73), *Thirty-Seventh Report: National Mineral Development Corporation Limited, Hyderabad* (New Delhi: Lok Sabha Secretariat, 1973), pp. 1–2, 63. For Australia, see McKern, *Multinational Enterprises*, pp. 206–15; and for South Africa, "Sishen-Saldanha Survey," *Supplement to Financial Mail*, Oct. 1, 1976, p. 11.

[12]In two cases, even at this early phase of the internationalization of the iron-ore industry, independent, unintegrated mining firms from the U.S. and Europe set up foreign ventures. These were the Marcona Mining Company—jointly owned by the U.S. mining firms Cyprus Mines and Utah International—in 1952, and Sweden's independent mining company Grangesborg, which began the LAMCO Joint Venture in Liberia in 1960.

[13]For the observations of others, see, e.g., M. M. Kostecki, "State Trading in Industrialized and Developing Countries," *Journal of World Trade Law* 12, No. 3; Monsen, "The Nationalized Firm: the Politicians Free Lunch?" *Columbia Journal of World Business* 12, No. 1 (Spring 1977): 95; and D. F. Lamont, *Foreign State Enterprises: A Threat to American Business* (New York: Basic Books, 1979).

[14]For an example of the developing countries' position, see United Nations, "Permanent Sovereignty over Natural Resources of Developing Countries," Economic and Social Council Resolution 1737, adopted May 4, 1973.

[15]See Stephen J. Kobrin, "Foreign Enterprise and Forced Divestment in LDCs," *International Organization* 34, No. 1 (Winter 1980): 65–88. For evidence in the oil industry, see Fariborz Ghadar, *The Evolution of OPEC Strategy* (Lexington, Mass.: Lexington Books, 1977), esp. pp. 20–33.

[16]See Peter Evans, *Dependent Development: The Alliance of Multinational, State and Local Capital in Brazil* (Princeton: Princeton University Press, 1979), pp. 89–90. See also John D. Wirth, *The Politics of Brazilian Development, 1930–1954* (Stanford: Stanford University Press, 1970), pp. 111, 112. For details of aborted international efforts to establish a Brazilian iron and steel industry, see Werner Baer, *The Development of the Brazilian Steel Industry* (Nashville, Tenn.: Vanderbilt University Press, 1969), pp. 64–75.

[17]Baer, *Development of the Brazilian Steel Industry*, pp. 75, 76.

[18]Next to CVRD, which shipped 48.7 million tons in 1978, the largest ore-mining operation is Mineracões Brasileiras Reunidas (MBR) with 1978 shipments of 13.5 million tons; Brazilian interests control 51 percent of MBR, and the U.S.-based Hanna Mining Company accounts for the other 49 percent. S.A. Mineracao da Trinidade (SAMTRI) is jointly owned by the European-based ARBED group, with the remaining 40 percent in the hands of private Brazilian interests. SAMTRI is also a partner in SAMARCO, a joint venture with the U.S. Marcona Corporation. Another private operation, Ferteco Mineracao, is wholly owned by a group of German steel firms.

[19]See Heribert Adam and Herman Giliomee, *Ethnic Power Mobilized: Can South Africa Change?* (New Haven: Yale University Press, 1979), esp. Chap. 6. See also David Kaplan, "The Politics of Industrial Protection in South Africa, 1910–1939," *Journal of Southern African Studies* 3, No. 1 (Oct. 1976): 70–91.

[20]For the Chilean experience, see Theordore H. Moran, *Multinational Corporations and the Policies of Dependence: Copper in Chile* (Princeton: Princeton University Press, 1974): for Mauritania, see "Senegal, Mauritania, Mali, Guinea," *Quarterly Economic Review*, No. 4, *Economist Intelligence Unit* (London, Mauritania, 1972); for Peru, see John Sheahan, "Peru: Economic Policies and Structural Change, 1968–1978," Center for Development Economics, Research Memorandum No. 72 (Williamstown, Mass.: Williams College, 1979), p. 10; and for Venezuela, see Argenis Gamboa, ed., *Nacionalizacion del hierro en Venezuela* (Caracas: Ediciones Centauro, 1974), pp. vi–xv.

[21]In 1947, the economic program of the All-India Congress Committee recommended that "in respect of existing undertakings, the process of transfer from private to public ownership should commence after a period of four years," and in 1955 the ruling Congress Party adopted a resolution calling for a "socialist pattern of society." See, e.g., G. C. Agrawal, *Public Sector Steel Industry in India* (Allahabad: Chaitanya Publishing House, 1976), p. 5.

[22]See Michael Kidron, *Foreign Investments in India* (London: Oxford University Press, 1965), p. 143.

[23]See Helen Lamb, "Business Organization and Leadership in India," in *Leadership and Political Institutions in India,* ed. Richard Park and Irene Tinker (Princeton: Princeton University Press, 1959), pp. 251–67.

[24]Ministry of Industry and Supply, Government of India, "Statement of April 6, 1948," in U.S. Department of Commerce, *Investment in India* (Washington, D.C.: U.S. Government Printing Office, 1961), pp. 193–95.

[25]See Asim Chaudhuri, *Private Economic Power in India* (New Delhi: People's Publishing House, 1975), pp. 36–37 and 161–65, and Laurence Veit, *India's Second Revolution: The Dimensions of Development* (New York: McGraw-Hill, 1976), esp. Chap. 9.

[26]For details of the obsolescing bargain, see Raymond Vernon, *Sovereignty at Bay* (New York: Basic Books, 1971), pp. 46–53.

[27]For details of foreign participation in the South African ore-export venture, see South African Iron and Steel Corporation, *Sishen-Saldanha Ore Export Project* (Pretoria, 1974), pp. 32–34. For Brazil, see "World's Largest Ore Port at Tubarão, Brazil," *Skillings Mining Review* 63, No. 39 (Sept. 28, 1974): 6–9.

[28]See Edward S. Mason and Robert E. Asher, *The World Bank Since Bretton Woods* (Washington, D.C.: Brookings Institution, 1973), pp. 150–51 and 371–74. According to Mason and Asher, World Bank restrictions on lending to nationalized industries were lifted in 1968. In general, the World Bank has sought government guarantees of loans to nongovernmental borrowers; see ibid., p. 190.

[29]Pooling their purchases in each country, Japanese mills in 1975 purchased 47.7 percent of noncaptive internationally traded iron ore. German mills bought a further 10.7 percent of the noncaptive internationally traded iron ore through two procurement companies, which coordinated their activities, Rohstoffhandel Gmbh. and Erzkontor Ruhr Gmbh. State-owned monopsonies handle all iron-ore imports for the British and Italians; their trade accounted for an additional 5.8 percent and 5.1 percent, respectively.

[30]CVRD accounted for 18.1 percent of noncaptive international supply in 1975. Two Australian mines, Hamersley Holdings and Mount Newman, produced 13.1 percent and 12 percent, respectively, of that supply; the Australian government sought to coordinate their sales strategy, but it is not clear how successfully. Malmexport A.B. accounted for a further 10 percent of the market; and Venezuela's Ferrominera Orinoco for a further 7 percent.

[31]Contracts that India signed with the Japanese in the early 1960s were of this kind; see Deepak Nayyar, *India's Exports and Export Policies in the 1960s* (Cambridge University Press, 1976), p. 364. In the early 1970s British Steel signed contracts specifying fixed prices for five years with the Canadian Carol Lake project and for three years with the privately owned MBR mine and state-owned CVRD, both in Brazil.

[32]An agreement between CVRD and the German steel-firm owners of the Ferteco Mineracao mine was of this type. The Germans agreed to tie their purchases from CVRD to the output of their captive Brazilian mine on a one-to-one basis if CVRD extended a railway to the captive source. Loans proffered to the Liberian LAMCO project were linked to long-term procurement contracts signed by German steel mills.

[33]Australian–Japanese long-term contracts permit price and volume flexibility; for instance, in typical contracts volume can vary 10 percent and price 7.5 percent around contracted levels; see Ben Smith, "Long-Term Contracts in the Resource Goods Trade," in *Australia, Japan and the Western Pacific Economic Relations,* ed. John Crawford and Saburo Okita (Canberra: Australian Government Publishing Service, 1976), pp. 299–325. Volume flexibility was also built into the long-term contracts between Venezuela's Ferrominera Orinoco and U.S. Steel, with prices pegged to the U.S. Mesabi base price.

[34]For a general review, see W. C. Labys, *Market Structure Bargaining Power and Resource Price Formation* (Lexington, Mass.: Lexington Books, 1980), pp. 163–195.

[35]By 1978, U.S. imports from Venezuela were less than 40 percent of 1974 levels, a level consistent with such commitments; American Iron and Steel Institute, *Annual Statistical Report, 1978* (Washington, D.C., 1979), p. 77.

[36]Smith, "Long-Term Contracts," p. 311.

[37]Information provided during interviews.

[38]CVRD *Annual Report,* 1975.

[39]CVRD has been engaged in arrangements with Mexico and China to swap iron ore for oil; *The Economist,* "Ore for Oil," Dec. 2, 1978, p. 86. For bilateral deals with Poland and Bulgaria, see "$2.5 bn Coal and Ore Pact Between Brazil, Poland," *Financial Times,* July 17, 1978, p. 3; "Rio Ore Deal Seen as Promising," *Financial Times,* July 24, 1978, p. 2.

[40]Details have been gathered from various sources, including interviews in Europe and Brazil and CVRD annual reports. See also "The Story of CVRD: Earth's the Limit," *Brazil,* (June 1978), pp. 14–18.

[41]The Carajas iron-ore project, which is targeted to come on-stream in the mid-1980s, has a planned capacity of at least 25 million tons.

[42]ISCOR, *Annual Report, 1974,* p. 19.

[43]See "U.S. Steel Bethlehem Agree with Venezuela on Plan for Take-over," *Wall Street Journal,* Dec. 18, 1974, p. 33; "Venezuela to Pay U.S. Steel Corp. and Bethlehem," *Wall Street Journal,* Nov. 29, 1974, p. 4; "Venezuela Sets Take-over on Ore," *New York Times,* Nov. 28, 1974, p. 53.

[44]Though the Industrial Policy Resolution of 1956 included the iron and steel industry in the state-dominated sector, it noted that "this does not preclude the expansion of the existing privately-owned units, or the possibility of the State securing the cooperation of private enterprises in the establishing of new units when the national interests so require." For a discussion of this resolution, see Francine Frankel, *India's Political Economy 1947–1977* (Princeton: Princeton University Press, 1978), pp. 129–30.

[45]With only one significant exception, all the large steel plants of India are state owned.

[46]Kudremukh Iron Ore Company, Ltd., *First Annual Report, 1976–77,* p. 6. Following the Iranian Revolution, Iran cut back its long-term commitment to buy Indian ore by 40 percent. See "Pitfalls of Selling Iron Ore," *Far Eastern Economic Review* 106, No. 47 (Nov. 23, 1979): 58.

[47]For a recent example, see "Ministries Differ on Ore Exports," *Economic Times,* Nov. 8, 1979, p. 1.

[48]Based on interviews with Goan exporters.

[49]Whereas in 1974 28.2 percent of ore consumed in U.S. steel mills emanated from outside North America, by 1978 the share of ores from outside North America had declined to only 14.4 percent. American Iron and Steel Institute, *Annual Statistical Report, 1978* (Washington, D.C., 1979), p. 77.

[50]See H. H. Newman, "Strategic Groups and the Structure-Performance Relationships," *Review of Economics and Statistics* 9 (Aug. 1978): 417–27.

[51]For a presentation of this argument in the context of the oil industry, see Raymond Vernon, "The State-Owned Enterprise in Latin-American Exports," *Quarterly Review of Economics and Business* 21, No. 2 (Summer 1981): 98–114; for a general discussion of the difficulties of establishing an effective cartel, see Richard E. Caves, "International Cartels and Monopolies in International Trade" in *International Economic Policy: Theory and Evidence,* ed. Rudiger Dornbush and Jacob A. Frenkel (Baltimore: Johns Hopkins University Press, 1978), pp. 39–69.

8
Uncertainty in the resource industries: The special role of state-owned enterprises

Since the remote era when King Solomon's slaves mined copper from the Negev desert, large-scale ventures in oil and minerals have produced intermittent periods of feast and famine for their owners. In the past hundred years, the owners of such enterprises, government or private, have engaged in unremitting efforts to reduce price fluctuations and stabilize the demand for their output. Some of these efforts have seemed at times to enjoy a certain success. The vast changes in the structure of the crude oil market from 1930 to 1960, for instance, were managed with remarkably few upsets. And until the last decade or two, the stability of the aluminum industry and the sulfur industry were legendary.

During most of those hundred years, the markets in oil and mineral ores were mainly dominated by private producers. Today, a significant part of the mining is done by state-owned enterprises. An obvious question is whether the participation of state-owned enterprises has altered the outlook for sellers and buyers. The answer suggested in this article is that the outlook has been greatly changed, and that the participants in the market will perceive their prospects as infused with a greater degree of uncertainty.

That conclusion is to be distinguished sharply from another issue, namely, whether state-owned enterprises in the raw material industries are a good thing for the countries that have established them. As we shall presently see, the motivations of countries in establishing such enterprises are complex; they have been created as a vehicle for reducing the influence of foreigners, for creating a *pole de croissance* in national development strategies, for fixing prices, collecting taxes, or distributing subsidies more effectively, and for a dozen other reasons. Measured against their purposes and against the alternative means of achieving those purposes, such enterprises may well score high marks. A heightened sense of uncertainty, however, is likely to prevail in the markets in which such enterprises dominate.

From *Risk and the Political Economy of Resource Development*, edited by David W. Pearce, Horst Siebert and Ingo Walter. © David W. Pearce, Horst Siebert and Ingo Walter 1984 and reprinted by permission of St. Martin's Press Inc. and The Macmillan Press, Ltd.

The struggle against uncertainty

Large-scale oil and mining undertakings, whether privately owned or state owned, face the prospect of substantial variations in price and output, variations that *ex ante* as well as *ex post* seem greater than those in most branches of industry. The reasons for that uncertainty are well enough understood; but they are worth reviewing very briefly.

Supply and demand

On the supply side the responses of producers to changes in market conditions are uncertain and poorly timed. One reason is the forbidding nature of the barriers to the establishment of new facilities. The barriers to entry have taken several different forms. Where private producers are involved, whether foreign or domestic, any new facility first requires the negotiation of complex agreements with governments. Once such agreements have been negotiated, they have typically been followed by a prolonged period of exploration and evaluation. Projects that survive that stage then confront the financing problem, which usually entails putting together a package of considerable size; these initial financial packages run from, say, $50 million for a small mining operation to $1,000 million for a large-scale undertaking.[1] Finally, there is a period of construction of extensive infrastructural facilities, including ports, rail lines, roads, and towns—and in recent years the design and construction of facilities for the protection of the physical environment. Therefore, from conception to realization, the process of entry in typical large-scale mining projects has characteristically consumed the best part of a decade if not longer.[2]

The barriers to exit from such industries have been no less formidable. The financing of these operations has generally been done on a fairly long-term basis and with fixed obligations, entailing a stream of anticipated payments over extended periods of time.[3] Besides, oil wells and mines have had a disconcerting propensity to appear in isolated areas, such as remote mountains and deserts; as a result, the support facilities created for their operation have had no obvious alternative use in the short run. Moreover, once in operation, such installations have tended to develop a large dependent population. When mines are located in agricultural communities, workers often abandon their farms for jobs more closely related to the mining operations, and when they are located in isolated locations migrants generally create new settlements nearby in order to serve the mines.[4] To add to the difficulties, in many cases a single mine or oilfield has come to occupy a major position in the economic life of a country, generating a considerable part of the country's foreign exchange and tax revenue. All these factors have deterred owners and governments from abandoning facilities that no longer offered much hope of profit. Even a temporary suspension of production has sometimes proved difficult because of the continued expenses that go with maintaining the shafts and equipment of nonoperating mines.

Suppliers in these markets, therefore, cannot be expected to tailor their entry or exit to the market's needs. And the supplier response has been made all the more difficult by the fact that the variable costs of production of the mines and wells are typically so low relative to their total costs; once on stream, therefore, it takes a very large movement in the price to justify a small change in production levels.

On the demand side, low price elasticities are also a problem. Estimates of such elasticities differ widely; but according to the available studies a doubling in the price of crude oil would only produce a 10 or 20 percent reduction in the use of the commodity within a year; the demand response would of course be much greater over a longer period, but meanwhile the upward price pressure would not be greatly alleviated by the shrinkage of demand.[5] Similar responses in demand to changes in price have been calculated for bauxite, copper, and iron ore.[6] On the other hand, the demand for oil and ores is quite responsive to changes in the business cycle. Such cycle-induced changes introduce an additional element of uncertainty to price and demand prospects.

Stability by horizontal agreements

Since the beginning of the modern history of oil and mineral ores, therefore, operators in these industries have made heroic attempts to reduce the uncertainties they confront. Those efforts have taken a number of different forms.

Cartels have been endemic, created through horizontal agreements among producers that attempted to control prices or production levels or both. The classic case of such an agreement, of course, was in oil, especially in the period from 1928 to World War II; but such agreements were even more common in the various metal ores. In aluminum, the first formal international cartel was formed in 1901, and with various interruptions operated in twenty-four of thirty-eight years following. In copper, three international cartels covered most of the period from 1918 to 1939. And in tin, a single cartel operated without interruption from 1929 to World War II.[7]

There were periods in which cartels managed to reduce the uncertainties that producers faced. Such arrangements, however, were able to go only a little way in bringing about the desired sense of assurance. Efforts to stabilize the price in the face of changes in demand collapsed from time to time, producing sharp discontinuities in the prices of some ores and metals. In addition, the actions of outsiders periodically rendered such agreements untenable. A persistent problem was created by the fact that U.S. producers were generally obliged to conduct their participation in ambiguous forms, in order to avoid a head-on collision with U.S. antitrust laws.[8] U.S. producers of oil, aluminum, copper, lead, and zinc repeatedly ran afoul of those laws because of allegations that they were engaged in restrictive international business practices. There were numerous indications that the need to limit their cooperation tended to weaken their reliability as cartel partners and to undermine the stability of the cartels that required their cooperation.

The obvious fragility of those horizontal agreements, when standing by themselves, has led producers to pursue other routes to stability, including the producer's consortium. These have been partnerships among otherwise independent firms, devoted to joint production at some specified site. From the viewpoint of producers, these partnerships have served several purposes at once: They have reduced the physical and political risks of each participant by allowing it to spread its production activities over a larger number of sites than it otherwise could support; and they have helped to create a common cost base for the various potential competitors, thereby reducing the risk of outbreaks of price competition. That kind of arrangement, common throughout the history of the oil and mining industries, is frequently encountered today. It is exemplified, for instance, by the Arabian American Oil Company (ARAMCO), which is a partnership of four American oil firms, and Compagnie des Bauxites de Guinee, whose partners include six producers from five different countries.

Stability by vertical integration

Even these measures, however, have not been sufficiently effective to satisfy the desire on the part of the raw-material producers to reduce their sense of uncertainty. In addition, therefore, firms in the raw materials industries have had a strong tendency to integrate vertically, linking their mines or wells to their downstream processors and even to industrial users of the processed raw materials. Such linkages have not reduced some of the main sources of market instability, such as the cyclicality of the demand for some metals and the barriers that impede the entry and exit of producers; but they have reduced or eliminated the uncertainties of the individual raw-material producers over their ability to retain their downstream outlets and the uncertainties of the processors over their supplies of raw materials.[9]

In oil and aluminum, the linkage has usually taken the form of direct ownership; but some links have consisted of more ambiguous arrangements. In copper, for instance, the privately owned refineries for many years attempted to maintain a following of faithful copper buyers by guaranteeing supplies to processors at a so-called producers' price; that price, it was understood, would be insulated from some of the instability that characterized the price quoted on the public metal markets, such as the London Metals Exchange. Accordingly, during the 1950s and 1960s, a considerable part of the world's business in refined copper, especially in the United States, took place at prices that were different from those quoted on public markets. Sometimes, the refineries benefitted from the differences; sometimes, it was the turn of the buyers. In iron ore, too, the vertical links between producers and users were strengthened by various informal arrangements. Although steel producers often had equity interests in the mines from which they drew their ores, the links between mills and mines were sometimes based on long-term associations of a less tangible sort, such as the historical ties between German steelmakers and Swedish ore producers, and similar links that have bound some U.S. steelmakers to certain Canadian mines.

State-owned enterprises in the market

In the past thirty years, state-owned enterprises have taken a commanding position in the international oil industry, as well as in all the major branches of mining, including bauxite, iron ore, copper, and the lesser ores.[10] Their appearance introduces fundamentally new factors in the prospects for such industries.

Factors behind their appearance

In a few countries of the world, notably the United States, the creation of a state-owned enterprise is seen as an exceptional measure, an aberration from the free-market norm. In most countries, however, the creation of state-owned enterprises fits comfortably into a tradition that allows for a considerable role on the part of governments in the creation and distribution of goods and services. The tendency to use government instrumentalities directly and extensively in the economy has been especially strong in developing countries, which have been responsible for much of the recent growth of the state-owned enterprise sector in the raw-material industries. Part of the tendency is rooted in history. Latin American countries for instance have strongly reflected their luzo-hispanic traditions of the dominant and responsible state; the francophone ex-colonies of Africa have exhibited the dirigiste preferences of their one-time European mentors; and even Britain's ex-colonies have carried over some of the tendencies of colonial officials as innovators and regulators. In addition, to the extent that such countries have borrowed from contemporary models offered by the more industrialized countries, most have leaned to the concept of a mixed economy, following the examples of Europe and Japan more closely than that of the United States.[11]

Against that background, the developing countries have not been hesitant to use the nationalization route whenever they saw it in their interest to dispossess the foreign firms that were operating their mines and oil wells. Even before World War II, an occasional extraordinary act of nationalization had occurred, such as Mexico's seizure of foreign oil companies in 1938. In the first decade after World War II, the nationalization of mines and oil wells occurred a bit more frequently, but was still a relatively rare event. By the 1960s, however, acts of nationalization were endemic, rising to a crescendo in the mid-1970s. By then, such acts appeared not only in nations that had just acquired their independence, located mainly in Asia, Africa, and the Caribbean, but also in older nations such as those in Latin America. The tendency even touched some more advanced countries, such as the United

Kingdom. The reasons for the shift have to be sought, therefore, in the special conditions of that period.

Perhaps the most striking condition that contributed to the change was the revolutionary improvement in international transportation and international communication, embodied in the jet aircraft, the intercontinental telephone, and the computer. These liberated the developing countries from their prewar isolation, allowing them to send large numbers of their people abroad for technical training, and greatly improving their ability to gather information about capital, technology, and markets.

While the developing countries were improving their ability to scan the rest of the world for their developmental needs, the organization of the petroleum and mining industries was beginning to loosen. In oil, the tight hold that three or four large companies had held on international markets from 1928 to 1950 began to give way to a more loosely structured industry that included a dozen or more vigorous "independents." In copper, the so-called Big Three of the U.S. market were being supplemented by five or six other mining and refining firms. In aluminum, the near-monopoly of the Aluminum Company of America was gradually giving way to an oligopoly with seven or eight important participants. The newcomers in each of these industries proved important for developing countries that were bent on acquiring an independent operation. In some cases, as in the aluminum oligopoly, the junior members of the oligopoly were sometimes prepared to provide technical and marketing assistance to developing countries without insisting on equity participation and control.

Similar liberating developments occurred during the 1960s with regard to capital. Those years saw the formation of the Eurodollar market, followed soon after by the radical internationalization of the world's major banks. At about the same time, the World Bank dropped its early hostility to loans for state-owned enterprises. The credits available from these sources were supplemented by those from the various regional banks that were coming into existence at the time, such as the Interamerican Development Bank, as well as from the various export-promoting official institutions that were being operated by the national governments of Japan, the United States, and the various European countries. When in the 1970s the big private commercial banks found themselves swimming in liquidity because of a flood of petrodollar deposits, the financial dependence of developing countries on foreign-owned oil and mining enterprises seemed forever gone. Indeed, lending to state-owned enterprises became so attractive from the viewpoint of the financial intermediaries that some governments took to using their state-owned enterprises as fronts for borrowing funds that were destined for the general use of government.

Having discovered that technology and capital could be obtained for their petroleum and mining ventures without giving up control to the multinational firms, governments in the developing countries still needed reassurance on one other issue, that of adequate access to markets. On that score, they were helped by various new elements in the situation. One of these, already mentioned, was the decline in the strength of the leaders in the industry and the concomitant decline in their power to control world markets. Another was the appearance of Japan as a major purchaser of raw materials. Fortuitously, Japan's policy during the 1950s and 1960s was to try to secure her needed raw materials through long-term purchase agreements rather than through vertical integration, a policy that nicely complemented the developing countries' desire to retain ownership and control. Still, some sort of trigger was often required before developing countries could bring themselves to take the momentous step of nationalizing foreign-owned properties. During the 1960s and 1970s, various triggering events occurred, from strikes in the copper mines of the United States to the oil embargo of 1973. These helped precipitate the various nationalizations mentioned earlier.

Those nationalizations left state-owned enterprises with a major stake in the international markets for oil, iron ore, and the nonferrous ores and metals. By the end of the 1970s, state-owned enterprises were marketing over 40 percent of the crude oil that appeared in international markets.[12] By that time, too, state-owned enterprises produced about 40 percent of the copper ore and 34 percent of the iron ore outside of the communist countries.[13] The private companies continued to hold a substantial position in some markets, but their raw-material activities were mainly concentrated in Australia, Canada, and the United States; and even in Canada, their prospects were under a cloud. Besides, the smelting and refining stage of the aluminum industry, which had been a bastion of oligopolistic strength for the private companies since the creation of the modern industry a century earlier, appeared headed for the early intrusion of state-owned enterprises on a large scale; a number of oil-producing countries with excess supplies of flare gas were gearing themselves up to conducting smelting and refining operations.

The entry of the state-owned enterprises in the 1960s and 1970s had various effects that bore directly on the future stability of the markets in oil and ores. For one thing, the number of entities engaged in these raw-material operations increased measurably. For decades, oil had been an industry in which six or seven international companies had controlled over 80 percent of the oil mining in international trade. But by the end of the 1970s, mainly by reason of the appearance of numerous state-owned enterprises, their share had been pushed below 40 percent. In various mining industries, as Figure 1 indicates, the concentration of world industry had also declined drastically, as measured by the standard Herfindahl index.[14] Only iron ore mining showed a tendency to reestablish its earlier pre-nationalization levels of concentration.

The entry of the state-owned enterprises not only reduced the concentration of the various industries concerned but also tended to cut off various upstream stages from the stages below in the vertical chains of the raw materials processing industries: the ownership of oil wells from that of refineries and chemical plants; iron ore mines from steel mills; and copper mines from copper refineries. Although I am not aware of any systematic measures that trace the changes in the degree of vertical integration in these industries, it is apparent that such integration declined measurably as a result of the takeovers of state-owned enterprises. For instance, in the case of the iron ore mining industry, whose concentration had uncharacteristically increased in the 1970s, the Australian and Brazilian mines that came to dominate the mining stage at that time had only tenuous connections with their Japanese and European steel mill customers downstream.

Figure 1
Herfindahl Indexes of Concentration of World Production in Three Industries

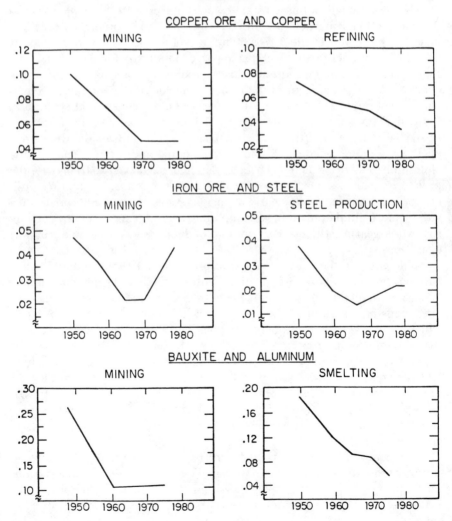

New efforts at stability

State-owned enterprises in most of the raw-material industries were not long in learning that their ownership of the producing properties gave them little added control over the price. In the case of the copper industry, which had experienced its principal acts of nationalization in the latter 1960s, the new owners found the 1970s bitterly disappointing; in iron ore and bauxite, for which the principal acts of nationalization came a few years later, the post-nationalization performance was also disappointing. Apart from a brief period of euphoria that coincided with the first OPEC oil embargo in 1973–74, the demand for ores continued to be uncertain. The price of copper on the London Metals Exchange, for instance, reached a peak of $1.42 per pound during 1974, but was back to 56 cents by the end of that year. In oil, the realization that demand and price might prove highly variable was slower in coming; but by 1981, a decade or so after the principal acts of nationalization, that point had become abundantly clear.

The efforts of the state-owned enterprises to gain a greater degree of control over the market predictably included various projects for the development of international agreements with other suppliers, in close imitation of the cartels that private enterprises had constantly been erecting in the same industries. OPEC, of course, had been created as early as 1960; it was therefore well placed in the 1970s to try to perform the price-raising function. CIPEC, the Conseil Intergouvernemental des Pays Exportateurs de Cuivre, was created in 1967 with similar aspirations on the part of some of its founders. IBA, the International Bauxite Association, came into being in 1974, with the hope in the minds of some of its members that the association could perform a similar purpose.

The existence of these institutions may have added a little to the capacity of producers to boost their prices or increase their taxes; that is a matter of some debate among observers.[15] But any hope that state-owned enterprises may have had of stabilizing the price and quantity of their sales of industrial raw materials was much weakened by the performance of the markets in such materials in the 1970s.

The efforts of state-owned enterprises to stabilize their earnings were not limited to those horizontal agreements, however. In all the raw materials, the enterprises made determined efforts to capture some of the advantages of vertical integration by arranging long-term deals for the sale of their materials. Such deals were commonly arranged between governments, operating through their respective state-owned enterprises. Indeed, in the cases of oil sales by Venezuela and Saudi Arabia, it has been official policy to discriminate in favor of state-owned buyers at the expense of private buyers, presumably in the hope of developing more durable arrangements.

But before the 1970s were out, it was evident that state-to-state deals were not a reliable answer. In some cases, it is true, these contracts did manage to provide the stability that sellers were seeking; France, for instance, was reported saddled with high-cost oil as prices fell during the early 1980s. But there were also occasional reports of governments attempting to escape from unfavorable commitments. More important, state-to-state arrangements proved vulnerable not only to some of the usual commercial hazards but to political disputes as well. For instance, reflecting such tensions, Iraq and Mexico broke off agreements with France for the sale of oil, Iran and India suspended a long-term arrangement for the sale of iron ore, and Jamaica, Trinidad-Tobago, and Mexico abandoned a long-debated project for a joint operation in bauxite, alumina, and aluminum.

With state-to-state deals offering only limited hopes for the reduction of uncertainty, state-owned enterprises have also toyed with the possibility of achieving their objective by vertical integration, that is, by acquiring downstream facilities to serve as captive customers. The urge of state-owned raw material producers to acquire downstream processing facilities may have been enhanced in some cases by the realization that some of the foreign producers whom they had dispossessed by nationalization were developing their own new sources of raw materials. In oil, for instance, expenditures to develop crude oil and natural gas in western Europe rose dramatically after the 1973–74 embargo, to more than triple the amount spent on similar activities in the Middle East;[16] that shift was the forerunner of a decline in the relative importance of Middle East oil, visible by the decade's end. Meanwhile, between 1970 and 1980, U.S. steel producers reduced their purchases of iron ore from "threatened sources" from 15.5 percent to 8.4 percent; in the same years, U.S. copper producers reduced their reliance on sources similarly classified from 13.0 percent to 4.3 percent; and aluminum producers reduced their reliance on sources so classified from 55.4 percent to 39.8 percent.[17]

State-owned enterprises have found it easy to contemplate downstream integration as long as the proposed processing facilities were located on home territory and as long as such facilities were designed simply to serve home demand. Protected from international competition, state-owned processing firms have managed to rely on the demand generated in home markets. If such downstream processing facilities are expected to subsist on the export of their processed products, however, governments are obliged to consider whether they can count on unhampered access to foreign markets. Recognizing this risk, some countries have sought to reduce the problem by taking foreign partners as joint venturers in the processing stage; that, for instance, has been Saudi Arabia's pattern in the development of a petrochemicals industry.

In a few cases, state-owned enterprises have been even more daring by seeking to develop a vertically integrated structure with subsidiaries located in foreign countries. In oil, such a strategy was already visible before the revolution that toppled the Shah in Iran, when the National Iranian Oil Company began to acquire distribution facilities abroad. Meanwhile, the state-owned enterprise of Abu Dhabi made similar arrangements in Pakistan, as did Mexico's Petroleos Mexicanos in Spain. The tendency picked up momentum in the 1980s, as the Kuwait Petroleum Company acquired interests in various refinery and engineering facilities in the United States. Similar strategies occasionally appeared in the mining and metals industries. In one of the few realized cases of that sort, Zambia acquired a 50 percent interest in a French casting rod plant, creating an outlet for some of its copper; in another, the Chilean state-owned enterprise, CODELCO, acquired a 40 percent interest in a German copper fabricating plant; and other possibilities also have been discussed.

Despite such cases, however, that strategy has not been pushed very far. Most countries—but especially developing countries—have found it difficult to authorize their state-owned enterprises to make extensive investments on foreign soil, particularly when the investments have entailed the establishment of industrial facilities.

So far, therefore, state-owned enterprises have not found a formula that greatly reduces the uncertainties that hang over the raw-material industries. It may be that the prospect will change with time. With more experience and more opportunity for experimentation, state-owned enterprises may perhaps feel more secure about the likely behavior of the market because of new forms of agreement and new types of consortia. But the disconcerting possibility is that certain inherent characteristics of state-owned enterprises will prevent them in the end from developing arrangements that offer any increased sense of security.

State ownership and instability

There are some relatively unique factors associated with state ownership of industrial facilities that exacerbate the sense of uncertainty of the participants in markets in which state-owned enterprises predominate.

Fixed costs and variable costs

One such factor is the effect of public ownership on the structure of costs. As a rule, state-owned enterprises look upon their initial capital costs and their prospective capital deficiencies with a viewpoint that distinguishes them from that of privately owned enterprises. The initial donation of capital from the state may be contributed with the expectation that loans will eventually be repaid and that interest and dividends will eventually be forthcoming. But so far as I am aware, there is no case on record in which a state-owned enterprise in the raw-materials field has been placed in bankruptcy for failure to pay its debt or otherwise to service its capital. To be sure, there have been occasional cases in which managerial heads have rolled for gross mismanagement; the case of Indonesia's Pertamina is especially well known. But the usual governmental reaction to an unplanned loss by a state-owned enterprise is to make up the deficiency in capital by an added capital contribution. One critical consequence of that fact is that state-owned enterprises are usually less concerned than private enterprises in balancing financial outflow with inflow; as a result, when demand falls off, the incentive of the state-owned enterprise to reduce output is not very strong. In the case of large-scale operations with a substantial workforce, that incentive is weakened even further by the near-universal desire of governments to use their state-owned enterprises as major sources of employment; governments prefer to retain the labor force even when production falls off.

When state-owned enterprises are engaged in the processing of a material that is domestic in origin, the cost structure of the firm is influenced by another important factor. In such cases, the processing facility—such as a petrochemicals plant or a copper refinery—is typically allowed to acquire its raw material at less than the export price to foreigners; accordingly, variable costs are reduced even further in importance.

The upshot is that state-owned enterprises characteristically see their variable costs as much lower than do the private enterprises that they displace. This is not to say that the managers of state-owned enterprises necessarily have an easier task than private managers. But it does mean that the financial incentive to adjust production levels to demand is blunted, and that the possibility of generating indigestible surpluses through overproduction is accordingly high.

The fact that state-owned enterprises have multiple goals, so often emphasized in the literature, adds to their difficulties in helping to stabilize the markets for their output. The multiple goals in the state-owned enterprise may include not only the goal of expanding employment but also that of maximizing foreign exchange, adding to government revenue, contributing to the development of feeder or derivative industries, or acting as a conduit for the distribution of subsidies. All of these goals tend to reduce the manager's desire to cut production in times of surplus, as compared with the responses of a profit-making firm. Maximizing foreign exchange, for instance, like the employment-maximizing objective, is likely to lead to a higher level of output in a declining market than maximizing profit.

Not enough experience exists as yet to say with certainty how these characteristics will affect the market behavior of the state-owned enterprises in the resource industries. They suggest, however, that for facilities that are already in place, the managers of state-owned enterprises will be slow to reduce production in the face of a decline in demand; for the short run, therefore, state-owned enterprises may tend to weaken prices with their unrestrained production. It is much less clear how the state-owned enterprise that is operating at capacity will respond to prospective increases in demand. On the one hand, a tendency to be pinched for capital may prevent such enterprises from pursuing the exploration and development activities that the market prospects would call forth from a private investor; on the other, however, the access of many such enterprises to official sources of credit without a severe market test may mean that exploration and development will not be hampered. This is a critical question for the longer term; and the answer in the end may prove to be quite complex.

Negotiating international agreements

There are a number of added reasons why the multiplicity of goals of the state-owned enterprise promises to inhibit the firms in these industries from developing international agreements that might reduce their sense of uncertainty. In an oligopoly composed of a limited number of profit-maximizing firms, as history has repeatedly demonstrated, private firms have proved capable at times of entering into tacit or explicit arrangements that are intended to stabilize the market. However, there are already indications, especially evident in the oil and copper markets, that the differences in the objectives of the various state-owned producing firms represent a formidable barrier to such agreements. Zambia's overwhelming reliance on copper sharply distinguishes it from Indonesia; Brazil's ebullient expectations for iron ore as a *pole de croissance* in remote areas offers a sharp contrast to Sweden's realization that its industry has a limited future; Mexico's desperate short-term need for foreign exchange in the sale of its oil offers a sharp contrast to Kuwait's position. This diversity stands in contrast to the situation in which five or six huge international oil companies found common ground in a relatively uncomplicated desire to achieve maximum profits and stability over the long run.

The increased role of the state in the negotiation of stabilizing agreements means also that political and security objectives begin to play a bigger role in determining the outcome. Conceivably, that factor could operate to facilitate agreement at times, as when the main producers see themselves collectively facing a common enemy. The greater probability, however, is that the lines of political alliance will run differently from the lines of economic interest, inhibiting effective economic agreements. The oil market is the obvious case in point. In that case, the hostility of the conservative Arab governments to the Libyan and Iranian radicals as well as the USSR has fractured the solidarity of the sellers, while the common interests between Saudi Arabia and the United States have linked sellers with buyers in complex patterns. Considerations of a similar sort have inhibited Australia from supporting the efforts of Jamaica and Guyana to elevate the price of bauxite. If the cartel arrangements in oil and aluminum were being proposed by private enterprises, almost irrespective of their nationality, the political implications of participation would have carried much less weight.

The political difficulties of state-owned enterprises lie not only in negotiating international cartel agreements but also in adhering to them once they enter into force. Private parties may continue to honor their agreements even while their governments are quarreling bitterly.[18] State-owned enterprises, on the other hand, are much more exposed to the possibility of political direction from the government. Indeed, even when governments would prefer not to interfere with the understandings and arrangements that their state-owned enterprises develop as members of an international oligopoly, they may feel obliged to do so for domestic political reasons. Such understandings characteristically demand compromise and restraint on the part of each of the participants, a willingness of each of them to forego profits in the short run in order to protect the collective rent of the group as a whole; accepting a ceiling on production, for instance, is a classic illustration of such restraint. But the willingness of any state-owned enterprise to restrain itself in accordance with an international agreement opens it to the charge at home of stupidity, corruption, or treachery; the temptation of the opposition to push such a charge is a persistent danger for many governments and their enterprise managers.

Vertical integration

As was pointed out earlier, state-owned enterprises have occasionally acquired subsidiaries abroad in an effort to secure captive customers or assured sources of raw materials. But for the state-owned enterprises of developing countries, such moves have been relatively rare, much less common than for the private enterprises that they have displaced. Such state-owned enterprises have been less prone to participate with other firms in producing consortia located in foreign countries, and less prone to establish foreign facilities on their own. In this case, too, the reason can be traced partly to factors that derive from the status of the enterprises as agents of the state. In developing countries, long accustomed to thinking of themselves as starved for capital, the idea of exporting capital selectively in order to improve the prospects of some of their enterprises understandably is slow in taking hold. Not only is it a novel possibility for most developing countries; it also runs counter to some quite fundamental—albeit quite naive—textbook rules of good economic behavior, such as the rule that capital-starved countries should be importing capital, not exporting it. Accordingly, any government of a developing country that gives serious consideration to such investment possibilities is treading on dangerous political ground.

All these factors add up to the fact that participants in the raw-materials market are likely to see themselves as confronting especially high levels of uncertainty. State-owned enterprises in those industries, as individual firms, will be inhibited from pursuing some of the risk-reducing arrangements that were for so long available to the privately owned firms that they displaced. These perceptions of heightened risk could reduce the tendency of suppliers to invest in the production of such materials over the long run, and may stimulate users of such materials to search for more attractive alternatives.

Notes

[1] For data on the point, see W. C. Labys, *Marketing Structure, Bargaining Power, and Resource Price Formation* (Lexington, MA: D. C. Heath, 1980), p. 79.

[2] For eight typical projects begun after 1961, the lag between commencement of exploration and production ranged from six to fifteen years, the median being ten years; see J. S. Carman, *Obstacles to Mineral Development: A Pragmatic View* (New York: Pergamon Press, 1979), p. 46.

[3] Southern Peru Copper's Cuajone project in 1975, for instance, entailed $627 million of financing, of which $411 million was in the form of debt, mainly in seven- to ten-year notes: "Southern Peru Copper Corporation and Mamouth National Bank," Case no. 9-279-091, Harvard Business School, Boston, 1979, pp. 4, 14. The Bougainville copper mine's 1972 financing was composed of $310 million in medium- and long-term debt and $160 million in equity. "Bougainville Copper Ltd. (B)," Case no. 9-174-104, Harvard Business School, Boston, 1974, pp. 5, 17.

[4] See for instance Carman, *Obstacles to Mineral Development*, p. 123.

[5] Estimates of demand elasticities for crude oil and its various products, gleaned from numerous studies, are reported in Robin C. Landes and Michael W. Klass, *OPEC: Policy Implications for the United States* (New York: Praeger, 1980), pp. 186–90.

[6] W. C. Labys, *Market Structure, Bargaining Power, and Resource Price Formation*, p. 19.

[7] Ervin Hexner, *International Cartels* (Chapel Hill, NC: University of North Carolina Press, 1946), pp. 216–48.

[8] Hexner, *International Cartels*, pp. 216-48, describes developments before World War II in some detail. Developments in the postwar copper market appear in the court records in *Reading Industries v. Kennecott Copper Corp. et al.*, U.S. District Court for Southern District of New York, June 12, 1979; see also "1958 Outlook: Copper," *Engineering and Mining Journal*, vol. 159, no. 2, Feb. 1958, p. 115. For oil, see J. E. Hartshorn, *Politics and World Oil Economics* (New York: F. A. Praeger, 1962), p. 154.

[9] The nature of these risks is described more fully in Raymond Vernon, "Organizational and Institutional Responses to International Risk," in Richard J. Herring (ed.), *Managing International Risk* (London: Cambridge University Press, 1983).

[10] Estimates for the various mineral industries are provided in Marian Radetzki, *State Enterprise in International Mineral Markets*, forthcoming.

[11] Peter Odell's comments in private correspondence served to remind me of the critical importance of these background factors.

[12] *Petroleum Intelligence Weekly*, vol. XIX, no. 8, Feb. 25, 1980, p. 4.

[13] For copper, calculated from American Bureau of Metal Statistics, Inc., *Non-Ferrous Metal Data, 1981* (New York, 1982), pp. 22–24. For iron ore, calculated from United Kingdom Iron and Steel Statistics Bureau, *International Steel Statistics, Summary Tables* (Croydon, England, 1980), pp. 4–5, and *Skillings Mining Review*, July 7, 1979, pp. 12–13.

[14] From Raymond Vernon, *Two Hungry Giants: The United States and Japan in the Search for Oil and Ores* (Cambridge: Harvard University Press, 1983), p. 49.

[15] The debate over the role of OPEC is summarized in Vernon, *Two Hungry Giants*, pp. 26–31; see also Ali D. Johany, *The Myth of OPEC Cartel: The Role of Saudi Arabia* (New York: John Wiley and Sons, 1980). IBA's role in aluminum is summarized in Douglas W. Woods and James C. Burrows, *The World Aluminum-Bauxite Market: Policy Implications for the United States* (New York: Praeger Publishers, 1980), pp. 100–101, 104–105; and Raymond F. Mikesell, *The World Copper Industry: Structure and Economic Analysis* (Baltimore, MD: The Johns Hopkins University Press, 1979), p. 205.

[16] Raymond Vernon, *Two Hungry Giants*, Table 2-3, p. 34.

[17] For definitions and sources, see Vernon, *op. cit.*, Table 3-3, p. 54.

[18] For the period leading up to World War II, see U.S. Senate, Committee on Military Affairs, Subcommittee on War Mobilization, *Economic and Political Aspects of International Cartels*,

Corwin D. Edwards (principal investigator) (Washington, DC: Government Printing Office, 1944), pp. 62–64. For more recent illustrations, the operations of U.S. oil companies in Angola and Libya are illustrative.

9

Linking managers with ministers: Dilemmas of the state-owned enterprise

The Issue

In the past decade or two, state-owned enterprises in the market economies of the world have multiplied in number, have diversified in function, and have come to account for a considerable proportion of the output and investment of those economies.[1]

To be sure, state-owned enterprises have a long history in many developing countries. But until a few decades ago, such enterprises were largely concentrated in industries that had the characteristics of national monopolies—in railroads, utilities, and the like. In the 1950s and later decades, however, most developing countries took to creating state-owned enterprises in manufacturing, banking, and trade. Some of these enterprises were created as part of a national program of import-substituting industrialization. Some came into existence as foreign-owned properties were nationalized on a massive scale, especially in oil and mining.[2] And for the most part, ideology seemed to play only a minor role; countries that emphasized the development of a private sector, such as Brazil, Korea, and Morocco, acted about as strongly to increase the state-owned sector as countries with a socialist bent, such as Algeria and India.

During these same decades, some of the more advanced industrialized countries also added substantially to their stock of state-owned enterprises, so that by the early 1980s, such enterprises had come to occupy a considerable place in their respective national economies. In some instances, the immediate motive was to gain public control of industries that occupied the economy's "commanding heights," that is, industries whose control was

This article was stimulated by an unpublished memorandum prepared by Richard Mallon. Jean-Pierre Nioche supplied invaluable material and comments. John Sheahan's perceptive criticisms of an earlier draft generated substantial revisions.

Reprinted with permission of the author from *Journal of Policy Analysis and Management*, vol. 4, no. 1, Fall 1984.

thought essential to the management of the economy. Britain's nationalization of its steel and coal industries was a case in point; so, too, was France's acquisition in 1982 of practically all French private banks as well as a dozen major manufacturing firms. But other motives occasionally appeared as well, including a desire of some governments to avoid foreign ownership of high-technology industries, as well as a desire to prevent some senescent industries from passing out of the scene too rapidly.

With the growth of state-owned enterprises all over the world, the problem of ensuring that such enterprises were appropriately managed became a major preoccupation with many governments. The long-term problems of assuring coherence and efficiency were exacerbated by short-term questions of solvency and liquidity. In Argentina, Brazil, Morocco, Sri Lanka, Algeria, Italy, France, and scores of other countries, state-owned enterprises were suddenly found absorbing great quantities of domestic funds and borrowing huge amounts from abroad. State-owned enterprises that were not banks commonly absorbed about one-third of the domestic credit of the economies in which they were located.[3] And from 1976 to 1983, state-owned enterprises raised over $80 billion through new bond issues offered on foreign markets.[4]

One conceivable response to the problem of controlling the state-owned enterprise might have been to integrate them more fully into the traditional ministries and bureaus of the government, on the theory that control would thereby be strengthened. But most governments were sensitive to the risk that some kinds of activities would be stifled if they were performed within the traditional ministries and bureaus. More particularly, the systems of incentives and rewards, the channels of command and control, and the provisions for accountability that were typical of government agencies seemed less than ideal for entities that were making and selling goods and services or processing investment loans.

Yet separating the state-owned enterprise from the ordinary machinery of government posed numerous novel problems. Although governments recognized the need for some autonomy on the part of managers, they also saw a need for responsiveness and accountability. To find the proper balance, governments experimented with various devices. Some created a special ministry for state-owned enterprises, which was expected to act as both a buffer and an advocate for such enterprises within the ministerial structure. Some attached each enterprise to an existing ministry—a *tutelle* in the jargon of French administrators. Some attempted, in addition, to develop explicit agreements or understandings between enterprise managers and ministry bureaucrats regarding the operations of the state-owned enterprise, hoping thereby to preserve both the autonomy and the responsiveness of the enterprises.[5] In India, for instance, a Bureau of Public Enterprises sought to develop a periodic "action plan" with the managers of each of the enterprises. And in France, a much more explicit and more detailed system of formal contracts between each state-owned enterprise and the national administration was developed. In the French case, three such contracts were consummated in the period 1971 to 1973, four in 1978 and 1979, and at least ten in 1983.[6]

In spite of the many imaginative efforts to create an effective link between ministers and managers, there has been widespread dissatisfaction with the results in practically every country in which state-owned enterprises have an important place in the national economy. As a first step in improving that link, therefore, it is necessary to look for the causes of that dissatisfaction.

Defining purposes

Some causes of that difficulty are painfully obvious: Governments have great difficulty in defining their purposes in a coherent, internally consistent manner. That incontestable fact, in turn, can be traced to several obvious causes.

Rival perspectives

In advanced industrialized countries, a number of different unreconciled views exist as to the appropriate function of the state-owned enterprise. For instance, some officials take the view that the principal justification for such an enterprise is as a means for overcoming some of the "imperfections" in the markets of the country. As they see it, some markets fail to perform efficiently because of especially high risks, imperfect information, external economies, monopoly, or any of the other well-known causes of such failure. State-owned enterprises, according to this view, can appropriately be charged with programs to overcome such failures. So, for example, the state-owned firm invests in backward regions where private firms are unwilling or unable to absorb the costs; and it receives capital from the state that the private market is not prepared to provide. But to the extent possible, it operates as if it faced an environment of prices such as an "efficient" market would generate, and it charges prices of a similar sort. According to this familiar view, any system of control that places less than total reliance on the discipline of the market tends to be labelled as a "second best" choice.

Although that view of the state-owned enterprise is sometimes pushed by influential officials in the key ministries, no government has been known to apply it very widely as national policy. In varying degrees, different governments introduce other factors in their desired policy mix. For instance even in the United States, bastion of the ideology that the market should be paramount, the few state-owned enterprises that exist are almost always restrained by statutory requirements that the prices they charge should be "fair" or "equitable" or "nondiscriminatory."[7] Moreover, the behavior of such enterprises is always circumscribed by procedural provisions that are intended to ensure that the enterprises will not be the sole arbiters of what those terms mean. The right of those affected to have a hand in the outcome by participating in hearings or appealing to the courts obviously represents a political value of high importance, without which there is a presumption that the result would not be fair. In addition, practically all countries, irrespective of their economic ideology, also subscribe to the proposition that state-owned enterprises should build some measure of cross-subsidization in their prices, commonly as a means of taking a little from the rich and giving to the poor.

We observed earlier, however, that governments had been known to create state-owned enterprises for various reasons other than to overcome the foibles of imperfect markets or to engage in cross-subsidization. These have included: forcing the pace of industrialization; occupying the commanding heights of the economy; preventing foreigners from preempting the opportunities that might otherwise be exploited by national interests; and slowing the exit of declining industries.

With so wide a range of objectives thought appropriate for the state-owned enterprise, one problem of fashioning an effective link between ministers and managers becomes clear. Any single enterprise at any given time has typically been the target of a number of commands from the various ministers, commands that stemmed from different sources and pointed the enterprise in different directions.

Who represents government?

The diversity of objectives that are urged on the managers of state-owned enterprises might not be so difficult to cope with if it were reasonably clear who in government were the legitimate masters of the managers. But the answer to that question is never free of ambiguity. Indeed, in the case of some countries, that ambiguity is deliberate. For instance, like some other countries that have developed a nationalized sector, the French are careful to distinguish between the instruments of the nation as a whole and those of the administration in power. Nationalized industries are thought of as belonging to the nation, not to the administration. The implications of that distinction, although not very precise, nevertheless run deep: Whatever the officials of any elected administration may attempt to do with such enterprises, the ultimate responsibility for defining the goals of those enterprises rests at some elevated level higher than the administration itself.

That ambiguity is deepened by a national view, prevalent not only in France but in many other countries, that workers in the enterprise are to have a special hand in managing the affairs of the enterprise.[8] To be sure, in actual practice, French employees of state-owned enterprises tend to concentrate on such issues as security of tenure and other worker benefits rather than on the right to share in general management powers;[9] but even in the French case, unions have been known to protest the overseas investments of state-owned enterprises such as Renault. And in countries such as Sweden, where the concept of worker participation is heavily stressed, the views of workers on the policies of the firms are even more frequently heard.

Factors such as these tend to reduce the ability of any administration to address managers as if the administration were the ultimate arbiter of what the nation wants. That ability is impaired a little further by the wide range of subjects that the administration and the enterprise are obliged to address. Because of that range, the French government sometimes designates two ministries rather than one to perform the tutelary role over an important state-owned enterprise—one ministry for "technical" matters and another for financial issues.[10] Indeed, in actual practice, managers have found themselves dealing with half a dozen ministers or more, each with some capacity to reward or punish.

In some cases, as in the de Gaulle era in France or the sultanate regime in Morocco, the diversities represented by the ministries and their ministers could be held in check by a strong personality at the head of the government. But even when such a personality dominates the government, it cannot be counted on to follow the flight of every sparrow in its domain. Ministers in the de Gaulle government, for instance, would be hesitant to bring their disputes over management and coordination to the attention of the head of state, for fear that the disputes may reflect on their reputation as managers. Moreover, even when a conflict between ministers has seemed too important to be ignored by a strong head of state, the head has often appeared reluctant to get involved.[11] In Mexico during the 1970s, for instance, at a time when no one could doubt either the ability or the need of the president to keep the country's national oil company in line, internecine warfare among the national oil company, the planning ministry, and the ministry of finance went on unchecked for a number of critical years.

In any event, democratic governments do not always produce strong heads of state. Where the democratic process produces coalition governments, as in Italy and Holland, the position of a head of state—whatever his personality—may be inherently weak. In fact, in coalition governments, the direction of individual ministries and even individual enterprises is often parcelled out among the various parties, witness the French Communist Party's special position with respect to Charbonages de France.

The limitations on the disposition of ministries to coordinate their views have some major implications for the management of state-owned enterprises. For one thing, the functional orientation of the ministries that are most directly involved in negotiating with the state-owned enterprise are bound to have a heavy influence on the content of any agreement with the managers of such an enterprise. In 1978, for instance, the contract entered into between the French government and Air France dealt almost exclusively with financial issues, such as limiting the cash needs of the airline; the financial emphasis, it is claimed, emerged for the simple reason that the contract was principally negotiated with the ministries of the budget and the treasury.[12] Agreements such as these court the risk that those ministries not involved in the development of the bargain may not feel themselves in any way bound by its terms.

Finally, the link between ministers and managers may prove weak not because of the intransigence of ministers but because of the independence of managers. The managers of state-owned enterprises stand a chance of becoming a political force in their own right. In the 1960s, Pierre Dreyfus, while chief executive officer of Renault, was widely recognized as having an independent political base, as was Enrico Mattei when he headed Italy's Ente Nazionale Idrocarburi (ENI) in the 1950s and 1960s.[13] In France, the collective political strength of the managers may prove particularly strong because of the ties that bind many of them through their common memberships in the *grands corps*; indeed, in one well-documented case, the officers of five French state-owned enterprises demonstrated their collective influence by bringing about the dismissal of a French minister of industry.[14]

Content of the interaction

Despite disagreement and confusion, considerable interaction between ministers and managers does take place. Obviously, the content of that interaction has to be understood if there is to be any hope of improving the link between ministers and managers.

Working toward strategic goals

In most countries, governments periodically review their strategic objectives and periodically restate their priorities, such as expanding exports, holding down inflation, and increasing productivity. When goals such as these have been explicitly targeted, governments with a well-developed private sector, such as Britain, France, Italy, and Brazil, are often found exhorting their private firms in much the same way as they exhort their state-owned firms. But some differences do exist: There is a tendency on the part of governments, for instance, to define the targets for the state-owned enterprises with somewhat greater specificity than for private enterprises. In the case of Air France, for instance, the French government's general desire for an increase in productivity is crystallized in target measures of performance, such as revenue per agent and technicians' costs per hour of flight.

The French government, more than most, has sought to cut through the conflict and confusion that typify democratic governments' efforts to define their national objectives, using the vehicle of the five-year national plan as its instrument for articulating a consensus. Each such plan has been drafted after a long process of consultation among the ministries, with the private sector, and with labor; and, when it is finally issued, the French plan does command a certain amount of authority and respect as an expression of governmental policy.[15]

After thirty years of French experience, however, it seems fairly evident that national plans can serve only a limited role as a guide for managers of state-owned enterprises. France's experience with national plans over the years has led it to recognize that the increasing openness of the French economy has placed severe constraints on the degree of specificity with which the country's development can be planned.[16]

To be sure, there are still some situations in which national plans can provide specific guidance. For instance, some projects or programs are so large and so vital to the national economy that national planners are obliged to consider them in detail. France's Seventh Plan, covering the years 1975 to 1980, contained twenty-five so-called programmes d'action prioritaires, large-scale capital-intensive projects of national significance. If a state-owned enterprise happens to hold a monopoly position in the execution of such a project, as in the case of the national telephone system, the guidance from the national plan for the enterprise can be quite considerable.

In market economies, however—especially in the market economies of large industrialized countries—such situations are quite exceptional. As a rule, only a small portion of the country's productive activities can be explored in detail at the level of the national plan. Even where goals in individual product lines are mentioned, it may prove difficult to distinguish the role of the state-owned enterprise from that of other firms. The role of state-owned Honeywell–Bull in France, for instance, cannot be well defined without considering the activities of foreign-owned IBM, while the chemical activities of state-owned Pechiney–Ugine–Kuhlmann cannot be defined independently of France's privately owned chemical companies. Accordingly, when the state-owned enterprises must share a market with other firms, whether a domestic market or an international market, the guidance provided by the national plan is bound to be highly conditional.

To be sure, effective linkage between national plans and enterprise operations is not impossible, as the case of Japan suggests. But that case also underlines how difficult it may be to achieve such linkage.[17] In that country, linkage between national policies and enterprise actions is promoted by an elaborate process of consultation that involves government ministries, government-controlled industrial enterprises, and private industry. Whether as a result of that process or as a result of factors that are more obscure, enterprises in the public sector operate in patterns that seem especially closely integrated with the policies of their ministries.[18] Firms in the private sector may occasionally refuse to participate in the system of consultation or resist the conclusions that the system produces; still, the conclusions carry considerable weight. The results have been highly visible in the country's pursuit of a number of major policy objectives, such as developing more secure sources of raw materials overseas[19] and reshaping the industrial structure of the home economy.[20] But Japan's ability to achieve that coordination has demanded some extraordinary institutions and habits of operation that have no close counterparts in other countries.

The difficulties involved in linking national objectives to the behavior of individual state-owned firms appear to trouble the developing countries at least as much as countries that are richer and more highly industrialized.[21] In some respects, in fact, the difficulties of the developing countries may be more acute. For instance, in many developing countries, technical weaknesses in the bureaucracy and a propensity of ministers to stress vertical more than horizontal relationships tend to inhibit the interactions that would be required to link enterprise activities with national plans.[22]

Moreover, neither developing countries nor developed countries can escape another problem that limits the influence of long-term official plans on the actions of state-owned firms. From time to time, governments are voted out of office or are driven from office by other means. In either case, changes in government are expected to bring about changes in national policy; and in most instances, those expected changes cannot fail to imply some shifts in the operations of state-owned enterprises. In France, François Mitterrand's socialist government took office in 1980, displacing a regime of a very different sort. As the head of a socialist government, Mitterrand could hardly allow the policies of the predecessor government to determine the behavior of the country's state-owned enterprises, even if those policies were to some extent embedded in contracts with such enterprises. A prime objective of the Mitterrand government was greatly to enlarge the state-owned sector; as France nationalized some of its largest firms, the existing enterprises of the state were plunged into a series of complex reshuffles of state-owned properties, maneuvers which absorbed much of the attention and energies of the state managers.[23] That source of potential instability to the contractual approach is presumably desirable—and in any case appears inescapable—in countries that are not locked into an unchanging authoritarian rule.

Regulating utilities

Apart from any national plan, practically every modern state is engaged in the piecemeal regulation of its public utilities. In many instances, as we noted earlier, those utilities prove to be state-owned enterprises.

Yet, curiously, state-owned enterprises in that position can sometimes exert greater power over the regulators than a private enterprise in the same situation might do. Governments that own their utilities often have a major stake in seeing to it that the utilities operate well—a greater stake in many instances than if the utilities were privately owned. But the efficient operation of some public utilities, such as railroads and power plants, may require special technical and managerial skills. That fact usually gives managers of state-owned enterprises a certain amount of bargaining power with their regulators; governments are usually not eager to shake up the management of a state-owned enterprise unless they can be sure that the new managers will be able to take over smoothly and expeditiously. Accordingly, the managers of state-owned enterprises usually have some room for maneuver, at least in the short run.

A second reason why state-owned enterprises may not respond attentively to the commands of the government agencies, as experience points out, is that even a monopolist is not altogether immune from changes in its business environment. Although the state-owned enterprise may be able to exercise tight control over the market for its output, it is still not impervious to the effects of variations in the aggregate demand for its services, a fact that has bedevilled France's railway system, SNCF. Besides, monopolists do not always control the price and supply of their inputs. When the price of oil rose dramatically in the winter of 1973–1974, for instance, it destroyed the basis of the contract between the government and Electricité de France. Facing contingencies such as these, state-owned enterprises are bound to try to retain some measure of flexibility.

There have been times when governments have tried to direct their state-owned enterprises to respond to governmental commands as if they were a national monopoly, despite the fact that those enterprises have faced actual or potential competition from other producers. In some of those instances, governments have quickly realized the limits of their regulatory powers and have had to back down. For instance, in a well-publicized dispute that lasted from 1974 to 1978, Air France managed to resist the French government's pressures to replace its aging Caravelle fleet with an inappropriate French-built Dassault product; eventually, Air France was authorized to lease thirteen U.S.-built Boeings, awaiting the time when the European-sponsored Airbus consortium could provide the desired aircraft.[24]

In other cases in which ministers have been obliged to recognize the limits of their powers, the state-owned enterprises concerned have been selling in international raw materials markets, including those in oil and copper. Ministers' efforts to direct those enterprises as if they were monopolies have usually proved either futile or costly to the countries concerned. The reasons have usually been obvious. In such industries, the marginal costs of most producers have typically been very much lower than their full costs. Managers selling in such markets have usually been aware that in the short run all of them faced a threat of price cutting, which would prevent them from recapturing their full costs. As a result, managers in such enterprises have commonly learned to be cautious in instituting any reductions in prices; the European managers of state-owned enterprises in the aluminum industry and the oil industry, for instance, have usually cooperated in tacit or explicit agreements on prices and markets, aimed at preventing an outbreak of price cutting. Although such arrangements have often seemed indispensable from the viewpoint of the managers, they have severely limited the extent to which managers could respond to ministers.[25]

The budgetary exercise

The governmental process that has had the most dramatic and immediate effects on state-owned enterprises, however, has been the budgetary exercise, a process that ordinarily occurs each year as governments try to maintain some tolerable relationship between income and expenditure. The chronic problem created by state-owned enterprises in this case is their propensity to run out of cash, making higher demands on governments than anyone had planned. That tendency, notorious among state-owned enterprises, is by now well documented.[26] As a result, fiscal authorities ordinarily try to develop restraints on how much each state-owned enterprise will be permitted to draw down from government sources or—more exceptionally— try to lay down goals representing the amounts that their enterprises will be expected to contribute to government revenues.

But governments have faced special difficulties in their efforts to control the cash flow of state-owned enterprises. Part of their problem has arisen from the fact that there are major advantages in distinguishing the income and expenditures of their state-owned enterprises from those of the government proper. The distinction serves numerous purposes. It helps make managers of such enterprises accountable for their performance and helps protect ministers from charges of profligacy; it creates a separate cache of resources in some instances, unavailable or unknown to public and parliament, that the government can draw on at strategic junctures; and it creates a separate international or domestic borrower, distinct from that of the government itself, whose resources nonetheless can be funneled into government accounts. In Mexico, for instance, 40 percent of the country's foreign borrowing in 1978 was done by state-owned banks and another 33 percent by other state-owned enterprises.[27]

Partly as a result of the separation of their accounts, state-owned enterprises often can develop cash crises without ministers being alerted in advance. Because the enterprises are separated from the ministries, information about the financial condition of the enterprise, as a rule, must come from the enterprise itself; and the enterprise is likely to have a natural and understandable urge to conceal a disappointing performance until the latest possible moment.[28] When the surprise is sprung and the enterprise is found short of cash, governments hesitate to force the enterprise to shut its doors. To be sure, a number of governments have adopted policies during the past few years of shrinking back the scale of unprofitable public enterprises and of selling some enterprises off to the private sector.[29] But there are numerous signs that the new policies have been encountering considerable resistance from forces both within and outside the government.[30] My assumption is that the tendency to shrink the financially unprofitable activities of the state-owned enterprises will not be very widespread or very resolute. As long as governments can print money, the temptation to keep open the doors of state-owned enterprises is likely to remain strong.

But the cash-flow problem is not limited to failing enterprises. Even state-owned enterprises that appear financially strong, such as the oil-exporting enterprises, can sometimes create cash crises for their governments. Governments commonly attempt to impose restraints on the ability of their enterprises to borrow abroad.[31] Firms with promising export opportunities are often well placed to urge governments to allow them to expand even faster than their internally generated resources will permit. Indeed, some of the notable balance-of-payment disasters of developing countries in the early 1980s could be traced to the uninhibited borrowing of relatively successful firms such as Pemex of Mexico and Pertamina of Indonesia.

As a result, the interactions between ministries and enterprises are bound to be permeated with struggles over the cash-flow issue, including questions about the rights of the enterprise to borrow and the obligations of the enterprise to pay taxes and dividends.[32] And when, as in the French case, contracts are developed between the government and the enterprise, undertakings that relate to cash flow almost always make up an important part of the contract. But these arrangements, as history demonstrates, have not eliminated the risks of the unexpected cash crisis.

Extracting special concessions

In the interactions between ministers and managers, another part of the traffic consists of the efforts of managers to secure some special rights or resources from their ministers, not available in the ordinary course. In some situations, the position of the managers is bolstered by the fact that their enterprises have been saddled with some costly responsibility for which compensation is being sought. Air France provides a striking illustration. When in 1974 Air France reluctantly agreed to shift its operational base from Orly airport to the just-completed Charles de Gaulle airport in Paris, it demanded and received official compensation for its increased operating costs.[33] And in the United Kingdom, British Rail's subsidy to support its services to loss-making rural locations offered an illustration of a similar type.[34]

At the same time, managers of such enterprises have sometimes demanded and received special privileges and subsidized resources to support their regular commercial activities. Special privileges may include, for example, a guaranteed monopoly on sales to another state-owned enterprise or protection from foreign imports. Subsidized resources can take many different forms. One common device is for the government to increase its equity in the state-owned enterprise on terms that the enterprise could not secure in the open market. Another is for the government to extend loans at concessionary terms; sometimes these are earmarked expressly for carrying out an authorized project, but at other times they represent an unrestricted source of capital.[35] Transactions of this sort are encountered in practically all countries with state-owned enterprises, and they constitute a major aspect of the financing of such enterprises.[36]

The outcome

In operational terms, then, the agreements that operate between managers and ministers usually consist of an eclectic mix—a mix that commingles long-term gains with short-term objectives, that changes frequently in content, and that is rarely tested for its internal consistency. When efforts are made to put such agreements in formal terms, as France has sought to do, they cannot fail to reflect those eclectic characteristics. The idea of a rational set of goals, responding to some coherent concepts of optimality and serving as a feasible measure of command and control, remains remote.

Next steps

The state-owned enterprise epitomizes a dilemma that has always existed for citizens who are lucky enough to live in a democratic state. On the one hand, the desire to use the full power of the state for important national purposes tilts the citizen toward endowing agencies with power and continuity. On the other hand, the emphasis on the democratic process pushes the citizen toward recognizing the legitimacy of rival value systems, acknowledging the rights of dissenters, and providing for the possibility of diversity and change. The relative strength of those two factors varies from one country to the next, and it changes over time in any given country. Those differences probably go some way toward explaining some of the differences in the prevalence and practices of state-owned enterprises.

In the United States, for instance, the desire of the electorate to prevent the state from preempting the rights of groups and individuals typically is stronger than its desire to use the power of the state for specified public purposes; the dominance of the first value over the second may explain why the United States typically avoids the creation of state-owned enterprises, deals with some natural monopolies through regulation, and deals with other monopoly problems by promoting competition among private enterprises.

The Japanese approach to the art of governance also recognizes the importance of accommodating the rights and interests of dissenting groups. But it achieves that accommodation in a very different way: by an unceasing process of negotiations between business, the bureaucracy, and the political parties, leading to a succession of marginal adjustments among the contestants. That process can make ready use of the state-owned enterprise, so long as it is incorporated in the bargaining process.

Other countries have found still other ways of reconciling national efficiency with individual rights. In France, the process is helped by a powerful network of graduates from France's elite schools and by the public's willingness—up to a point—to leave technical economic decisions in the hands of specialists. In India, Brazil, Mexico, and Korea, one sees still other patterns for reconciling national objectives with individual rights, each reflecting the different values and institutions that prevail in the four countries.

Even where a nation's value system allows for developing and enforcing an unambiguous long-term strategy for the state-owned enterprise, however, it is doubtful that agreements can remain valid over any long term. This is not to say that state-owned enterprises will find long-term planning to be useless. On the contrary, such planning usually has some positive pay-off even in an uncertain and uncontrollable environment—the size of the pay-off depending on the extent to which action under the plan is irrevocable, the frequency with which the plan is reexamined, and the cost of the planning process. The period covered by any agreement between ministers and managers, however, may still have to be relatively short. All signs so far point to the proposition that, even under relatively stable conditions and even where a well-articulated plan for the enterprise exists, the terms of any agreement cannot usefully cover a period of more than two or three years at the outside. In France, the provisions of contracts have proved intolerable or irrelevant after a year or two and the contracts have been renegotiated or abandoned. Obviously, one can try to reduce the risk that a contract will rapidly be rendered obsolete by external events, simply by laying down the terms of the agreement that would be applicable under various alternative scenarios.[37] But the limits of the approach are quickly reached. To be relevant, the approach must encompass a considerable range of contingencies, singly and in combination. In that case, however, the combinations soon multiply to unmanageable proportions.

But the more fundamental reason why long-term commitments will not work has already been well explored in the literature of political science. Because of the multiplicity of the objectives that governments constantly pursue and because of the high degree of ignorance and uncertainty with which governments are obliged to pursue those objectives, policymakers in government find it impossible to make their decisions in large optimizing exercises; instead, such policies are formulated by small increments, with constant feedback and adjustment.[38] That conclusion, of course, builds on propositions that have long been articulated by economists such as Herbert Simon and his principal associates with regard to the behavior of large firms. According to that school, large firms cannot fail to pursue a number of different goals, to search constantly for information bearing on those goals, and to move incrementally in their efforts to achieve those goals.[39]

When the state-owned enterprise interacts with government, it is usually the case of a large firm interacting with a large bureaucracy. The enterprise operates according to multiple objectives, some originating from inside the firm, some from without; the influence of the various objectives on the behavior of the state-owned enterprise varies with time; and the environment in which the enterprise operates usually contains substantial elements of instability. Besides, operating in markets that are strongly oligopolistic in character, such enterprises must be in a position to engage in behavior that is far removed from the assumptions or prescriptions of the competitive model, behavior that will sometimes involve cooperation with their rivals.[40]

An analysis of this sort is inevitably anticlimactic, offering more obstacles than solutions. But it does contain some guidance for those who would predict or prescribe the relations of a state-owned enterprise in any country to its government. There is no optimum applicable to all countries; each arrangement must—and inescapably will—reflect the values of the country concerned. That conclusion, however, may still leave considerable room for choice. When some choice remains, anyone who is charged with predicting or prescribing for the enterprise must constantly keep in mind the compelling demands that derive from operating in oligopolistic markets, from responding to multiple objectives, and from accommodating to uncertainty and change.

Notes

[1]Data on the relative importance of state-owned enterprises are not complete. But, except for the United States, they typically account for 5 percent to 25 percent of the output of market economies. Relevant data appear in: Mary M. Shirley, "Managing State-Owned Enterprises," World Bank Staff Working Papers, no. 577, Washington, 1983, pp. 5, 18. See also UNIDO, Division of Industry Studies, "The Changing Role of the Public Industrial Sector in Development," Vienna, June 3, 1983, pp. 68, 96, 100, 104.

[2]Raymond Vernon, *Two Hungry Giants* (Cambridge: Harvard University Press, 1983), pp. 27–28, 46–47.

[3]Shirley, "Managing State-Owned Enterprises," p. 15.

[4]*World Financial Markets*, Morgan Guaranty Trust Co., New York, January 1984, p. 6.

[5]The efforts of various countries are briefly summarized in Shirley, "Managing State-Owned Enterprises," pp. 23–38, 77–87.

[6]The contracts of 1971–1973 and 1978–1979 are well described in Jean-Pierre Anastassopoulos, *La stratégie des entreprises publiques* (Paris: Dalloz, 1980), pp. 161–83. Eight of the ten contracts of 1983 are described in "Analyses des Contrats de Plan par Firme," Notice 7, *Supplément Aux Cahiers Français No. 212, July–Sept. 1983*, la Documentation Française, Paris, 1983, and in "Politique Industrielle et Contrats de Plan en 1984," Notice 8 in the same source.

[7]For an example involving the pricing of U.S. postal services, see William B. Tye, "The Postal Service: Economics Made Simplistic," *Journal of Policy Analysis and Management*, vol. 3, no. 1, Fall 1983, pp. 62–73.

[8]See for instance Peter Hall, "Socialism in One Country," in Philip Cerny and Martin Schain (eds.), *Socialism, The State and Public Policy* (London: Frances Pinter, 1984); Theodore Geiger, *Welfare and Efficiency* (Washington, DC: National Planning Association, 1978), pp. 38–107.

[9]Jean-Pierre Anastassopoulos, *La stratégie des entreprises publiques*, pp. 149–57.

[10]Anastassopoulos, *The Strategic Autonomy of Government-Controlled Enterprises*, p. 87. The same source, pp. 97–105, contains interesting details of the operations of Electricité de France under its first contract, signed in 1970.

[11]Anastassopoulos, "The French Experience: Conflicts with Government," in Raymond Vernon and Yair Aharoni (eds.), *State-Owned Enterprise in Western Europe* (London: Croom Helm, 1981), p. 111.

[12]Jean-Pierre Nioche, "Les entreprises publiques et la planification," C.E.S.A., April 1981, pp. 9–10.

[13]Øystein Noreng, "State-Owned Oil Companies," in Raymond Vernon and Yair Aharoni, *State-Owned Enterprise*, pp. 139–40. The same author in *The Oil Industry and Government Strategy in the North Sea* (London: Croom Helm, 1980), pp. 148–49 notes similar tendencies in the managers of Norway's Statoil.

[14]For a description of the *grands corps*, see E. Suleiman, *Elites in French Society: The Politics of Survival* (Princeton: Princeton University Press, 1978); for their representation in French state-owned enterprises, see Jean-Pierre Jarvenic and Maurice Chenevoy, "Les Dirigeants des

Entreprises Publiques," in *Revue Française d'Administration Publique*, no. 4, Oct.–Dec. 1977, pp. 103–108; and "Socialism Means Nationalizing the Gaullists' Mistakes," *The Economist*, July 16, 1983, p. 86.

[15]Stephen Cohen, *Modern Capitalist Planning; The French Model* (Berkeley: University of California Press, 1977), p. 21 *passim*; John Zysman, *Governments, Markets and Growth* (Ithaca, NY: Cornell University Press, 1983), p. 106.

[16]An excellent account of the place of the planning function in the Mitterrand administration during the early 1980s appears in Peter A. Hall, "Socialism in One Country," in Philip Cerny and Martin Schain (eds.), *Socialism, the State and Public Policy in France* (London: Frances Pinter, 1984).

[17]For background, see Chalmers Johnson, *Japan's Public Policy Companies* (Washington, DC: American Enterprise Institute, 1978), especially pp. 81–100, 141–48; also by the same author, *MITI and the Japanese Miracle* (Stanford, CA: Stanford University Press, 1982), pp. 35–82, 198–274,

[18]Chalmers Johnson, *Japan's Public Policy Companies*, p. 102; Kiyohiko Yoshitake, *An Introduction to Public Enterprise in Japan* (Beverly Hills: Sage Publications, 1973), p. 270.

[19]Raymond Vernon, *Two Hungry Giants*, pp. 89–106.

[20]See for instance, Ira C. Magaziner and Thomas M. Hout, *Japanese Industrial Policy* (London: Policy Studies Institute, 1980), pp. 57–58, 66–67.

[21]A remarkable analysis of the problems encountered by the Moroccan government is found in *Rapport Général: Relations Etat-Entreprises Publiques*, Royaume du Maroc, December 1980, pp. 18–32. A suggestion of similar problems in the Mexican context, presented in a narrower framework, appears in Jorge Ruiz Dueñas, *Eficacia y eficiencia de la empresa pública mexicana* (Mexico City: Editorial Irillas, 1982).

[22]I am not aware of any systematic studies in support of this generalization. For a typical allusion to the phenomenon, see Merilee S. Grindle, *Bureaucrats, Politicians, and Peasants in Mexico* (Berkeley, CA: University of California Press, 1977), p. 173.

[23]"Nationalization without Tears," *The Economist*, December 19, 1981, p. 69; and "Shuffling the Pack," *The Economist*, September 17, 1983, p. 71. An irony of these reorganizations is that they undermine the contracts that the same Mitterrand government had previously negotiated with some of the same state-owned firms.

[24]The incident is recounted in Anastassopoulos, "The French Experience," pp. 100–102. A broad-ranging review of the French experience appears in Jean-Pierre Anastassopoulos and Jean-Pierre Nioche, *Entreprises Politiques: Expériences Comparées* (Paris: f.n.e.g.e., 1982).

[25]For a striking illustration, see R. B. Stobaugh, "The Oil Companies in the Crisis," in Raymond Vernon (ed.), *The Oil Crisis* (New York: W. W. Norton, 1976), pp. 189–90.

[26]See for instance Shirley, "Managing State-Owned Enterprises," pp. 10–17.

[27]Jeff Frieden, "Third World Indebted Industrialization: International Finance and State Capitalism in Mexico, Brazil, Algeria, and South Korea," *International Organization*, vol. 35, no. 3, Summer 1981, pp. 411–12.

[28]The most notorious incident of this kind involved Indonesia's state-owned oil company, Pertamina. See Seth Lipsky (ed.), *The Billion Dollar Bubble* (Hong Kong: Dow Jones Asia, 1978), pp. 1–41.

[29]Shirley, "Managing State-Owned Enterprises," pp. 55–61, recounts some recent liquidations and divestitures. See also "Ca Marche, 20 Years on," *The Economist*, August 14, 1982, p. 33; "Reprivatisation," *The Economist*, October 8, 1983, p. 86; and "Privatisation: The Government's Troubles Begin," *The Economist*, January 7, 1984, p. 43.

[30]Illustrative of such resistance is the case of Thailand, where proposed programs for the sale of state-owned enterprises to the private sector have made almost no headway. See "The Lame Duck Legacy," *Far Eastern Economic Review*, April 21, 1983, pp. 63, 64.

[31]The United Kingdom, for instance, has pushed this approach very far; see, for instance, "Nationalized Industries," *The Economist*, April 8, 1978, pp. 103–104, and "How Short is an Arm's Length?," *The Economist*, December 8, 1979, p. 93. For Brazil, see Dennis J. Mahar, "Destabilization in Brazil," in Howard J. Wiarda and Janine T. Perfit (eds.), *Changing Dyna-*

mics in the Brazilian Economy (Washington, DC: American Enterprise Institute, 1983), pp. 46, 49.

[32]Anastassopoulos, *The Strategic Autonomy of Government-Controlled Enterprises*, pp. 133–39, 202–17, 274–82. For Britain, see "Nationalized Industries: No Free Lunch," *The Economist*, Dec. 12, 1981, p. 64; and "Britain: Nationalized Industries," *The Economist*, March 6, 1982, p. 39. For Morocco, see Royaume du Maroc, *Rapport Général*, pp. 22–42.

[33]Anastassopoulos, "The French Experience," pp. 102–103.

[34]Richard Pryke, *The Nationalized Industries: Policies and Performance Since 1968* (Oxford: M. Robertson Publishers, 1981), pp. 108–10. For a more extended account of the British government's relations to British Rail, see Richard Pryke, *Public Enterprise in Practice* (London: MacGibbon and Kee, 1971), p. 42 passim.

[35]See for instance Royaume du Maroc, *Le Financement des Entreprises Publiques*, Rabat, September 1980, pp. 7–82.

[36]For France, see Jean-Pierre Anastassopoulos, *The Strategic Autonomy of Government-Controlled Enterprises in a Competitive Economy* (Ann Arbor, Michigan: University Microfilms, 1977), pp. 210, 278–79; for Brazil, Thomas J. Trebat, *Brazil's State-Owned Enterprises* (New York: Cambridge University Press, 1983), pp. 201, 216. See also Shirley, "Managing State-Owned Enterprises," pp. 29–30.

[37]The approach has been used in long-term contracts between governments and foreign mining companies. See James K. Sebenius, *Negotiating the Law of the Sea* (Cambridge, MA: Harvard University Press, 1984).

[38]See for instance G. Majone and A. Wildavsky, "Implementation as Evolution," in J. L. Pressman and A. Wildavsky, *Implementation* (Berkeley: University of California Press, 1979), pp. 192–94.

[39]The classic statements are contained in J. G. March and H. Simon, *Organizations* (New York: John Wiley and Sons, 1958), pp. 169–204; and R. M. Cyert and J. G. March, *A Behavioral Theory of the Firm* (Englewood Cliffs, NJ: Prentice Hall, 1963), p. 112. See also Oliver E. Williamson, *Corporate Control and Business Behavior* (Englewood Cliffs, NJ: Prentice Hall, 1970), pp. 168–75. For a related approach to the behavior of state-owned enterprises, see Renato Mazzolini, *Government Controlled Enterprises* (New York: John Wiley and Sons, 1979), especially pp. 249–314.

[40]See F. M. Scherer, *Industrial Market Structure and Economic Performance* (Chicago: Rand McNally, 1970), pp. 158–212, 443–53.

Part 4

Trade with the Soviet Union

10

Soviet commodity power in international economic relations

The issue

The debate over the size of the Soviet Union's "commodity power" has been with us for a long time. The question can hardly be avoided. A nation of 265 million people with a gross national product exceeded only by that of the United States has centralized its decisions on the production, export, and import of its commodities. Few other countries leave such decisions wholly to the vagaries of the market place. But the Soviet Union stands out in two respects. Apart from the People's Republic of China, it is by a considerable margin the largest of the nations that has made the choice to centralize. And its centralizing controls, without important exceptions, are the most rigorous on earth.

Assume, then, that the Soviet Union has centralized its buying and selling of commodities for the purpose of maximizing its power outside of the home economy. Has that step in fact endowed the USSR with any significant amount of power? And if so, to what end will such power be used?

Judging from the expressions of concern of observers outside the USSR, one can distinguish three possibilities. First, the Soviet Union might see some advantage at times in upsetting—or in threatening to upset—the international economic system of the non-Soviet world, as a tactical step in the rivalry between competing ideologies. Second, the USSR might see possibilities for using its commodity power to influence the political behavior of individual nations. Third, commodity power might be used by the USSR to capture the lion's share of the economic gains that arise from ordinary international trade. How seriously is one to take any of these alternatives?

Upsetting the system

The fundamental fact that needs to be remembered in exploring all of these alternatives is that, measured against world aggregates, the Soviet

From *The Soviet Impact on Commodity Markets*, edited by M. M. Kostecki. © M. M. Kostecki 1984 and reprinted by permission of St. Martin's Press Inc. and The Macmillan Press, Ltd.

Union is a dominant seller of only a few commodities, such as chromite, manganese, and platinum, and a dominant buyer of practically nothing. Yet the experience of the past few years, notably in petroleum and in grains, suggests that the position of a country does not need to be overwhelming in order to create a measurable short-term effect on world markets.

The reason for the Soviet Union's ability to affect some commodities in which it does not appear to have a dominant position is evident. In the short run, the price elasticities of supply and demand for many products, including oil and grains, are very low; increased prices neither reduce consumption very much nor generate very large increases in production. Moreover, the Soviet Union projects an image abroad of imperturbability regarding its needs to buy or to sell the products concerned, while the sellers and buyers that it confronts scramble to persuade their respective governments that the prospective sales or the prospective purchases are a matter of life or death. In such circumstances, the bargaining position of the USSR may be strong, at least in the short run.

The corollary to this general observation is that the USSR may be capable of influencing inflationary and deflationary movements in countries with open economies, out of all proportion to the size of the country's place in world markets. Whether the USSR actually realizes that potential depends in part on how the inflationary and deflationary waves in those economies are generated. Some economists view short-term ripples in the world price of any given commodity, whatever the commodity's importance, as largely irrelevant to the world's inflationary cycles. These are thought to be determined by other kinds of factors, notably, the supply of money. Changes in the supply of money in turn are regarded as stemming from factors that have little to do with the decisions of any one buyer or seller with regard to a commodity or two.

However, other economists, including myself, are prepared to entertain the possibility that a change in the price of some key factor such as oil or grain can trigger a series of price increases over a broad front. Short-term disequilibria, such as were experienced in grain in 1972 and in oil at various times in the 1970s, provoke an inflationary push in all other commodities, until eventually the relative prices of the various products are brought into line again. If the object of a purposeful intervenor were simply to generate inflation in world markets and if the expectations of the rest of the world were ripe for a follow-up, according to this argument, it would need no very large intervention in the market to produce the amplifying response.

I doubt that the USSR has ever used its commodity power with any such general purpose in mind. That would be ascribing to the USSR more subtlety of purpose and more control in the execution of buying and selling strategies than seem warranted. And from the lack of exploration of this possibility on the part of my collaborators, I detect a general assent that this contingency carries a low probability in their minds as well.

Influencing individual nations

It is another matter altogether when one considers the possibility that the USSR may be hoping to use its commodity power to influence the political behavior of other nations.[1] In the Soviet view, trade and politics are inseparable in foreign policy. Accordingly, if intent could determine effect, there would be no question that the trade of the Soviet Union represented an instrument for the exercise of political power.

To be sure the USSR is not alone in linking trade to politics. In some degree, all nations conduct their foreign trade with an eye to politics. For instance, since the end of World War II, the United States and western Europe have maintained special restrictions on their trade with eastern Europe, based upon political and security considerations. With these same considerations in mind, the west also imposed embargoes or restrictions from time to time on other countries, such as Southern Rhodesia and Cuba. Moreover, both the United States and Europe in other ways have linked the nature of their trade regime to their political objectives. The United States has used the General Agreement on Tariffs and Trade to support its aspirations for the development of an open interdependent trading world; and Europe has used the European community as its vehicle for reducing the risk of conflict among its members and for maintaining special links to former colonies and to selected countries in the Mediterranean area.

Still, the USSR can be distinguished from Europe and the United States in the way it has used trade for political ends. The USSR conducts its foreign trade on the principle that no trade is justified unless it makes a contribution to the nation's objectives. The economies of western Europe and North America conduct their trade on the principle that any trade is permissible unless it is explicitly adjudged harmful to the nation's objectives. In practice, the two courses of action converge toward one another; yet the remaining gap between them is vast. In the case of the market economies, if the trade benefits some significant group within the economy, that is usually enough to protect the trade from arbitrary cut-off for political purposes; U.S. sales of grain to the USSR represent a striking case in point. In the case of the USSR, the state's screening of its trade for the achievement of the state's objectives appears much more rigorous.

What is more, as part of its control system over international trade, the USSR prefers where it can to develop deals in which payments are explicitly matched with receipts. The various means by which that is achieved are of course well known and fully documented.[2] In some cases, the matching is achieved by deals with individual firms in the west, deals in which the firm eventually receives payment for its sales in the form of specified products; in other cases, the matching is done by government-to-government agreements that specify in greater or lesser degree the goods that are to be exchanged.

A priori, agreements of this sort executed under the USSR's system of trade controls offer some potential for the USSR to exercise coercion. Just how much coercion, however, depends critically on a number of factors regarding the relative situation of the two trading partners. A nation that badly needs the imports or exports it undertakes—that is, a nation that would assume a high cost if it failed to undertake the trade—can hardly be said to have much commodity power. Moreover, a nation that hopes to exercise commodity power by withholding its exports must be able to count on the inelasticity of supply from other sellers; if other sellers are prepared to fill a void created by the power-seeking seller, the seller's objective will be thwarted. (A parallel statement, of course, can be made for the power-seeking buyer.) Finally, the country seeking market power must confront trading partners on the other side of the transaction whose discretionary power in the market is limited; if the buyer is as centrally organized as the seller and also has as much choice as the seller about the size and timing of its purchases, then the capacity of each to manipulate the other is indeterminate.

On these criteria, the USSR appears to be a strong candidate for the exercise of political power. Various CMEA countries look to the Soviet Union as their principal source of raw materials, a relationship that the USSR has fostered in some instances at considerable cost to its economy. Cuba relies on the USSR to absorb its sugar; in the short run, the costs would be staggering for Cuba if the USSR were to suspend its purchases of sugar, whereas the inconvenience to the USSR would be slight. (Ironically, the U.S. embargo in this case increases Cuba's perception of its costs and hence enhances the power of the USSR.)

In other cases, the coercive power of the USSR may be less clear. Germany's importation of Soviet gas will carry little coercive power as long as Germany's gas users are in a position to turn easily to alternative sources of fuel. In still other cases, the coercive capabilities of the USSR can only be marginal. U.S. reliance on Soviet chromium and platinum, for instance, presumably bestows little coercive power on the USSR, inasmuch as the United States draws on a number of other sources and has the option of expanding its strategic stockpiles if the problem seems serious enough.[3]

Nevertheless, the power of the USSR is not to be belittled. In any given commodity, one can usually find a country with a higher level of aggregate purchases or sales than the Soviet Union; but not as a rule, under a central control.

Finally, the USSR stands out from most other nations in the degree of secrecy surrounding its demand and supply situation in individual commodities. Lacking information, the USSR's trading partners find it difficult to evaluate the USSR's bargaining strengths and bargaining weaknesses. Once the USSR begins to show its hand, the risk of exaggerating its strength is relatively high.

It is a serious question, therefore, whether the USSR is in a position to use its commodity power in order to extend its influence beyond the CMEA. On this score, the various commodity studies that follow should cast a little light.

Capturing the gains from trade

The bilateral approach to international trade places large countries in a position not only to influence the political behavior of some of their trading partners but also to capture the lion's share of the gains from trade. Although the suspicion has often been voiced that the Soviet Union may have been motivated partly by that objective in choosing the bilateral balancing approach, the evidence on that score is equivocal; some bilateral relationships, as we have suggested earlier, seem costly to the USSR in economic terms.

Here and there, however, the possibility persists; it is especially plausible for transactions in which the USSR has agreed to provide raw materials to foreign buyers in compensation for their supplying the capital equipment that will produce the materials. In this case, the USSR is in a position to mobilize all its oligopoly strength, such as it is, to shift the risks onto the buyer. But a great deal more analysis of such deals will be needed before the USSR's power in this regard can be assessed.

Another way in which the USSR might conceivably be expected to try to enlarge its share of the gains from trade would be to form an international cartel in the products that it exports or to join one that already exists. In a sea of uncertain conjecture, this is one possibility on which the signals are fairly clear. The USSR is no joiner. In part, this may be because of the identity of the countries it would have to join: for gold, South Africa; for asbestos, Canada; for cotton, the United States. In part, too, it may be because of the USSR's overwhelming penchant for secrecy and control. In any case, in the range of alternative possibilities to be considered, this one takes a low priority.

Finally, we are left with the possibility that the USSR might exercise its oligopoly or oligopsony power as best it can in open world markets. This is the kind of question with which economists and commodity analysts feel most at home.

The future structure of markets

Yet one is entitled to wonder if studies of individual commodity markets can go very far in answering the central questions of this symposium. Such studies, after all, are based largely on history. And history in this case may be providing an imperfect guide for the future. Some changes in the organization of the world's commodity markets in recent years suggest that the power of a country organized on the lines of the USSR may increase in the future.

In oil and the various nonferrous metals in particular, some portentous changes in market structure have been taking place over the past several decades. Those changes can be described in three rather distinct stages: a period of control by the multinationals in the period immediately following World War II; a second period in which that control was weakening, accompanied by some decline in the degree of concentration of the industry in world markets; and finally, a period in which state-owned enterprises appeared as sellers, leading to a market that was more diffuse and more fractionated than in the past.

With the end of World War II, a very considerable part of world production and trade in each of these industrial raw materials was concentrated in a handful of large western firms, operating in a market structure that protected their oligopoly rents and promised a certain stability. In oil, seven leading international companies controlled nearly 90 percent of the internationally traded product;[4] in aluminum, six firms controlled about 85 percent of the world's smelting capacity.[5] Only in iron ore was the world industry reasonably diffuse in structure; in this case, the different national steel industries had few interlocking links. But even in this case, the principal producers of some important countries, including the United States and Japan, managed to maintain some strong links to their foreign sources of ore, using vertical integration, long-term contracts, and monopsony arrangements to maintain control.[6]

During the first period in which the big multinational enterprises typically were in control, their profit-making objectives were largely expressed in efforts to achieve stability and security of supply. As long as they were left in tolerably peaceful possession of their mines and oilfields and as long as their contractual arrangements were not being disturbed by demands for renegotiations or threats of nationalization, host countries heard very little from the enterprises. One index of the strength of these enterprises lay in the fact that when the USSR was involved in the export of any commodity in which the multinationals dominated, the Soviet sellers rarely showed any disposition to play an independent role in the market. In tin and aluminum they coordinated their sales with that of the western leaders,[7] while in oil they tended to shade their prices with care, cutting them only enough to secure the necessary market penetration.[8]

The "commodity power" of the multinationals was not exposed to any real test until the second period, when the host countries decided to try to overturn existing arrangements. Incidents of that sort occurred continuously in oil and occasionally in the nonferrous metals from the 1950s on. When they did, it grew clear that the power of the companies and their governments was quite circumscribed after all. In the early 1950s, to be sure, in response to Mossadeq's takeover of Iranian oil, the oil companies did succeed in preventing the Iranians from assuming an independent position in world oil markets by mobilizing the economic and political power of Britain and the United States. But that situation was exceptional, being based mainly on the fact that Iran's geographical position made control of the area appear critical in the pursuit of the cold war.[9] There were numerous other occasions both before and after the Mossadeq affair in which the willingness and ability of the United States to support its multinational oil companies were put to the test. The earlier oil nationalizations in Bolivia and Mexico and the subsequent ones in Indonesia, Peru, and elsewhere, provided such occasions. The support that the oil companies were able to muster on these occasions was characteristically sporadic, episodic, and ineffectual.[10]

In copper, iron ore, and bauxite, the story was very much the same.[11] All that the companies could do in response to expropriation and threats of expropriation was to turn to safer areas for their subsequent expansion.[12] This response on the part of the multinational companies did represent commodity power in a sense; but its coercive effect was largely negated by the fact that the state-owned enterprises that absorbed the properties of the multinationals were free to borrow in world capital markets.

With the decline in the power of the multinationals during the second and third stages, the markets for many non-agricultural commodities have taken on some new characteristics. As in the past, these markets continue to be fairly concentrated in structure, in the sense that a considerable part of the production lies in the hands of a few sellers and a considerable part of the consumption is accounted for by a few buyers. The threat of instability, therefore, continues to hang over these markets, as it has in the past. What has changed, however, has been the nature of the equilibrating mechanisms that once operated in these markets. As long as the multinationals dominated, they acted as intermediaries in the system. In that role, they matched supply with demand in their vertically integrated structures, they swapped supplies and markets with one another to cover temporary unbalances,[13] and they resorted to various institutional devices to avoid periods of overproduction or shortage for world markets as a whole.[14]

With the decline in the power of the multinationals, governments and their enterprises have assumed a greater measure of power in such decisions. But the ability or willingness of governments to coordinate such decisions among themselves have, on the whole, been considerably less than the ability and willingness of the multinationals to perform those roles.[15]

Governments, therefore, appear to be in the position of having more responsibility for deciding to whom they shall sell and from whom they may buy. At the same time, however, they are exercising that responsibility in markets which have been changing in character. With weaker coordinating devices among the producers, the markets are more prone to the appearance of transitory surpluses or shortages than in the past; and with weaker means for swapping among producers, they are less effective in balancing supplies and markets at any moment in time. Balance will be achieved after the fact; but it is likely to entail more frequently than in the past external adjustments in the marketplace rather than internal adjustments within the multinational systems. In practice, this could mean more frequent breaches of contract as well as more vigorous swings in spot prices.

As tendencies of this sort grow in any market, there is a presumption that a purposeful seller or a purposeful buyer, bent on using their buying or selling power for specific ends, will encounter more opportunities for the exercise of that power. If sudden shortages and surpluses prove more common in these markets, the purposeful seller that can fill the shortage and the purposeful buyer than can absorb the surplus presumably find a larger stage for their operations.

What this change suggests is that, in a new era of less stable commodity markets, the commodity power of the Soviet Union could well increase.

Notes

[1]For an extended theoretical discussion of the factors affecting such influence, see A. O. Hirschman, *National Power and the Structure of Foreign Trade* (Berkeley: University of California Press, 1969), especially pp. 13–52.

[2]See for instance J. Quigley, *The Soviet Foreign Trade Monopoly* (Columbus: Ohio State University Press, 1974), pp. 103–107, 127; L. J. Brainard, "Soviet Foreign Trade Planning," in U.S. Congress, Joint Economic Committee, *Soviet Economy in a New Perspective* (Washington: Government Printing Office, 1976), pp. 695–708.

[3]See for instance L. L. Fischman, *World Mineral Trends and U.S. Supply Problems* (Baltimore: Johns Hopkins University Press, 1981), pp. 483–89; U.S. Department of Interior, Bureau of Mines, *Minerals Yearbook Preprints: Platinum-Group Metals* (Washington: Government Printing Office, 1979); U.S. Department of Interior, Bureau of Mines, *Minerals Yearbook Preprints: Chromium* (Washington: Government Printing Office, 1979).

[4]Federal Trade Commission, Report to the Subcommittee on Small Business, U.S. Senate, *The International Petroleum Cartel* (Washington: Government Printing Office), pp. 124–25.

[5]Compiled in Charles River Associates, "An Economic Analysis of the Aluminum Industry," Cambridge, Mass., 1971, Table 3-4, pp. 3–50, xeroxed, based on yearbooks of American Bureau of Metal Statistics, U.S. Bureau of Mines, and W. R. Skinner.

[6]Raymond Vernon and Brian Levy, "State-Owned Enterprises in the World Economy: The Case of Iron Ore," in Leroy P. Jones (ed.), *Public Enterprise in Less-Developed Countries: Multidisciplinary Perspectives* (Cambridge: Cambridge University Press, 1981).

[7]Zuhayr Mikdashi, *The International Politics of National Resources* (Ithaca: Cornell University Press, 1976), p. 121; and Zuhayr Mikdashi, *A Comparative Analysis of Selected Mineral Exporting Industries* (Vienna: OPEC), xeroxed, pp. 13–15 and 134–35.

[8]See for instance Marshall Goldman, *The Enigma of Soviet Petroleum* (London: George Allen and Unwin, 1980), pp. 68–69, 83; and A. J. Klinghoffer, *The Soviet Union and International Oil Politics* (New York: Columbia University Press, 1977), pp. 66–88.

[9]S. D. Krasner, *Defending the National Interest* (Princeton: Princeton University Press, 1979), pp. 120–21; C. D. Goodwin (ed.), *Energy Policy in Perspective* (Washington: Brookings Institution, 1981), pp. 116–17.

[10]S. D. Krasner, *Defending the National Interest* p. 186–88, 238; Mira Wilkins, *The Maturing of Multinational Enterprise* (Cambridge: Harvard University Press, 1974), pp. 367–68. Also G. M. Ingram, *Expropriation of U.S. Property in South America* (New York: Praeger, 1974), pp. 93–94.

[11]Krasner, *Defending the National Interest*, pp. 227, 234, 241; P. E. Sigmund, *Multinationals in Latin America* (Madison: University of Wisconsin Press, 1980), p. 153; Zuhayr Mikdashi, *The International Politics of National Resources* (Ithaca, NY: Cornell University Press, 1976), p. 113. Also G. M. Ingram, *Expropriation of U.S. Property in South America* (New York: Praeger, 1974), p. 321.

[12]S. Moment, "Long Term Associations of Developing Countries with Consumers of Bauxite, Alumina and Aluminum," United Nations Industrial Development Organization, Vienna, 1978, pp. 24–36.

[13]R. B. Stobaugh, "The Oil Companies in Crisis," in Raymond Vernon (ed.), *The Oil Crisis* (New York: W. W. Norton, 1976), pp. 186–88; Commission of the European Community, "Report by

the Commission on the Behavior of the Oil Companies in the Community during the period from October 1973–March 1974," Brussels, 1974, p. 162.

[14]Zuhayr Mikdashi, *The International Politics of National Resources*, pp. 82–117, 187, 232–33.

[15]For a description of the Aramco formula for determining output, see M. A. Adelman, *The World Petroleum Market* (Baltimore: Johns Hopkins University Press, 1972), published for Resources for the Future, pp. 85–89. And for a description of prewar aluminum consortia formulas for determining output see Charles River Associates, "Economic Analysis of the Aluminum Industry," Cambridge, Mass., 1971, pp. 3–24, xeroxed. In the postwar period, overlapping joint ventures have provided an informal means of pooling information and maintaining desired price and supply policies. See Charles River Associates, "An Economic Analysis of the Aluminum Industry," Cambridge, Mass., 1971, pp. 3–45, xeroxed.

11

U.S. economic policies toward the Soviet Union

MARSHALL GOLDMAN AND RAYMOND VERNON

There are special difficulties that hamper the United States in any effort to formulate a set of effective economic policies toward the USSR. One set of difficulties arises from the intimate tie in our relations with the Soviet Union between economic policies on the one hand and political or security policies on the other; whereas in relations with most other countries, these fields of policy can be somewhat insulated from one another, in relations with the USSR that distinction has proved in practice impossible to maintain. Another set of difficulties has been due to the profound incompatibility of the Soviet system of trade and payments with the open global system that U.S. interests would like to see maintained and strengthened; an expansion of trade with the USSR encourages the growth of trading practices that threaten the system. Moreover, the controls maintained by the USSR over its trade open up the possibility that the gains from trade will be captured mainly by the Soviet Union. Whereas in relation with most other countries, such differences usually can be managed within the existing world system of trade and payments, in the case of the USSR those differences are so vast as to pose special problems of vulnerability for countries that maintain a market economy. Finally, there have been the well-known differences in political institutions and political processes in the two countries, differences that have pitted a closed and controlled political process against one that is fractionated, diffuse, and open.

The policies reviewed

Partly as a result of these factors, U.S. policy toward the Soviet Union has appeared vacillating and complex, shifting among a number of different

This chapter was titled "Economic Relations" in *The Making of America's Soviet Policy*, Joseph Nye (ed.), New Haven: Yale University Press, 1984, and is reprinted by permission of the publisher.

goals. These have been pursued singly or in combination, changing their identity and their weights according to shifts in U.S. political and military policy, and according to the needs of domestic politics.

The Stalinist era

The end of World War II marked the end of a decade in which U.S. policy toward the USSR had gone through a number of extreme stages, from cautious contact in the early New Deal days, to implacable hostility over the Finnish invasion and the Hitler–Stalin partnership, to wartime support and alliance.

With the onset of the cold war in 1948, the U.S. government instituted a special set of controls over transactions with the Soviet Union and eastern Europe. Some were aimed at curbing Soviet growth and limiting its supplies of hard currency in order to restrain Stalin's war-making potential; some were smuggled into U.S. law for domestic protectionist purposes. When the Soviet Union emerged as North Korea's supporter in the Korean war, the U.S. Congress responded by including a provision in the Trade Agreement Extension Act of 1951 that denied most-favored-nation (MFN) tariffs to Soviet imports. As a result, Soviet exports to the United States became subject to the very high tariffs enacted under the Smoot–Hawley Tariff Act of 1930, making such exports relatively unprofitable. At the same time, imports of some products such as various furs and crabmeat were banned from the United States entirely.

U.S. exports to the USSR were similarly encumbered. Under the terms of the Export Control Act of 1949, prospective exporters of most strategic goods to the Soviet Union were required to obtain licenses from the American government. At the time, western Europe and Japan were still recovering from the war's destruction, and the United States was the undisputed industrial and technological leader of the non-communist world. U.S. restrictions on the sale of technologically sophisticated goods to the Soviet Union therefore carried a considerable bite. In addition, most of the countries of western Europe joined the United States in 1949 to form the Consultative Group Coordinating Committee, COCOM; Japan would join a few years later. COCOM was charged with the task of coordinating the embargo of strategic goods to the Soviet Union. Although exports from the Soviet Union to western Europe were not subject to similar controls, these were inhibited by the import restrictions that most countries in western Europe had adopted in order to strengthen their foreign exchange positions.

These early measures restricting transactions between the United States and the USSR were probably more important for their symbolic import than for their direct substantive effect. It is not at all clear that during this period the USSR was much interested in increasing its imports and exports with the west; under Stalin's orders, there was a marked shift in the trade flows of eastern Europe and the Soviet Union away from western Europe toward one another. In any event, the denial of western markets, products, and technology during the Stalin era did not seem to affect Soviet economic and military growth. The late 1940s and early 1950s were years of very rapid growth for the USSR.

With the death of Stalin, political relations between the two countries took a turn for the better. But with the legacy of the cold war still strong, most Americans approached the period of detente with an understandable wariness. Trade with the Soviet bloc had never been of much importance to the U.S. economy. Accordingly, very few champions were to be found in the United States, prepared to fight for a less restrictive set of trade policies toward the USSR.

An initial opening

Nevertheless, as the years passed, the western attitude toward the Soviet Union and the Soviet attitude toward the west did begin to change. In part this was because Khrushchev in 1958 embarked on a program designed to liberalize the Soviet Union from within and to increase interaction with the outside world.

For the first time in the postwar era, the Soviet Union seemed to be seriously interested in making significant purchases of industrial machinery from the west. Khrushchev's effort to increase the productivity of Soviet agriculture required greatly increased use of chemical fertilizers. However, the Soviet Union had almost no chemical industry and no industry that built chemical process plants. Between 1959 and 1961, the Soviet Union ordered approximately fifty chemical plants from abroad. This resulted in a brief surge in machinery exports from western Europe, a surge that ended in 1963; at that time, a particularly disappointing grain harvest obliged the USSR to divert its foreign exchange to grain purchases, while Khrushchev's ouster brought an end to some of his liberalizing policies.

Even in the brief period of expanded Soviet trade, however, the volume of Soviet purchases of foreign goods was still small, not great enough to interest U.S. manufacturers. Exports from Germany, for instance, totalled only about $200 million a year and those from the United Kingdom, France, Italy, and Japan amounted to even less. Not surprisingly, the main emphasis of American economic policy toward the Soviet Union continued to be one of restraint. Surveys among American businessmen at the time indicated a continuation of the cautious attitude toward trade with the Soviet Union.[1]

In the mid-1960s, however, more changes of atmosphere occurred. In April 1966, Premier Kosygin announced that in an effort to speed up economic growth, the Soviet Union would henceforth increase significantly its purchases of foreign technology and machinery.[2] This policy declaration was followed in August 1966 by the signing of a contract with Fiat to build a $1.5 billion automobile plant. Soon thereafter, the USSR unveiled a shopping list of major industrial projects whose import component would come to approximately $5 billion in 1969 prices. That the USSR was serious at the time is reflected by the fact that almost all the plant imports that were then listed were actually realized in later years.

With the accelerated pace of Soviet imports, the interest of U.S. businessmen quickened. By 1968, Germany doubled its 1962 exports to the USSR, raising the total to over $400 million; and the Japanese and the Italians were not far behind. Observing these lost opportunities, members of the American business community and Congress began to reexamine the effectiveness and wisdom of existing policy.[3] Gradually, the mood changed from one of restraint in the approach to Soviet trade to one of outright encouragement of such trade.

The shift in the position of U.S. businessmen and the Congress at this stage raises the usual question whether profit once more had managed to rise above principle. That conclusion, however, would be too simple. After 1963 the prevailing mood in east–west relations was one of detente. The new mood was exposed to considerable stress in 1968, with the Soviet Union's invasion of Czechoslovakia and its continued support of North Vietnam. Factors such as these served to postpone the time when the quickened interest of U.S. business in Soviet trade would actually be translated into a less restrictive U.S. policy, demonstrating that political factors still played a major role in determining such matters. Finally, in 1972, the switch to a liberalized policy occurred, generated at least in part by the interest of U.S. businessmen in sharing in a growing Soviet market.

An era of linkage

As the mood toward trade with the Soviet Union began to change, the U.S. government acknowledged the change by drastically relaxing its controls over east–west trade. But the relaxation was not unconditional; instead it was linked to Soviet political behavior. "Linkage," as Secretary of State Kissinger came to call his policy, tied the liberalization of restrictions on trade, technology, and credits to the Soviet Union's demonstrating a commitment to restrained international conduct, a willingness to help settle concrete issues including those of Vietnam, Berlin, and the Middle East, and a willingness to negotiate a SALT Treaty.[4]

It is difficult to assess how much the USSR actually modified its foreign policy in response to these trade pressures during the few years in which linkage was practiced. Henry Kissinger, who was the President's Assistant for National Security Affairs in 1972, was of the view that the Soviet Union tempered its behavior in the Middle East at the time and made other small concessions in response to the linkage policy. There is, however, a sense of uncertainty on this critical point. On the other hand, the USSR did respond in substantial ways to U.S. pressures in the human rights field, directed mainly at changing internal Soviet practices.[5] *Refusniks* who had been imprisoned for seeking to emigrate were sometimes released from jail, and a large percentage of those for whom emigration was requested were allowed to leave.

Similarly, a repugnant education tax levied on emigrants was removed. In much the same way, pressure from the west Europeans pushed the Soviets into agreeing to a human rights clause in the 1975 Helsinki Agreement; this later became the source of considerable embarrassment for the Soviet Union.

Concurrently, the U.S. government shifted its emphasis from hampering trade to promoting it. Under the terms of the U.S.–USSR trade agreement of October 18, 1972, the two countries agreed to take specific measures to facilitate a sharp increase in trade between the two countries. For instance, the American side agreed that the president would go to Congress to seek a change in the 1951 Trade Agreement Extension Act which denied MFN treatment to Soviet goods. As part of the same package, the Soviet Union for its part agreed to resume payment of its Lend–Lease debt incurred during World War II; it undertook to make three token payments totalling $48 million between October 1972 and July 1975. Future annual payments would be made contingent on the restoration of MFN status by the United States. As a byproduct, with the resumption of Lend–Lease payments, the Soviet Union would again become eligible for loans from the United States Export–Import Bank. Under the trade agreement, the United States also agreed to the formation of the U.S.–USSR Commercial Commission, consisting of senior government economic officials, to ensure that there would be high-level attention to any trade problems that might arise.

In accordance with the spirit of the detente era, the United States did what it could to facilitate the sale of grain in 1972 and again from 1975 to 1979, after the U.S.–Soviet grain agreement was signed. In the same spirit, U.S. laws governing export controls were altered so that the burden of proof no longer lay with the American exporter to explain why such trade should be allowed. Instead export controls were not to be applied unless the Department of Commerce showed that the sales of such goods would threaten American national security or that similar goods were unavailable in the west or in Japan.[6]

It was in this period that some of the incompatibilities generated by the differences in the trading systems of the two countries began to surface. All foreign trade of the USSR is conducted by the state, operating through designated foreign trade organizations. We shall shortly be exploring some of the implications of that arrangement; but it is sufficient at this point to observe that the Soviet government acts as a monopsonist when it buys from foreign sellers. At times, that power is ineptly used. But in 1972 the USSR was able to complete one of the largest grain purchases in history up to that time without causing a noticeable increase in the price of grain. Only after the Soviet purchasing agents had completed their mission did word of what happened reach the market; then the prices tripled. It turned out that officials in the U.S. Department of Agriculture were informed of what was happening, but did nothing with the information. The incident had considerable impact on the U.S. public, contributing to the souring of the trading atmosphere that was to follow.

A return to tension

The period of a positive U.S. trade policy toward the Soviet Union was relatively short-lived, covering only three or four years. While it is hard to assess blame, the Soviets argue that the U.S. government did not live up to its agreement to provide MFN treatment and access to Export–Import Bank credits. Led by Senator Henry Jackson and Congressman Charles Vanik, the U.S. Congress not only refused to revoke the 1951 Trade Agreement Extension Act which denied MFN treatment to Soviet goods, but it passed the so-called Jackson–Vanik Amendment to the Trade Act of 1974 which conditioned the extension of MFN status upon Soviet willingness to allow a substantial flow of immigrants from the Soviet Union. Continued Soviet harrassment of potential immigrants and dissidents plus the arrest in 1978 of J. Crawford, a Moscow representative of International Harvester, insured popular as well as congressional support for such punitive legislation. In the years to follow, the United States would complain about Soviet expansionism in Africa, the invasion of Afghanistan, and interference in Poland. Unlike the containment era of the 1940s and 1950s, however, the post-1975 restraints on trade with the Soviet Union were made by selective denials of export licenses on critical items rather than by more sweeping prohibitions.

During this period, the U.S. government received constant reminders of its own limited capacity to act effectively unless there was collaboration from other industrialized countries. The perennial competition of exporting countries to sell their machinery to the USSR kept generating frictions. Cases commonly arose in which the U.S. government was prevented from denying the USSR some useful technology, simply because the same technology or something very much like it could be obtained from other sources. In the most spectacular effort of the U.S. government to impose such a denial—the case of turbines for the Soviet gas pipeline to Germany—the limitations of the U.S. capacity to prevent such movements became palpable.

The competition for sales to the Soviet Union also led western exporters to undercut one another by offering heavily subsidized credit terms. Periodically, the exporting countries would agree to place a floor on interest rates charged the USSR and just as often the agreement would be violated. The most recent attempt at credit restraint was made in 1982, with uncertain results.

The policies reviewed

Looking back on the three and one-half decades in which the U.S. government has shaped and reshaped its economic policies toward the USSR, one can discern a number of different approaches, never fully juxtaposed or reconciled, that have motivated U.S. actions. At one extreme, there has been the view that transactions with the USSR should be held to an absolute minimum, in the hope of increasing the general stress on the Soviet economy; such increased stress, according to extreme versions of this view, might eventually change the nature of the Soviet system and reduce its warlike potential. A second view has been more restrained in its objective: the object has been to retard the Soviet's build-up of its military capability by selectively denying it strategic materials, hoping thereby to maintain or widen the U.S. lead. A third view has been to use economic restrictions as a way of punishing or rewarding the USSR, hoping thereby to modify its aggressive behavior. And a fourth, in various degrees and variations, would positively encourage economic contacts with the USSR, in the hope that its people would develop a taste not only for western products but also for western ideas.

Although U.S. government policy has vacillated among the various objectives, its behavior has been consistent in certain basic respects.

One consistent characteristic has been the deepseated ideological preference of the United States to hold down the direct transactional role of government in trade and investment. In spite of the importance that the U.S. government has attached at times to the management of its economic relations with the USSR, the government's direct transactional role has been kept to a minimum: The introduction of new economic initiatives and the execution of economic transactions have by and large been left to the private sector, to a degree unmatched by other countries.

Another characteristic of U.S. policy has been the tendency to use general rules, formal procedures, and publicized decisions in the administration of its various policies toward the USSR, once again in sharp contrast to the approaches of other countries. Here too, the style of the U.S. government has been typical of the application of its governmental powers in general.

A third characteristic reflects the fact that governmental powers over foreign economic policy are so widely diffused within the U.S. government. Numerous studies have emphasized the point that the U.S. decision making process is almost unique among nations in the extent to which such governmental powers are shared among the various units of government. Within the executive branch, the defense establishment is constantly at odds with the State Department, while Commerce and the White House provide added points of view. Moreover, as the various studies indicate, each of these units as a matter of course makes complex alliances with congressmen and their staffs in an effort to carry their positions in the executive branch. To add to the complexities, both the president and the Congress are obliged at times to bow to the courts, as individuals and groups exercise their rights of judicial initiative and appeal.

With a structure of that sort, policy initiatives and actions to block policy initiatives can come from a dozen different quarters. Where special interests are concerned, therefore, the U.S. process offers a picture of frenetic activism, with results that are often both unpredictable and inconsistent in direction; the export restrictions relating to the Soviet gas pipeline and the offers to sell grain to the USSR are only the latest illustrations of such contradictions. As a result, it has been especially hard for the executive to conduct a policy of linkage in relations with the USSR; neither the executive's power to punish nor its power to reward has been secure.

All those characteristics promise to some extent to typify U.S. behavior in the future. That prospect obviously places some powerful restraints on the kinds of policies that realistically can be considered.

The merits of U.S. policies

Deciding on the right U.S. policy for east–west trade relations turns not only on what is feasible but also on what will produce the appropriate benefits. To calculate the costs and benefits of various policies, however, entails some difficult judgments. In the first place, how will restrictions on the export of strategic goods and technologies affect the behavior and performance of the USSR and its COMECON partners? A second group of questions addresses the non-communist countries and the enterprises within their borders: Are there common policies with which these countries can be expected to agree? In the absence of agreement, how can they and the industries within their borders be expected to behave toward the USSR and eastern Europe? Finally, there are the judgments relating to the United States: What economic difference will the presence or absence of restrictions have on the U.S. economy?

Judgments of this sort are difficult in any case, requiring not only an estimate of the existing situation but also estimates of various counterfactual possibilities; and not only estimates of the immediate impact of any given restraint, but also estimates of the adjustments that the USSR might ultimately undertake. If the question, for instance, is whether to deny the Soviet Union some important U.S. export, such as blades for the turbines of giant gas compressors, it is not enough to establish the fact that the denial will be painful to the USSR; it is necessary also to determine if, after the USSR has made its various adjustments to the embargo, it will be in a better or a worse position than if the denial had not occurred. By the nature of the question, exploring the consequences of any policy becomes an exercise in projection far beyond the point at which hard data are still relevant. It demands an extensive understanding of how the economy of the USSR is structured and how it operates under stress; judgments such as these rest on fact and speculation that extend far beyond the individual case, requiring generalizations about the Soviet system as a whole.

Increasing the stress

Perhaps the most important judgments regarding the wisdom of the west's export restrictions have to do with their overall effects on the strength of the USSR and its COMECON partners.

Those who would limit economic contacts with the USSR to an absolute minimum usually see the added costs as likely to create a more restless and less governable Soviet populace. With more difficulties at home, according to this set of views, Soviet leaders are likely to be less adventuresome abroad.

Those who support added contact also hope to reduce the aggressiveness of the USSR by such a policy.

The two views are not necessarily contradictory; both could be right. The important point to be recognized is that propositions such as these are altogether conjectural; no hard data exist as a basis for choosing between them.

Yet, one must realistically recognize that, right or wrong, it is certain that our allies will not buy the restrictive approach. The gulf between the United States and Europe on the subject has been very wide at times in the past few years, particularly because of the disputes over the gas pipeline from the Soviet Union. And as long as the United States pursues highly restrictive policies based primarily on political and security factors, the prospects of finding a working consensus with the Europeans on this basic subject seem close to zero. Without the support of Europe, a U.S. effort to curtail economic contact with the USSR is almost meaningless. The U.S. government's choices, therefore, are more limited, ranging from a policy of aloofness and selective denial to one of the aggressive promotion of contact between the two camps.

Restraining a war-making capacity

To restrain the USSR's capacity to make war, U.S. analysts regularly identify products and technologies that the USSR would have difficulty in providing for itself, and seek to withhold such products or technologies. The object has been to exacerbate the bottlenecks in the system, place obstacles in the way of the Soviet learning process, and thereby extend a U.S. technological lead.

After thirty-five years of pursuing such a policy with varying degrees of intensity, however, there is no hard evidence that on balance it has had its intended effect. The difficulty with such a policy is obvious: Sometimes denial slows up forward movement; sometimes it stimulates the target to find effective substitutes or to find ways of doing without. In the Soviet case, there are instances in which it is reasonable to assume that restriction has slowed the growth of Soviet capabilities, and instances in which it is reasonable to assume the opposite. As a result, we cannot exclude the possibility that the extensive control system of past decades in some respects may actually have improved the Soviet Union's present capacity to make war.

At first blush, these conclusions may seem counterintuitive. But a little reflection will indicate why they are quite consistent with similar conclusions regarding the effects of restrictions in somewhat analogous situations. Consider, for instance, the industrialization processes of developing countries. A number of such countries have deliberately refrained from importing technologically advanced products from more industrialized countries in order to stimulate their own enterprises to master difficult production problems; India's outstanding success in the field of large-scale electrical generators and Brazil's equally striking success with the manufacture of executive aircraft illustrate the strategy.[7]

In the case of the Soviet Union, there are special reasons for supposing that U.S. denials of strategic products may have galvanized the country to overcome its vulnerabilities. To understand the basis for that conclusion, one has to begin with some appreciation of the sluggishness and insensitivity of the Soviet planning process. Exceedingly strong signals are needed for a significant redirection of resources on the part of the system. Every so often, vast elephantine shifts do occur: a movement to rural electrification, to the use of chemical fertilizer, to the mechanization of agriculture, to the development of gas reserves. But these initiatives are a reaction to visible failings in the system too obvious to be disregarded.

Picture a situation in which the USSR is unequivocally vulnerable with respect to some critically important item—vulnerable in the sense that its supplies come from foreign sources, that the sources could conceivably be cut off for political reasons, and that the development of replacement sources would take considerable time or entail considerable cost. The original decision to import is generally made at lower levels of the Soviet hierarchy, and the upper levels are usually involved only on high-priority matters. Our judgment is that as long as the critical supplies are small in amount and as long as they continue to be available from foreign sources without interruption, the vulnerability can go "uncorrected" for extended periods of time. Indeed, managers in the USSN that rely on such imported goods as inputs generally have strong incentives not to interrupt the flow, inasmuch as any shift to domestic sources will introduce new uncertainties over their plan fulfillment.

In a system of that sort, U.S. export restriction lists offer Soviet planning authorities a convenient monitoring device, a dry run on their vulnerabilities. Soviet authorities hardly need a list of that sort to tell them that they are still incapable of producing satisfactory mainframe computers, large aircraft engines, or oversized steel pipe. But for hundreds of less obvious deficiencies, the U.S. export restriction lists serve to by-pass the clogged lines of internal communication, to galvanize the Soviet planning process, and to speed up the reaction time of the USSR to its strategic weaknesses. The CIA report of the middle 1970s that the Soviet Union and its allies would become importers of large quantities of petroleum by 1985 had just that effect. After having ignored the repeated appeals of their own specialists for increased investment in the Soviet petroleum industry, Soviet political leaders finally bestirred themselves after the issuance of the CIA report.[8]

To be sure, the USSR will not always find an acceptable replacement for a foreign product that has been denied it. For instance, it was shaken by the U.S. denial of spare parts for its Kama River truck plant following the invasion of Afghanistan and it is being shaken by the U.S. denial of various products required for its gas pipeline projects. But even in these cases, U.S. denials have prodded Soviet planners into attempting to overcome vulnerabilities at a time when the burden of the adjustment could reasonably be met. It is in this sense that U.S. denial efforts give the USSR a dry run on its vulnerabilities and a chance for substitution and learning, thus reducing rather than increasing U.S. capacity to squeeze the country in an acute emergency. The dangers of advertising Soviet vulnerabilities well in advance of the outbreak of hostilities are apparent and the potential costs of such advertising are obvious. The hope of those that press for a strict system of restrictions is that the retarding and bottleneck-creating effects of such restrictions will more than offset their stimulative and learning effects.

There is no doubt that individual cases exist in which the costs of developing a substitute source for an embargoed product or the costs of doing without such a product impose a burden on the Soviet economy. But the assumption that the aggregate costs to the USSR generated by the restrictions is enough to offset the advantages that the Soviet Union gets from them is no more than a guess. And certain characteristics of the Soviet economy suggest strongly that the guess may be wrong.

The strength of a policy of denial depends on its ability to create bottlenecks and scarcities. In the USSR, there is no doubt that acute bottlenecks do exist from time to time, often for reasons that have little to do with the U.S. denial policy. For instance, the absence of chemical machine-building equipment, machine tools used to produce miniature ball-bearings, ammonia plants, geological exploration systems for petroleum, sophisticated drill-bit plants, pipe-laying equipment, and computers has retarded Soviet economic and military growth. However, by far the more common problem for Soviet planners is not the lack of capital and human resources but their misapplications throughout the system. Foreign technology and foreign machines sometimes help break bottlenecks; but they are commonly misplaced and misused, sometimes putting off the development of more appropriate solutions.[9] The same tendency toward lack of coordination and misapplication in the system means that equipment and labor are underutilized, while industrial materials are wasted. For example, because of various wasteful practices, expenditures of fuel per ton of open-hearth steel is considerably higher in the Soviet Union than it is in the United States and Japan. Similarly, the expenditure of fuel per kilowatt of electricity generated is higher in the Soviet Union than it is in the United States. The Soviet Union also uses more metal per unit of engine power than comparable engines in the United States.[10] These results are mainly due to inadequate incentives and coordination, and they generate a level of factor productivity for the Soviet economy that is about one-half that of the United States.[11]

In our judgment, the poor coordination and wasteful use of resources that typify normal Soviet industrial performance provide a cushion for Soviet planners when the upper levels of the bureaucracy have been alerted to the need to correct some specific vulnerability in the economy. Some of the slack resources that are to be found throughout the system can be mobilized if the priority is high enough. In some cases, to be sure, the effort may be slowed up because a critical technological ingredient is missing. But more generally, engineers and technicians can be rounded up for the relatively uncomplicated task of cutting, pasting, fitting, and testing that makes up much of the activity associated with imitative industrial innovations. (Indeed, the number of persons classified in the USSR as scientists and engineers is about twice that of the United States, suggesting slack in this category as well.) Specialized materials that are being stockpiled or used in the civilian economy, once they are located, can readily be diverted to the higher priority project. This capacity to draw on slack resources, we believe, is why the USSR has been able to produce extraterrestrial satellites, submarines, nuclear reactors, and high-performing fighter aircraft, all with considerable speed and of acceptable quality, as the need has arisen.

The effectiveness with which the USSR responds to the information it gains from U.S. denial lists depends in some cases on the country's ability to produce the needed products from heretofore improperly utilized domestic resources; but it depends in other cases on the country's ability to find other foreign suppliers of the proscribed technologies or products. Judgments on the ineffectualness of U.S. embargoes come mainly from unsystematic and anecdotal evidence. But cumulatively the evidence is persuasive. And it points to several key conclusions.

Since World War II, the technological links between the U.S. economy and facilities located in foreign countries have been growing at a quite staggering rate. There has been a rapid growth in the number of foreign subscriptions to technical journals in the United States, as well as a rapid increase in the number of foreign graduate students enrolled in technical fields in U.S. universities. In addition, there has been an extensive internationalization of U.S. engineering and other technical firms, partly through licensing agreements with independent producers outside the United States, partly through the creation of foreign subsidiaries by U.S. firms. The number and intimacy of the foreign technological links that the U.S. economy has created suggest that efforts to restrict the flow of technology are highly vulnerable and that they are getting more so. U.S. technology has become increasingly accessible in foreign jurisdictions, sometimes through channels that are quite legitimate in character, sometimes by illegal means. And as the U.S. government has pressed its efforts to embargo strategic items, the USSR has acquired increasing experience in the art of ferreting out alternative sources of supply.

Besides, even when the United States can guard the precise specifications needed to duplicate a new technological capability, it has much greater difficulty concealing the fact that the capability exists. Often, the knowledge that the capability has been achieved is enough; the history of scientific research and industrial innovation suggests that once scientists and engineers are aware that a given capability has already been achieved, they proceed in their search with a much higher expectation of success. Accordingly, where the flow of technological information is concerned, restrictions applied at the U.S. border have lost a considerable part of their meaning.

In addition to the fact that the U.S. border has grown more porous, there is also the fact that in many of the industries that encompass critical technological areas U.S. technology no longer enjoys a commanding lead. Accordingly, the technology originating in other nations is often quite good enough to serve Soviet needs.

Agreement among the industrialized countries, therefore, is necessary for any serious effort at denial; when other industrial countries fail to go along with a U.S. attempt to withhold technology or products, the likelihood that the U.S. effort will have much effect is considerably reduced. But such agreements unfortunately entail a cost for the United States. Over the years, justifiably or not, other countries have come to think of these agreements as something that the Americans want and that the other countries concede; the United States is seen as securing the benefits of the undertakings while the other countries assume the burdens. Just how divisive the issue can be has been amply demonstrated in the battle over the building of the Urengoi natural gas pipeline. To the west Europeans, the pipeline not only meant an additional source of energy supply, but exports and jobs in a recession. To U.S. policymakers, however, the pipeline was an example of selling the hangman a rope: a case in which the west finances the Soviet export of a crucial commodity that provides the Soviet Union with badly needed hard currency and that some day may be used for political blackmail. The result of the quarrel has been that the United States has managed to convert what should be an east–west issue into a west–west issue, in which the only clear winner is the Soviet Union.

The difference in view between Europe and the United States stems partly from the fact that U.S. interests have had relatively little economic stake in the maintenance of east–west trade. Only in 1975 and 1976 did U.S. machinery exports to the USSR substantially exceed a half-billion dollars. For the most part, therefore, the United States is not giving up much when it urges an embargo on machinery exports to the Soviet Union. As a consequence, the United States has jockeyed itself into a position of appearing to impose undue costs on the rest of the alliance while escaping similar costs for itself. This is made all the more apparent by the fact that the United States, which does have a major stake in agricultural exports to the Soviet Union, has awarded itself an exception from its own policy of denial. To add insult to injury, the exception is justified by a transparently feeble rationalization, namely, that the USSR's purchase of the grain will reduce its economic strength by reducing its foreign exchange resources.

It will be objected, of course, that the reaction of the other members of COCOM to U.S. proposals for strategic export controls is unreasonable, that the U.S. desire to enforce a web of COCOM restrictions is intended for the benefit of all the alliance members. The others have characteristically replied, however, that their desire for security against the Soviet threat is no less than that of the United States; that if they thought the sale of technology and goods to the USSR or the purchase of goods from the USSR weakened the relative position of the west, they would be foolish to allow it; and that their ability to make such judgments is at least as good as that of the United States. Irrespective of the merits of the debate, the strains that it places upon the unity of the west are considerable.

All told, therefore, the efforts of the United States to restrain the USSR's war-making capacity by restricting exports are having consequences that are altogether uncertain; they may even be having the opposite of their intended effects. By strengthening the USSR's autarchic capabilities and by weakening our NATO ties, the effort could be tipping the war-making scales in favor of the USSR.

Signalling displeasure

More difficult to evaluate is the question whether it is useful to use trade restrictions from time to time as an expression of disapproval of the political or military behavior of eastern countries, such as on the occasion of the Afghanistan invasion.

The objectives of the U.S. government in expressing displeasure over some objectionable policy of the USSR are usually quite complex. One purpose—perhaps the most important purpose—is simply to find some vent for U.S. frustration, in cases in which the U.S. government has no way of striking back. Barely distinguishable from that motivation is the desire of U.S. leaders to signal their U.S. constituencies in some cases that they are not indifferent to Soviet policies. Another objective, however, is to stiffen the backs of groups outside the United States—of the victims themselves, or of third countries. And yet another is to try to persuade the USSR to change its policies.

There is a respectable case for the view that the USSR is sensitive to manifestations of displeasure. We have already observed that the USSR was prepared to go a little way to meet U.S. demands during the linkage period. Moreover, the world's outcries after the Afghanistan invasion, some contend, has been partly responsible for the USSR's seemingly ineffectual pursuit of Afghan guerrillas, as well as its muted role in Poland and the Middle East.

But these cases suggest that manifestations of displeasure on the part of the United States will only work in some cases: if they are attached to some quid pro quo, as in the case of the linkage era, or if they are joined by a large number of other countries. But the capacity of the United States, under its diffuse system of governance, to manage a policy of linkage is very limited; that was amply demonstrated by the disruptive impact of the Jackson–Vanik amendment on Secretary Kissinger's linkage policy. And the ability of the U.S. government to secure the cooperation of other countries to any set of strongly restrictive measures is also limited.

In practice, therefore, there will be only a very occasional instance in which the signalling device will produce results.

Protecting the western trade regime

One type of threat to the west that is associated with the growth of east–west trade is mentioned only infrequently—the possibility that such growth may help to weaken the existing trade regime within the west itself. Operating mainly through the rules of the General Agreement on Tariffs and Trade and the European Community, the Atlantic alliance countries have managed over this past thirty-five years to create a remarkably open system among them for the movement of industrial goods. The system is, of course, riddled with exceptions: limitations on the movement of steel, automobiles, and textiles are illustrative. Still, the system is remarkable for its vitality, and it presumptively produces major economic gains for the west.

Trade with the east, on the other hand, is conducted along the lines that centrally directed economies require, which differ profoundly from the western system in two important respects. First, as noted earlier, the eastern authorities begin with a principle that is the obverse of the western rule. Whereas the west assumes that all trade is permitted unless the state intervenes, the east assumes that no trade occurs until the state initiates it; that is why the state can act as a monopsonist in the acquisition of technology and grain. But it is the second principle that creates the real source of conflict. Authorities of the eastern countries typically try to set up their trade arrangements in a way that guarantees a balance between their imports and their exports in each separate segment of their trade. Germany sells the steel and related equipment for gas pipelines and is paid off eventually in deliveries of gas; Pepsico trades soft drinks for vodka; and so on.

From the viewpoint of the west, a system that forces a balance between imports and exports in the trade of every country or every firm undermines the trade regimes developed in the west under the GATT and the European Community. In order to achieve the required bilateral balance, each country or each firm is obliged to take the goods of the other in amounts sufficient to bring about balance. The countries participating in the GATT or the European Community will be obliged to reserve corners of their national markets for the products of their eastern partners, irrespective of the competitive quality of products being offered by trading partners in the west. The economic gains from trade for the west are accordingly sharply reduced.

This fundamental incompatibility between the east's trading system and that of the west has always existed. But east–west trade has been sufficiently limited in amount up to now so that the occasional awkwardnesses created by such trade could be handled as special cases. Accordingly, the aborted trade agreement between the United States and the USSR that was negotiated in 1972 contained an ambiguous clause that simply allowed each party to ban imports from the other whenever it felt that such goods would "cause, threaten or contribute to the disruption of the domestic market." At present levels of east–west trade, western governments could presumably go on, without great loss, sweeping problems of this sort under the rug. But if there were ever a substantial increase in such trade, it would place new stresses on the existing trade arrangements within the west, imperilling the substantial economic and political advantages that have been derived from the present system.

Problems such as these suggest a need for a more effective set of economic policies toward the USSR. But the policies appropriate for dealing with this problem, although they might entail restrictions in some circumstances, would be quite different in objective from the restrictions embodied in the present U.S. system of security export controls, and could readily be distinguished from such controls.

Capturing the gains from trade

There is a related area in which worries over economic interations with the USSR do seem to be based on solid considerations. Overall, present patterns of trade between east and west probably generate gains for both sides. But given the present institutional structures and ground rules under which east–west trade is conducted, the odds seem overwhelming that the east captures most of the gains from trade. Indeed, the possibility is not to be excluded that, when measured in social-welfare terms, there are a significant volume of transactions in which the gains to the west are negative.

The tilt in that direction is suggested by a number of different factors. One factor pointing to the likelihood that the east captures the bulk of the gains is the fact that, apart from the items subject to security controls, the level and composition of the trade between east and west are determined by the official policies of the east, not by those of the west. In principle, unless the appropriate authorities in the east have determined that there are gains to be made for their economies from a given transaction, the transaction does not take place.

On the western side, on the other hand, no similar screening occurs; any proposal from the east that a private buyer or seller in the west wishes to pursue can presumably take place, unless it is blocked by security controls. Besides, no effective coordination of buying or selling power takes place on the western side. There may be occasional coordination among the buyers or sellers of a single nationality, such as the French or the Japanese; but there is rarely collaboration of buyers or sellers of different western nationalities such as the gas pipeline deal produced.

If private gain were the equivalent of social gain, the fact that the judgment was in private hands rather than in the hands of government authorities might not matter a great deal. But discrepancies between the two are common, especially in east–west trade.

One source of the discrepancy is the role of public subsidies in such trade. Grain figures heavily in the west's exports to the USSR; and grain production is subsidized to some degree by agricultural research and extension services, by price support programs, and by the government loans. Another part of the westward flow is capital equipment. Such equipment is commonly financed by the east through long-term loans offered by the west; and these loans are typically subsidized by western governments. In addition to capital equipment, the east also imports considerable quantities of technology from the west; these too are subsidized heavily by western governments.

The fact that the east can exert some means of monopsony or monopoly power in its transactions with western enterprises adds to the risk that the east may be seizing an undue share of the gains. In most products, to be sure, the gains that the USSR an eke out from its monopsony or monopoly power are probably not very large.[12] But there are important exceptions to that generalization, including notably sales of technology. A western seller of technology, when selling to a centrally directed economy, does not have any of the usual alternatives that normally exist in the foreign markets of the west: Failing to license the technology, the western seller does not have a substantial possibility of exporting products to eastern markets that incorporate the technology; nor does the western seller have the ready possibility of setting up a producing subsidiary in the east. From the seller's viewpoint, therefore, if there is to be any profit from the use of the technology in eastern economies, the license is usually the only alternative. And because the technology is already in being, any licensing fees received from the east represent almost clear profit. With the bargaining conditions set up in this way, eastern buyers will almost certainly manage to extract a much better price for the technology than a western buyer for the same information.

The key lessons

Some fundamental propositions are suggested by this analysis that should be governing in the development of east–west economic relations. First, the relationship of the United States to other non-communist industrial countries must be a central consideration in the choice of policy. Without joint actions, the U.S. capacity to develop an effective trade policy toward the Soviet Union is quite limited; this conclusion applies both to U.S. efforts to deny the Soviet Union goods that are useful for her military potential and U.S. efforts to generate gains from trade with the Soviet Union. Second, the advantages that the United States gains from holding back strategic goods are advantages of uncertain value; indeed there is a substantial risk that they are actually counterproductive. By giving the USSR a dry run on its vulnerabilities and by reducing the USSR's dependence on external resources for critical items, the restrictions produce complex results whose net effects on Soviet war-making capabilities are quite uncertain.

Managing east–west economic relations

The national context

In developing its economic policies toward the Soviet Union, the United States is unlikely to stray very far from the fundamental constraints that are imposed by its ideology and its institutions. Its preference for limiting the direct transactional role of the U.S. government in trade and investment will surely continue, leaving such activities largely to the private sector. Moreover, consistent with the U.S. preferences for restraining the role of government, U.S. policies will continue to lean toward developing rules of the game that are non-selective in application, such as the nondiscriminatory application of tariffs and the mechanistic application of quotas pursuant to explicit transparent formulas.

And despite those preferences at the level of principle, the U.S. system will continue to leave plenty of room for narrower interests in the country to attempt to improve their positions within any general program that the government may devise. These enduring characteristics are likely to shape any policies that the U.S. government may adopt.

Relations with third countries

Where the U.S. government has been at its best in the development of effective economic policies has been in promoting general regimes among nations that limit the direct operational role of government. That kind of regime has governed relations between the United States and its principal allies since the end of World War II. It was noted earlier that any considerable increase in trade with the USSR under the rulkes of the game that the USSR prefers would weaken such a regime. An important corollary is that the weakening of the existing regime—epitomized in the General Agreement on Tariffs and Trade and by various other agreements in support of an open competitive market—will concurrently increase the willingness of those countries to accept the USSR's terms for doing more business. The German gas deal, for instance, can be seen in part as the country's response to the fact that it could not rely on economic arrangements outside the Soviet bloc for assuring supplies of energy, as well as to the more pervasive fact that the existing system was not producing full employment for Germany. If the GATT system weakens much further and if the open-market system which the United States has promoted begins to falter, the ability of the United States to frame effective economic policies toward the USSR will weaken as well.

Practically speaking, for those who are concerned with maintaining an effective set of economic relations toward the USSR, U.S. efforts to strengthen an open trading system for the world offer the most feasible area for action. Restrictive provisions designed explicitly to deal with the USSR seem much less promising, given the characteristics of the U.S. system of governance, because they constantly require the U.S. side to address individual cases in a context that is highly politicized and involves strong special interests, and in a context that demands the active cooperation of other countries to support individual cases.

Bilateral policies

If a special restrictive regime toward the USSR is infeasible or ineffectual, are there other possibilities for special policies toward the USSR that might produce constructive results? One possibility suggested earlier was that of deliberately expanding our economic contacts with the USSR in the hope that increased contacts will have the effect of reducing the ability and propensity of the USSR to engage in destructive foreign policies. That line of policy may be worth pursuing. If it were followed, however, a number of critical points would have to be taken into account in its implementation.

First, the principal advantage by far to be gained from such a policy is that it will reduce the gap between the United States and its allies, and therefore increase the probability of cooperation and joint actions over the forms and limits of increased contact with the USSR.

Second, the spirit in which the United States invites increased economic contact with the USSR is of critical importance. On this point, Khrushchev's formula for justifying increased east–west contact could conceivably be adapted for U.S. use. In seeking an expansion of economic contacts, we should be expressly and openly seeking an opportunity for competition. And we should be voicing the confident expectation that in the competition, the Soviet system will be buried.

If that approach can be struck and maintained, it will have several major advantages for the United States. If the Soviet Union holds back, as it very well may, the advantage will be with the United States. If the Soviet Union does not hold back, the U.S. position may help to explain to an uncertain or resistant U.S. Congress and U.S. public why increased economic contacts between the two countries are desirable even though political hostility remains high. Accordingly, it may reduce the domestic pressures that have derailed U.S. policies toward the Soviet Union in the past. It will reduce the risk that the president may be obliged to use unproductive trade restrictions as a gesture of the country's displeasure whenever the USSR engages in some unfriendly act. And it will reduce a risk of quite another sort—the risk that an increase in the level of trade may be misinterpreted in the United States as a decline in the level of military risk.

Third, in the exceptional case in which a U.S. transaction would contribute directly to the military capabilities of the USSR for conducting large-scale hostilities, we should not hesitate to restrict the export. But such controls must be used sparingly and with great selectivity. Where military objectives are concerned, the cases that best merit such controls are those that satisfy two conditions: The USSR is already fully alert to its military vulnerability and will not profit from the U.S. denial signal; the USSR's efforts to fill its lack from alternative sources will entail considerable delays or high costs in terms of military capabilities. A limited number of such cases of this sort clearly exist; but any effort significantly to enlarge the list would be a threat to the policy as a whole.

Finally, if the objective were to increase economic contact with the USSR, we could not altogether overlook the risk that the USSR might continue to capture the lion's share of the gains from trade between us. Accordingly, measures that might help to redistribute those gains should be considered, such as those mentioned below.

Realistically, it must be recognized that any steps to redistribute the gains from trade would be difficult to implement. U.S. controls over trade with the USSR have for so long been determined by strategic military considerations and domestic politics that it will be difficult at first for the United States to establish the critical fact that it intended thenceforth to be guided primarily by economic objectives. Recognition that such a shift had occurred could not be achieved by any single presidential pronouncement nor over a short period of time. The spirit in which the necessary measures were sought and carried out, therefore, would probably be as important as the substance; particularly important would be a constant sensitivity to the point that the cooperation of other friendly countries is indispensable. Some joint curbs would be needed on the use of countertrade and other bilateral balancing devices, along with joint limits on the use of subsidies. The countries of the west would also have to agree on a process for fixing upset prices in exceptional transactions, in order to prevent excessive discriminatory pricing in favor of the USSR by western exporters; and the U.S. government would have to arm itself with the powers and procedures for participating in such a process. That power would prove especially important in selected transactions involving the sale of technology.

As befits measures intended for the economic improvement of the western position, however, it would be important to ensure that the needed coordinating machinery did not have the furtive and clandestine quality of COCOM undertakings; if it retained that quality, it could not escape being regarded as primarily for security purposes. The coordinating process would have to be overt and non-conspiratorial, a simple effort to redress a balance in negotiation brought about by institutional differences between the two systems. There may even be a time when the USSR can be invited jointly with the west to explore the problem of the institutional imbalance, possibly with a view of reaching joint solutions.

In the end, such efforts could fail. Even if they did not, the U.S. government could well find that its endemic inability to conduct a program that demanded consistency and subtlety in the handling of individual cases prevented its following an effective policy especially designed for the USSR relationship. In that case, it might be pushed back to the one remaining line of policy that offers some hope—the task, difficult enough in its own terms, of building the most effective possible system for the economic linking of the non-communist market economies.

Notes

[1]U.S. Senate Committee on Foreign Relations, *East–West Trade* (Washington, DC: U.S. Government Printing Office, 1964), 88th. Cong., 2nd. sess., parts I, II, III; Marshall I. Goldman and Alice Conner, "Businessmen appraise east–west trade," *Harvard Business Review*, January/February 1966, p. 6.

[2]*Pravda*, April 6, 1966, p. 7.

[3]U.S. Senate Committee on Banking and Currency, *East–West Trade* (Washington, DC: Government Printing Office, June 1968), 90th Cong., 2nd. Sess.

[4]Henry Kissinger, *Years of Upheaval* (Boston: Little, Brown and Co., 1982), p. 247.

[5]Kissinger, pp. 204–205, 247, 252, 995–96.

[6]Franklin D. Holzman, *International Trade Under Communism* (New York: Basic Books, 1976), pp. 151, 159.

[7]For the Indian case, see Ravi Ramamurti, "Strategic Behavior of Effectiveness of State-Owned Enterprises in High Technology Industries: A Comparative Study in the Heavy Engineering Industry in India," Harvard University, unpublished D.B.A. thesis, 1982, Chapter 6; for the Brazilian case, see *Air Transport World*, vol. 18, no. 3, March 1981, "Airlines Have 1100 Planes on Firm Order: U.S. Hold on Market is Slipping," pp. 64–65; *Aviation Week and Space Technology*, June 27, 1977, "Brazil Seeking New Aircraft Markets," pp. 63–65.

[8]See Marshall Goldman, *Enigma of Societ Petroleum: Half Emptor Half Full* (Boston: Allen and Unwin, 1980), p. 178.

[9]Thane Gustafson, *Selling the Soviets the Rope? Soviet Technology Policy and U.S. Export Controls* (Santa Monica, CA: Rand Corporation, April 1981), p. 6.

[10]T. Khachaturov, "Prirodyne resursov i planirovanie narodnogo khoziaistva" [Natural Resource and National Economic Planning], *Voprosy ekonomiki*, Moscow, August 1973, p. 25.

[11]Abram Bergson, *Productivity in the Social System—The USSR and the West* (Cambridge, MA: Harvard University Press, 1978), p. 101.

[12]M. M. Kostecki (ed.), *Soviet Impact on Commodity Markets* (London: Macmillan Press, 1983).

12

The fragile foundations of East–West trade

If wishing can make it so, the trade between the advanced industrialized countries of the West and the command economies of the East will be growing rapidly in the years ahead. The Soviet Union has made no bones about its strong desire to expand the scope of East–West trade. Businessmen, bureaucrats, and politicians in the Western countries have been only a little more equivocal. Some countries have made an occasional effort to screen out technologies with important military application, while the United States has also sought to break down Soviet restrictions on the emigration of Russian Jews. But the West, too, has been on the side of expanded trade.

All told, the drive on both sides for more East–West trade had had its effect. Over the past fifteen years, the annual trade of the USSR and its COMECON partners with the advanced industrialized countries has managed to grow tenfold from about $3.5 billion to over $35 billion. What I suggest is that if such trade continues to grow at a rapid pace, frictions and obstructions will appear with increasing frequency. Under the existing institutions and rules of the game, increased East–West trade will strain the trading relations among the Western states, and will distribute the economic benefits of trade disproportionately to the East. As these effects become apparent, they will raise serious questions about the value of such trade for the West.

Yet it makes very little sense for the United States or any other country to attempt to suppress the growth of East–West trade. If appropriate rules of the game can be devised and adopted, such trade can bring economic benefits to both sides. Besides, if the United States were to attempt a policy of suppression, the effort would almost surely fail. But before it failed, it would generate major political costs both within the Western community and in relations with the East.

The challenge, therefore, is to devise a set of institutions and procedures that is compatible with a growing volume of East–West trade—but one that responds adequately to the interests of both sides. If my analysis is correct, any such regime will be difficult to put together. Some considerable consen-

Reprinted with permission of the publisher from *Foreign Affairs*, Summer 1979.

sus will have to be developed among Western countries as to the nature of the problem and the direction of the appropriate remedy. As part of the appropriate response, the United States may be obliged to give up its sporadic efforts to use trade in order to extract political concessions from the USSR. Effective action may even require the tacit understanding of the Soviet Union itself.

As realists, of course, we must face up to the chance that none of these steps will prove possible. In that case, we may have to sit by until the increasing frictions and mounting obstructions eventually convey the necessary message.[1]

If Adam Smith were observing the nations of Western Europe and North America today, he would see little to connect them with the ideal open markets of his *Wealth of Nations*. Yet these Western economies still are predominantly market economies, in which market-determined prices, costs, and profits play a key role. Some observers assume that these traits will be comprised over time, and that the West will develop an international system which is much more highly regulated. They point out that Western governments already conduct their trade in food, oil, gas, shipping, aviation, armaments, and various raw materials under special rules not wholly consistent with the open market system. Moreover, wherever big, one-shot deals have been involved, such as the sale of ten B-747s or of a billion-dollar steel mill, these have been arranged under rules *sui generis*. Today, these aberrations are supplemented by an expanding number of bilateral "voluntary" export agreements, especially with the new crop of industrializing developing countries. If most of the trade among the so-called market economies comes to be conducted on the basis of such "state" arrangements, it would not be very difficult for those countries to deal with the special problems of East–West trade.

What is a plausible projection, then, of the future economic patterns inside the Western economies and of the trading system that is likely to prevail among them? Such a projection, it seems to me, is an indispensable preliminary step in trying to puzzle out what the effects would be of greatly increased trade between the West and the Soviet Union.

The odd thing is that almost any projection of Western economic patterns and of their future trade relations seems prima facie implausible. To begin with, it is implausible to assume that the important role played by the market inside such economies and among such countries will continue with the same strength in the future; the demands of one special group or another for protection from the rude impact of open competition seem greater than ever. Yet it is just as implausible to assume that the Western economies will greatly control the operations of the open market, whether in their internal structures or in trade among them. The ideological and economic interests that would resist any such curtailment seem formidable; indeed, the economic interests that have a stake in maintaining an open market have never been so large. Moreover, any country that takes a substantial step toward closing its borders is exposed to retaliation, on a scale unmatched in history.

My expectation, therefore, is that the Western economies will back into a new set of relationships, one that tries to retain some considerable measure of national and international market freedom accompanied by some substantial capability for responding to the demands of their threatened sectors. The only such set of relationships I can envisage entails a tightening of the ties among a relatively limited number of Western countries that are historically committed to the extensive use of the market mechanism, a grouping that seeks to achieve its measures of economic adjustment by joint action. This begins to sound like a modified free-trade area among some subset of advanced industrial countries of the OECD: an area in which monetary, fiscal, agricultural, industrial, and conjunctional policy are developed and applied with some measure of coordination; and an area with some common economic policies toward outsiders.[2]

But if such a system actually developed, the economies of its members would still remain substantially different from that of the USSR. For the West, the underlying rule would still be that any trade can take place unless a government prevents it; while for members of COMECON, and especially for the USSR, the rule would be that no trade takes place unless the state initiates it. Inside the Western economies, firms would still be buying inputs at something resembling an open market price and selling their outputs at such a price; and internal prices would still be linked directly to foreign prices by comparatively low trade and payment barriers plus a convertible currency.

Meanwhile, inside the Soviet Union internal prices and costs would only be linked to foreign prices and costs to the extent that the central planning process chose to make the linkage. Any direct or automatic linkage would be prevented by: a prohibition of international trade and payments except when conducted by authorized intermediary agencies; a requirement that internal producers deliver designated goods for export or accept foreign goods through intermediary Soviet agencies, without regard to price; and a domestic currency that has no value outside the USSR.[3]

These differences would mean, among many other things, that the Soviet Union could restrict its trade (as it does today) simply by failing to act; whereas any restriction on the Western side would require (as it does today) some visible restrictive measures.

The differences between any future regime that may be foreseen among the market economies and the inherent features of the Soviet system are apparent not only in international trade but also in foreign direct investment. Under present conditions, it seems somewhat farfetched to think of substantial foreign direct investment on the part of the Soviets. Nevertheless, if the foreign trade of the USSR should expand very much—especially if it should expand in manufactured products—the country will be pushed to set up servicing and assembling facilities in some of its overseas markets. Soviet authorities, for instance, have talked more than once about expanding their exports of Lada automobiles from the present trickle to something more substantial. But that step is hard to contemplate unless the Soviet Union or its agents are prepared to set up substantial facilities in some of the markets to which Ladas are exported.

Among the market economies, governments are gradually beginning to face up to the issues associated with the operations of multinational enter- prises in their respective economies.[4] It is already fairly clear that, as this type of business structure grows in relative importance in the market econo- mies, the countries concerned will have to find new ways of sorting out the jurisdictional frictions among them; subjects such as taxation, restrictive business practices, security controls, political activity, and labor relations, among others, could well be involved in such discussions. In general, the home countries of such enterprises are likely to find themselves increasingly restrained by international agreement whenever they contemplate reaching out to control the foreign subsidiaries of their firms.

For the USSR, on the other hand, the tie between the home government and the overseas subsidiaries of Soviet firms will probably always be strong. On command from the ministries of the USSR, for instance, Soviet firms would be expected to withdraw from any country declared to be non grata; or to make their liquid business assets available to the Soviet Union; or to discriminate in the choice of customers and suppliers. For the present, how to integrate such actors into the Western system seems unclear.

The means by which the two systems seek to gain from international transactions are thus markedly different. The Soviet system is based on the proposition that social gain is maximized by the state's commands. The American system, like the system of most Western countries, is fashioned on the proposition that as individuals pursue their private gain, the benefits for the country will exceed its costs, yielding a social gain.

The fact is, however, that private gain to the American parties in any individual transaction does not correspond to U.S. social gain. The private parties in the transaction may be subsidized from the public sector, through Export–Import Bank loans or through research subsidies. Even when not subsidized, their otherwise profitable transactions may have implications for inflation or unemployment or national defense which turn private gain into social loss. The classic case, of course, was the Great Grain Robbery of 1972; but other less spectacular cases are sometimes cited as well. Nevertheles, as far as U.S. policies and practices are concerned, private gain in any given transaction is both a necessary condition and a sufficient condition for any trade or investment. Social gain alone is neither necessary nor sufficient.

As long as an American is engaged in trade or investment with another Western country, the gap between private gain and social gain is fairly toler-

able. In the case of those countries, the situation in theory is broadly recipro-
cal. That is, the private firms of any Western nation engage in trade or
investment with those of another nation in the group whenever they see an
opportunity for private gain, irrespective of the social economic consequences of their transactions for their home economies as a whole. (That
proposition is less true of trade or investment with Japan—a fact that explains in part the underlying tensions in the West in economic relations with
that country.)

Of course, Soviet traders do not always manage to capture a social gain
for their own country. Decisions may be taken in the Soviet Union out of fear
or ignorance or stupidity or the narrow interests of some portion of the Soviet
bureaucracy. But it would be prudent to assume that the USSR would not sell
any product to the West if the sale entailed any obvious social loss for the
Soviet Union. At the same time, the point should not be lost that Moscow can
readily block any transaction that might entail an obvious social gain for the
West.

Accordingly, trade and investment relations between the West and the
USSR are conducted on a chancy basis. In some transactions, to be sure, both
sides may find themselves gaining in social terms. For instance, the Soviet
Union may sell the United States much-needed oil while we sell them badly
needed grain; the chief advantages to us may be a dampening of inflation, and
to them a dampening of political discontent. In other transactions, however,
the Soviets may gain while we lose in social terms: the USSR may gain some
new technology, while the United States acquires a new competitor in international markets. In sum, a lopsided relationship exists that should qualify
our enthusiasm for an expansion of trade and investment with the Soviet
Union, as long as these transactions are conducted through existing institutions and ground rules.[5]

A more familiar concern with regard to Soviet economic relations with
the West is that the USSR is in a position to exercise its power as sole supplier
or sole purchaser in trading transactions with competing Western businessmen, thus capturing most or all of the gains from trade.

This argument has been repeatedly advanced and repeatedly pooh-
poohed by some economists familiar with the structure of East–West trade.[6]
The counter-argument has been that, as buyers, the Russians are not all that
important to the West; and as sellers, they contribute only marginal quantities of any given product to the West. Accordingly, they are seen as price
takers, unable to determine the level of market prices, rather than as giant
forces determining the prices in such markets.

It is important not to exaggerate the extent of Soviet economic power.
But it is wrong to assume that such power is trivial. The trade relations of the
Soviet Union and COMECON with various European countries, for instance,

are substantial. Besides, our concern here is not with the existing level of trade and investment, but with a substantially expanded level. Finally, there are some peculiarities of pricing on both the buying and the selling side of Soviet trade that merit substantial concern.

Sales by the West to the USSR in recent years have included a considerable amount of technology; sometimes these sales have been associated with the sale of capital equipment, sometimes not. It is customary to think of sellers of technology as monopolists or oligopolists, capable of exacting a rent from buyers. But, of course, practically all sellers of modern technology confront competitors or near-competitors offering some alternative technological approach.

Where such competition exists, the USSR appears to be in an excellent position to exploit that fact. First of all, few sellers to the Soviets are interested in making an isolated sale, however large that sale may be; most sellers are aware that firms with a prior record in the Soviet Union have an inside track for the future. Accordingly, there is good reason in the interest of future sales to price the technology low. To be sure, this tendency is not unknown in Western markets. But the difference is an important one of degree. In Western markets, the sellers can ordinarily hope to make multiple sales of a given technology; in the USSR, just one. In Western markets, the seller has his eye on developing a privileged position with one buyer if he can; in the case of the USSR, his eye is on access to a whole economy. Accordingly, the temptation to cut prices may be commensurately stronger.

That temptation is strengthened by still another factor. If a Western firm fails to sell its technology to the Soviet Union, it cannot hope to exploit the technology inside the USSR by other means, such as exports or licensing or production through subsidiaries. When the firm sells it technology, therefore, it gives up nothing in the way of alternative opportunities. This means that a floor price, which would exist if the Western sellers were making their offers in a market economy, is not present in sales to the Soviets. Inasmuch as the added costs to the firm of generating the technology for sale to the USSR is usually zero or near zero, there is almost no restraint on how deeply the seller can cut the price.

Taken together, these factors seem likely to create a powerful downward push on sales prices. Inasmuch as the actual facts in the case are not well known, this conclusion can only be stated as surmise. Nevertheless, the surmise seems sufficiently plausible to justify a certain amount of caution while gaining a better grasp of the facts.

As for the pricing of goods and services exported by the Soviet Union, this, too, has certain peculiarities. The mix of products and services offered by the Soviets for sale in the open market will be determined by the national economic plan, supplemented from time to time by items that have been overproduced in the USSR or acquired in barter with other countries. The sales goals will often be stated in physical units, and the rewards to the selling agency will depend heavily on whether its physical targets are met. Since the

Soviet Union separates internal costs from external prices, such costs need not serve as much of a constraint. Instead, the foreign price fixed for these products and services will characteristically be the closest competitor's price, discounted just enough to meet the sales target.

Another price problem associated with Russian trade stems from the fact that many East–West transactions are barter trades that characteristically swap Soviet goods for Western technology or goods. These swaps take a number of different forms. One consists of straight barter of specified quantities of goods, such as American soft drinks for Russian vodka; another more generalized form allows the Western partner to choose from a shopping list; a third consists of barter that pays off the Western partner with future output from a specified plant—so-called compensation deals. The swap in its various forms has peculiarities that place its control largely in Soviet hands. For instance, the volume of goods to be sold by the foreigner in the USSR is always under Soviet control, simply because the state controls the distribution channels; so are the quantity and character of the goods available in return, which are mediated by the export ministries.

Some forms of swap arrangements also exacerbate the problem of marginal pricing to a degree that elevates the problem to major proportions. In compensation deals, for instance, there is commonly a long interval between the time when the Western partner delivers a plant or other capital goods to the USSR and the time when it receives some of the resulting output as compensation. When such an interval exists, the Western partner receives its return long after its own costs are only a matter of memory. At that stage, the Western partner may be willing to accept any price in the resale of the Soviet merchandise received. Occidental Oil's recent sales of Russian ammonia in the U.S. market raise many of these issues.

One response of the market economies to this group of problems in years past has been to try to apply the rules of the market economy by analogy to trade with command economies. If this approach were ever applied, however, the markup of state trading importers would be analogous to a tariff and would be subject to negotiation; importers would be duty-bound not to discriminate among different sources of supply, and so on.[7] Any approach of this sort is a nonstarter. Because the internal prices of the USSR have been totally insulated from foreign prices, the market analogy is meaningless.

To be sure, the Soviet Union has undertaken in bilateral agreements with the United States and with various European countries to provide a response of sorts. The USSR undertakes in such cases to cease exporting products to a given market which the importing partner feels will "cause, threaten, or contribute to the disruption of its domestic market." Although this formula no doubt is offered in good faith by the Russian side, it nevertheless lays all the political onus on the West. The Soviets can limit the entry of Western goods without taking any overt act—simply by failing to buy. The Western partner, on the other hand, must explicitly invoke the disruption clause, a step that cannot avoid having political overtones. Similarly with export restrictions: the USSR can limit the export of its producers simply by failing to sell; but the Western partner will have explicitly to restrain its sellers in order to achieve the same result. The hesitation of Europe to invoke this kind of clause because of political considerations has been palpable in the past year or two.[8] Although there has been widespread distress over mounting imports of steel products and textiles, disruption clauses have not been invoked. Accordingly, we are far from having achieved a balanced basis for bilateral trade.

In any case, the problems of any Western country with respect to the USSR's trading practices commonly involve third-country markets as well as those of the country itself. This involvement takes several different forms.

One major problem arises out of the Soviet Union's strong preference for conducting its foreign trade on a balanced bilateral basis. In their most restrictive form, the arrangements that are fashioned to maintain such a balance extend well beyond the barter-type transactions mentioned earlier. In such arrangements, the authorities agree on some target bundle of imports and exports of more or less equal value that they envisage will be bought and sold by the traders of the two nations over a given period, say a year. A pair of clearing accounts is set up, maintained by the respective central banking authorities of the two countries concerned. As individual transactions are arranged, each country pays off its exporters in its home currency, and receives in its home currency the payments due from its importers. The object is to finish each trading period with a zero balance in both national accounts; in that way, neither country is obliged to pay any foreign exchange to the other.

During the period of the agreement, of course, one nation or the other may find itself with a surplus in the clearing account, generated by the fact that its exporters will have sold more than its importers have bought. In that case, the deficit country will exhort its partner to buy more. When that happens, the partner is expected to find ways of discriminating in favor of the deficit country. For example, if one of the partners is a mixed economy with a substantial contingent of state-owned enterprises or heavy governmental purchases, such as Brazil, it is likely to correct an imbalance by directing its enterprises and government offices to buy Soviet products whenever they can, irrespective of price.

Where a bilateral agreement exists and where an imbalance needs to be righted, the temptation of the partners to manipulate an import licensing system is hard to resist. Even if no such agreement exists, the propensity for discrimination will be high wherever the trade has been placed on a barter basis. Not surprisingly, one hears occasional complaints that West European countries tolerate the imports of steel and textiles from Eastern Europe while barring similar imports from Japan and the developing countries.[9]

So far, these practices have not been of earthshaking importance in the trade of West European countries. True, such practices have been inconsistent with various commitments to other Western countries, but they have covered only small quantities of trade. If trade is greatly increased, however, there is a risk that countries will disregard their commitments to nondiscrimination, epitomized in the General Agreement on Tariffs and Trade, the Common Market treaty, and various other treaties, to a degree that could imperil the commitments themselves.

The problems posed by the growth of the Soviet Union's trade involve third-country relationships in other ways. The market-disruption clause to which the USSR is prepared to subscribe in bilateral agreements, it should be noted, does not apply to Soviet sales made to third countries. Where such sales displace U.S. exports or the exports of other market economies, it is for the importing country to decide whether to take measures to redress the balance. For instance, if the USSR were to sell its Lada automobiles in Canada at extraordinarily low prices, as it might well have to do in order to build up an adequate volume of sales, the third-country problem would surface in an especially acute form.

The security export controls of the United States pose a special set of problems for the growth of East–West trade. These controls have little or nothing to do with the economic problems associated with such a trade, which is the center of the concern I am expressing here. Instead, they are intended to prevent certain selected exports with direct military application from going to the USSR.[10]

As long as the U.S. government applies such controls with great care and selectivity, their contribution to U.S. interests cannot seriously be questioned. I have always had considerable reservations, however, about the utility of attempting to apply such controls beyond the occasional exceptional case. The recent shift in emphasis from restricting goods to restricting technology generates the same reservations on my part, and they are widely shared by others. One reason for such reservations is the judgment of many Western experts that the USSR has the capability of closing (or at any rate of substantially narrowing) most technological gaps in the military field if it considers them serious. Another is that the imposition of overt controls from the West at times helps the ponderous Soviet bureaucracy in its efforts to highlight any weaknesses in Soviet military capabilities, and helps that bureaucracy generate higher internal priorities for an effective response.

If the application of a general system of security export controls is of dubious value to the United States, as I think is the case, any costs that are incurred in applying such a system seem especially misplaced. One obvious cost is incurred whenever the United States finds itself obliged to put pressure on unwilling allies in order to make some U.S.-initiated embargo effective. Some of that pressure is exerted through COCOM, an international organization in which the United States seeks to generate common lists of products and processes to be embargoed for security reasons. Other U.S. government pressures, even more costly in political terms, are exerted via the U.S.-based multinational enterprises, and target the subsidiaries of such enterprises located in third countries.

The stringency of these controls has varied over time, according to the temperature of relations with the Soviet Union. The number of instances in which the United States feels obliged to put pressure on its allies, however, is a function not only of the degree of stringency of the controls but also of the general level of East–West trade. Accordingly, as such trade increases, the United States is likely to be found exerting its pressures with increasing frequency, thereby adding to the political costs of garnering the questionable benefits of the export control program.

Related to the use of security controls in East–West trade is the question of whether the United States should use its economic leverage with the USSR, such as it is, to try to achieve political ends. Of course, any basic aspect of the relationship between the United States and the Soviet Union cannot fail to be shaped by some fundamental political calculation; the superpower status of the two countries virtually compels both countries to weigh their relationship in political terms. The question here, however, is whether the United States should attempt to link specific economic concessions to specific political goals. The Jackson-Vanik Amendment of 1974 compels the president to make the linkage in the case of Soviet emigration policies. The approach could easily be extended in principle to issues such as Soviet military support to South Yemen and Ethiopia.

The case to be made on either side of the issue involves the subtle questions of strategy and tactics. On relatively simple grounds, however, case-by-case linkage is not desirable. There are two reasons for my conclusion.

First, as suggested earlier, the situations in which the United States alone can exercise significant leverage are rare; at best, therefore, the gains in such an overt policy can only be small. The reasons for the relative impotence of the United States have already been suggested. In order for the United States to exert effective leverage, the costs to the USSR of doing without American grain or American technology, for instance, must be fairly high. Experience suggests that such cases are not common, because the Soviet Union can generally redeploy its own internal capabilities to narrow the gap or to find a near-substitute for American products and processes in other countries.

The second point is that on any issue that relates to the Soviet Union, U.S. negotiators are in an extraordinarily weak position for effectively handling a linkage strategy. Such a strategy demands great flexibility in choosing both when to link and when to delink. The fishbowl in which the executive branch ordinarily conducts its relations with the USSR is a grossly unpromising environment in which to pursue such a policy.

Besides, once the American negotiators have chosen—or have been pressed—to link economic benefits to political objectives, they can no longer use their economic power to pursue other needs. If my argument is right, the economic needs may well prove to be compelling, demanding all the economic leverage the United States can muster.[11]

It hardly needs saying that the other advanced industrialized countries of the West have both economic and political interests in common with the United States in their dealings with the Soviets. These other countries so far have resisted the development of a common trade policy toward the Soviet Union based on common political interests. But they have never been strongly tested on whether common *economic* interests might be allowed to shape their trade policy toward the USSR.

So far, the failure to develop such cooperation has not been very costly, simply because East–West trade has not been very great. If such trade should very much increase under existing ground rules and existing institutions, however, the cost could prove substantial.

Nevertheless, shifting our trade strategy with the Soviet Union from one based on military security and politics, narrowly construed, to one based on economics will be difficult. The atmosphere is already conditioned by twenty-five years of debate in COCOM, where the United States has argued its case principally on political or military grounds. Still, the shift in emphasis may be possible. Europe today is more preoccupied with the potentially disruptive economic effects of East–West trade than before, worrying about dumped manufactures and hard competition in shipping from Soviet sources.[11] Moreover, the fact that the European Community under the terms of the Rome Treaty has now assumed the responsibility for East–West trade policy (at least in the formal sense) opens up possibilities for coordination that did not exist earlier.

To achieve the necessary cooperation, the market economies would have to come to share the key judgment suggested earlier: that high volumes of trade between them and the USSR could imperil the relations of the market economies with one another unless some improved rules of the game can be devised; and that the uncoordinated approach of the market economies could allow the USSR to capture the larger portion of the gains from trade. Not all market economies could be persuaded to consider these propositions seriously; most developing countries, for instance, would draw back from such consideration. But the principal countries to be persuaded in any case would be those in the Organization for Economic Cooperation and Development.

In order to increase the receptivity of OECD countries, the first requirement would be to pursue the subject outside of COCOM, thereby emphasizing the changed basis for the discussion. The second would be to limit the formality of any organizational structure, for fear of straining the political tolerance of the Europeans. OECD consultative procedures, for instance, might be as far as one would want to go at first.

At least as difficult would be the problem of convincing the Soviet Union itself that changes in the trading framework were being dictated by economic considerations, not by cold-war tactics. On that score, the United States and the other Western countries suffer from the initial disadvantage of having allowed the USSR for so long to go unchallenged in some of its key contentions as to what constitutes "reciprocity" and fair-trading relationships. So far, the market economies have tacitly tolerated the lopsided idea that any failure on the part of the Russians to trade with them is a neutral nonpolitical act, a manifestation of an inherent right of the USSR not to trade unless it sees its interests being served; whereas the unwillingness of the market economies to trade is seen by the Soviets as an aggressive political act, even in circumstances in which such trade might incur a social loss for such economies. The Soviet Union must be persuaded that these long-unchallenged assumptions have always been indefensible, and that if greatly increased volumes of trade are to take place, such assumptions will have to be abandoned.

The objective, therefore, is to develop a regime among the advanced industrialized countries in which trade and investment with the Soviets can comfortably expand. In the best of circumstances, such a regime will be difficult to create. It will be impossible to create, in my view, if the United States insists on retaining the right to use its trade with the USSR as a lever for the attainment of political conditions; in that case, other advanced industrialized countries would want to maintain considerable distance from U.S. policy. Such a regime, therefore, might well require the United States to give up its independent approach to East–West trade, including the use of political conditions to determine whether unconditional most-favored-nation treatment and Export–Import Bank loans should be granted to the Soviet Union.

What would such a regime include?

One basic principle would be for the Western states to claim the right to apply the same presumption that the USSR applies, namely, that no trade should be expected to take place unless it contributes a net economic benefit to the market economies as a group. Agreement on the principle is more important, in my opinion, than its rigorous application. Indeed, any effort to judge many individual transactions by that criterion could rapidly be turned into a bureaucratic nightmare. But the principle would be important for two purposes: first, to remind both sides of the fundamental point that both must be in a position to benefit in a social sense if trade is to continue and to expand; second, to snag the occasional large isolated transaction which, by its terms, seems to threaten the aggregate economic interests of the West.

A second principle would be to multilateralize, as far as possible, the participation of the advanced industrialized countries in trade with the Soviet Union. Under this heading, bilateral clearing accounts and government-supported barter would be curbed; provisions for the sharing of raw materials sold by the USSR would be set forth, to be applied in periods of acute scarcity; and quantitative goals for aggregate Soviet imports from the cooperating market economies would be developed, goals that might be reached by a process of negotiation with the Soviet Union.[12]

Another element in such an approach would be the development of joint policies among the market economies on various technical issues that relate to trade with the Soviet Union, such as the terms of credit to be extended to Soviet buyers. This is an old chestnut, on which cooperation has not been notably successful in the past; on the other hand, agreements in this field have always been pursued in a vacuum, outside of any larger economic framework for trade with the Soviets. It may be that, as one plank in a more coordinated approach, such agreements would have a greater chance for success.

Finally, there is the possibility of developing joint economic demands that would involve the intangible aspects of trade and investment. For example, one could conceive of the Soviets being asked to improve the rights of visitation of Western businessmen to a number of branches of Soviet industry in which such businessmen had a technological interest. Under a regime of this sort, it is conceivable that the privilege of Soviet representatives to visit, for instance, the steel plants of the West would be balanced by the right of Western businessmen and technicians to visit designated groups of plants in the USSR. Steps such as these would be needed to right the lopsided character of existing arrangements.

These possibilities are suggested only illustratively. The important underlying point is to recognize that the present basis for trade and investment is lopsided; that if East–West trade greatly increases, a form of Gresham's law may push the market economies further from their own preferred basis for trading with one another; and that any solution to that problem is likely to require greater cooperation among such economies.

Desirable as this recognition may be, one must soberly entertain the possibility that it will not come about. The individual states of Western Europe and Japan are already tied up in so many complex deals with the USSR—the United States with grains, Italy with oil, Germany with gas, and so on—that the world may well have reached the point at which a cooperative effort is beyond the collective capabilities of the advanced industrial nations. As a result, we may find ourselves impotent to right the imbalance between the West and the USSR, and unable to mitigate the threat to our present international economic systems that appears to be associated with increasing economic relations with the Soviets under the existing rules.

Even in that case, however, a heightened sensitivity to the problems of such trade will serve some purpose. It will serve to remind us that, under the present rules of the game and under existing institutions, any expansion of trade with the Soviet Union may entail some significant costs, and that the benefits to be derived ought to be clearly superior to those costs.

Notes

[1] Of course, if the USSR proves incapable of expanding its foreign trade very much in spite of the desires of its leaders, as some experts think, the problem may be put off. See Richard Portes, "East, West, and South: The Role of the Centrally Planned Economies in the International Economy," Discussion Paper No. 630, Harvard Institute of Economic Research, June 1978.

[2] The twenty-four member countries of the Organization for Economic Cooperation and Development are Australia, Austria, Belgium, Canada, Denmark, Finland, France, the Federal Republic of Germany, Greece, Iceland, Ireland, Italy, Japan, Luxembourg, the Netherlands, New Zealand, Norway, Portugal, Spain, Sweden, Switzerland, Turkey, the United Kingdom, and the United States. The European Communities and Yugoslavia have limited participant status.

[3] For a recent description, see E. A. Hewett, "Most-Favored-Nation Treatment in Trade Under Central Planning," *Slavic Review,* March 1978, pp. 25–39.

[4] See my article, "Multinationals: No Strings Attached," *Foreign Policy,* Winter 1978, pp. 121–34.

[5] The idea is hardly new. See my article "Apparatchiks and Entrepreneurs: U.S.–Soviet Economic Relations," *Foreign Affairs,* January 1974, pp. 249–62.

[6] See, for instance, *Economic Relations Between East and West: Prospects and Problems,* Washington, D.C.: Brookings Institution, 1978.

[7] See, for example, *Havana Charter for an International Trade Organization,* Articles 29, 30, and 31, adopted by the Economic and Social Council of the United Nations conference in Havana, Cuba, November 14, 1947–March 24, 1948.

[8] See, for instance, European Parliament, *Report on the State of Relations Between EEC and East European State-Trading Countries and COMECON, Document 98/78, May 11, 1978.*

[9] *Ibid.*

[10] See Jonathan B. Bingham and Victor C. Johnson, "A Rational Approach to Export Controls," *Foreign Affairs,* Spring 1979, pp. 894–920.

[11] See, for instance, "Chemicals in the East Explode West," *The Economist,* February 10, 1978, p. 84.

[12] Some additional interesting suggestions appear in E. A. Hewett, "Most Favored-Nation Treatment in Trade Under Central Planning," *supra,* footnote 3.

Index

A

B

C

J

N

U